James Thomas Fields

Good company for every day in the year

James Thomas Fields

Good company for every day in the year

ISBN/EAN: 9783337414412

Printed in Europe, USA, Canada, Australia, Japan

Cover: Foto ©Lupo / pixelio.de

More available books at **www.hansebooks.com**

FOR EVERY DAY IN THE YEAR.

"Good company . . . . . . well approved in all."

SHAKESPEARE.

BOSTON:
TICKNOR AND FIELDS.
1866.

Entered according to Act of Congress, in the year 1865, by
TICKNOR AND FIELDS,
in the Clerk's Office of the District Court of the District of Massachusetts.

UNIVERSITY PRESS: WELCH, BIGELOW, & CO.,
CAMBRIDGE.

CONTENTS.

	Page
JOHN G. WHITTIER: Yankee Gypsies	1
JAMES RUSSELL LOWELL: Dara	16
THOMAS CARLYLE: Cromwell	19
T. WESTWOOD: Little Bell	86
ROSE TERRY: The Mormon's Wife	89
JOHN GIBSON LOCKHART: Beyond	109
JOHN MILTON: Autobiographical Passages	110
WILLIAM ALLINGHAM: Wakening	117
EDMUND LODGE: John Graham	118
W. EDMONDSTOUNE AYTOUN: The Burial-March of Dundee	128
GOETHE: Mignon as an Angel	134
MRS. GASKELL: The Cage at Cranford	136
EDMUND SPENSER: Verses on Sir Philip Sidney	150
GEORGE TICKNOR: Prescott's Infirmity of Sight	152
DANTE: Beatrice	168

CONTENTS.

ROBERT SOUTHEY: A Love Story 170

BAYARD TAYLOR: The Mystic Summer . . . 236

MRS. JAMESON: Two of the Old Masters . . . 239

FREDERICK TENNYSON: The Poet's Heart . . 261

GIORGIO VASARI: Character of Fra Angelico . . 265

WILLIAM BLAKE: Songs 267

J. HAIN FRISWELL: Upon Growing Old . . . 277

R. W. EMERSON: The Titmouse 284

NATHANIEL HAWTHORNE: Little Pansie . . . 288

H. W. LONGFELLOW: Palingenesis 305

SIR WALTER SCOTT: My Childhood 308

YANKEE GYPSIES

By JOHN G. WHITTIER.

"Here's to budgets, packs, and wallets;
Here's to all the wandering train." — BURNS.

I CONFESS it, I am keenly sensitive to "skyey influences." I profess no indifference to the movements of that capricious old gentleman known as the clerk of the weather. I cannot conceal my interest in the behavior of that patriarchal bird whose wooden similitude gyrates on the church spire. Winter proper is well enough. Let the thermometer go to zero if it will; so much the better, if thereby the very winds are frozen and unable to flap their stiff wings. Sounds of bells in the keen air, clear, musical, heart-inspiring; quick tripping of fair moccasoned feet on glittering ice-pavements; bright eyes glancing above the uplifted muff like a sultana's behind the folds of her *yashmack*; school-boys coasting down street like mad Greenlanders; the cold brilliance of oblique sunbeams flashing back from wide surfaces of glittering snow or blazing upon ice-jewelry of tree and roof. There is nothing in all this to complain of. A storm of summer has its redeeming sublimities, — its slow, upheaving mountains of cloud glooming in the western horizon like new-created volcanoes, veined with fire, shattered by exploding thunders. Even the wild gales of the equinox have their varieties, — sounds of wind-shaken woods, and waters, creak and clatter of sign and casement, hurricane puffs and down-rushing rain-spouts. But this dull, dark autumn day of thaw and rain, when the very clouds seem too spiritless and languid to storm outright or take themselves out of the way of fair weather; wet beneath and above, reminding one of that rayless atmosphere of Dante's Third Circle, where the infernal Priessnitz administers his hydropathic torment, —

> "A heavy, cursed, and relentless drench, —
> The land it soaks is putrid"; —

or rather, as everything, animate and inanimate, is seething in warm mist, suggesting the idea that Nature, grown old and rheumatic, is trying the efficacy of a Thompsonian steam-box on a grand scale; no sounds save the heavy plash of muddy feet on the pavements; the monotonous, melancholy drip from trees and roofs; the distressful gurgling of water-ducts, swallowing the dirty amalgam of the gutters; a dim, leaden-colored horizon of only a few yards in diameter, shutting down about one, beyond which nothing is visible save in faint line or dark projection; the ghost of a church spire or the eidolon of a chimney-pot. He who can extract pleasurable emotions from the alembic of such a day has a trick of alchemy with which I am wholly unacquainted.

Hark! a rap at my door. Welcome anybody just now. One gains nothing by attempting to shut out the sprites of the weather. They come in at the keyhole; they peer through the dripping panes; they insinuate themselves through the crevices of the casement, or plump down chimney astride of the rain-drops.

I rise and throw open the door. A tall, shambling, loose-jointed figure; a pinched, shrewd face, sunbrown and wind-dried; small, quick-winking black eyes. There he stands, the water dripping from his pulpy hat and ragged elbows.

I speak to him; but he returns no answer. With a dumb show of misery quite touching he hands me a soiled piece of parchment, whereon I read what purports to be a melancholy account of shipwreck and disaster, to the particular detriment, loss, and damnification of one Pietro Frugoni, who is, in consequence, sorely in want of the alms of all charitable Christian persons, and who is, in short, the bearer of this veracious document, duly certified and indorsed by an Italian consul in one of our Atlantic cities, of a high-sounding, but to Yankee organs unpronounceable, name.

Here commences a struggle. Every man, the Mahometans tell us, has two attendant angels, — the good one on his right shoulder, the bad on his left. "Give," says Benevolence, as with some difficulty I fish up a small coin from the depths of my pocket. "Not a cent," says selfish Prudence; and I drop it from my fingers. "Think," says the good angel, "of the poor stranger in a strange land, just escaped from the terrors of the sea storm, in which his little property has perished, thrown half naked and helpless on our shores, ignorant of our language, and unable to find employment suited to his capacity." "A vile impostor!" replies the left-hand sentinel. "His paper, purchased from one of those ready writers in New York who manufacture beggar credentials at the low price of one dollar per copy, with earthquakes, fires, or shipwrecks, to suit customers."

Amidst this confusion of tongues I take another survey of my visitant. Ha! a light dawns upon me. That shrewd, old face, with its sharp, winking eyes, is no stranger to me. Pietro Frugoni, I have seen thee before. *Si, signor*, that face of thine has looked at me over a dirty white neckcloth, with the corners of that cunning mouth drawn downwards, and those small eyes turned up in sanctimonious gravity, while thou wast offering to a crowd of half-grown boys an extemporaneous exhortation in the capacity of a travelling preacher. Have I not seen it peering out from under a blanket, as that of a poor Penobscot Indian who had lost the use of his hands while trapping on the Madawaska?

Is it not the face of the forlorn father of six small children, whom the "marcury doctors" had "pisened" and crippled? Did it not belong to that down-east unfortunate who had been out to the "Genesee country" and got the "fevernnager," and whose hand shook so pitifully when held out to receive my poor gift? The same, under all disguises — Stephen Leathers, of Barrington — him, and none other! Let me conjure him into his own likeness: —

"Well, Stephen, what news from old Barrington?"

"O, well I thought I knew ye," he answers, not the least disconcerted. "How do you do? and how's your folks? All well, I hope. I took this 'ere paper you see, to help a poor furriner, who couldn't make himself understood any more than a wild goose. I thought I'd just start him for-'ard a little. It seemed a marcy to do it."

Well and shiftily answered, thou ragged Proteus. One cannot be angry with such a fellow. I will just inquire into the present state of his Gospel mission and about the condition of his tribe on the Penobscot; and it may be not amiss to congratulate him on the success of the steam doctors in sweating the "pisen" of the regular faculty out of him. But he evidently has no wish to enter into idle conversation. Intent upon his benevolent errand, he is already clattering down stairs. Involuntarily I glance out of the window just in season to catch a single glimpse of him ere he is swallowed up in the mist.

He has gone; and, knave as he is, I can hardly help exclaiming, "Luck go with him!" He has broken in upon the sombre train of my thoughts and called up before me pleasant and grateful recollections. The old farm-house nestling in its valley; hills stretching off to the south and green meadows to the east; the small stream which came noisily down its ravine, washing the old garden wall and softly lapping on fallen stones and mossy roots of beeches and hemlocks; the tall sentinel poplars at the gateway; the oak forest, sweeping unbroken to the northern horizon; the grass-grown carriage-path, with its rude and crazy bridge, — the dear old landscape of my boyhood lies outstretched before me like a daguerrotype from that picture within which I have borne with me in all my wanderings. I am a boy again, once more conscious of the feeling, half terror, half exultation, with which I used to announce the approach of this very vagabond and his "kindred after the flesh."

The advent of wandering beggars, or, "old stragglers," as we were wont to call them, was an event of no ordinary interest in the generally monotonous quietude of our farm life. Many of them were well known; they had their periodical revolutions and transits; we could calculate them like eclipses or new moons. Some were sturdy knaves, fat and saucy; and, whenever they ascertained that the "men folks" were absent, would order provisions and cider like men who expected to pay for it, seating themselves at the hearth or table with the air of Falstaff, — " Shall I not take mine ease in mine own inn?" Others, poor, pale, patient, like Sterne's monk, came creeping up to the door, hat in hand, standing there in their gray wretchedness with a look of heartbreak and forlornness which was never without its effect on our juvenile sensibilities. At times, however, we experienced a slight revulsion of feeling when even these humblest children of sorrow somewhat petulantly rejected our proffered bread and cheese, and demanded instead a glass of cider. Whatever the temperance society might in such cases have done, it was not in our hearts to refuse the poor creatures a draught of their favorite beverage; and was n't it a satisfaction to see their sad, melancholy faces light up as we handed them the full pitcher, and, on receiving it back empty from their brown, wrinkled hands, to hear them, half breathless from their long, delicious draught, thanking us for the favor, as " dear, good children "! Not unfrequently these wandering tests of our benevolence made their appearance in interesting groups of man, woman, and child, picturesque in their squalidness, and manifesting a maudlin affection which would have done honor to the revellers at Poosie-Nansie's, immortal in the cantata of Burns. I remember some who were evidently the victims of monomania — haunted and hunted by some dark thought — possessed by a fixed idea. One, a black-eyed, wild-haired woman, with a whole tragedy of sin, shame, and suffering written in her countenance, used often to visit us, warm herself by our winter fire, and supply herself with a stock of cakes and cold meat; but was never known to answer a question or to ask one. She never smiled; the cold, stony look of her eye never changed; a silent, impassive face, frozen rigid by some great wrong or sin. We used to look with awe upon the "still woman," and think of the demoniac of Scripture who had a "dumb spirit."

One — I think I see him now, grim, gaunt, and ghastly, working his slow way up to our door — used to gather herbs by the wayside and call himself doctor. He was bearded like a he-goat and used to counterfeit lameness, yet, when he supposed himself alone, would travel on lustily as if walking for a wager. At length, as if in punishment of his deceit, he met with an accident in his rambles and became lame in earnest, hobbling ever after with difficulty on his gnarled crutches. Another used to go stooping, like Bunyan's pilgrim, under a pack made of an old bed sacking, stuffed out into most plethoric dimensions, tottering on a pair of small, meagre legs, and peering out with his wild, hairy face from under his burden like a big-bodied spider. That "man with the pack" always inspired me with awe and reverence. Huge, almost sublime, in its tense rotundity, the father of all packs, never laid aside and never opened, what might there not be within it? With what flesh-creeping curiosity I used to walk round about it at a safe distance, half expecting to see its striped covering stirred by the motions of a mysterious life, or that some evil monster would leap out of it, like robbers from Ali Baba's jars or armed men from the Trojan horse!

There was another class of peripatetic philosophers — half peddler, half mendicant — who were in the habit of visiting us. One we recollect, a lame, unshaven, sinister-eyed, unwholesome fellow, with his basket of old newspapers and pamphlets, and his tattered blue umbrella, serving rather as a walking-staff than as a protection from the rain. He told us on one occasion, in answer to our inquiring into the cause of his lameness, that when a young man he was employed on the farm of the chief magistrate of a neighboring State; where, as his ill luck would have it, the governor's handsome daughter fell in love with him. He was caught one day in the young lady's room by her father; whereupon the irascible old gentleman pitched him unceremoniously out of the window, laming him for life, on the brick pavement below, like Vulcan on the rocks of Lemnos. As for the lady, he assured us "she took on dreadfully about it." " Did she die?" we inquired anxiously. There was a cunning twinkle in the old rogue's eye as he responded, " Well, no, she did n't. She got married."

Twice a year, usually in the spring and autumn, we were honored with a call from Jonathan Plummer, maker of verses, pedler and poet, physician and parson, — a Yankee troubadour, — first and last minstrel of the valley of the Merrimac, encircled, to my wondering young eyes, with the very nimbus of immortality. He brought with him pins, needles, tape, and cotton thread for my mother; jackknives, razors, and soap for my father; and verses of his own composing, coarsely printed and illustrated with rude woodcuts, for the delectation of the younger branches of the family. No lovesick youth could drown himself, no deserted maiden bewail the moon, no rogue mount the gallows without fitting memorial in Plummer's verses. Earthquakes, fires, fevers, and shipwrecks he regarded as personal favors from Providence, furnishing the raw material of song and ballad. Welcome to us in our country seclusion as Autolycus to the clown in Winter's Tale, we listened with infinite satisfaction to his readings of his own verses, or to his ready improvisation upon some domestic incident or topic suggested by his auditors. When once fairly over the difficulties at the outset of a new subject his rhymes flowed freely, "as if he had eaten ballads and all men's ears grew to his tunes." His productions answered, as nearly as I can remember, to Shakespeare's description of a proper ballad — "doleful matter merrily set down, or a very pleasant theme sung lamentably." He was scrupulously conscientious, devout, inclined to theological disquisitions, and withal mighty in Scripture. He was thoroughly independent; flattered nobody, cared for nobody, trusted nobody. When invited to sit down at our dinner-table, he invariably took the precaution to place his basket of valuables between his legs for safe keeping. "Never mind thy basket, Jonathan," said my father; "we sha'n't steal thy verses." "I'm not sure of that," returned the suspicious guest. "It is written, 'Trust ye not in any brother.'"

Thou too, O Parson B., — with thy pale student's brow and rubicund nose, with thy rusty and tattered black coat overswept by white, flowing locks, with thy professional white neckcloth scrupulously preserved when even a shirt to thy back was problematical, — art by no means to be overlooked in the muster-roll of vagrant gentlemen possessing the *entrée* of our farm-house. Well do we remember with what grave and dignified courtesy he used to step over its threshold, saluting its inmates with the same air of gracious condescension and patronage with which in better days he had delighted the hearts of his parishioners. Poor old man! He had once been the admired and almost worshipped minister of the largest church in the town where he afterwards found support in the winter season as a pauper. He had early fallen into intemperate habits; and at the age of threescore and ten, when I remember him, he was only sober when he lacked the means of being otherwise. Drunk or sober, however, he never altogether forgot the proprieties of his profession; he was always grave, decorous, and gentlemanly; he held fast the form of sound words, and the weakness of the flesh abated nothing of the rigor of his stringent theology. He had been a favorite pupil of the learned and astute Emmons, and was to the last a sturdy defender of the peculiar dogmas of his school. The last time we saw him he was holding a meeting in our district school-house, with a vagabond pedler for deacon and travelling companion. The tie which united the ill-assorted couple was doubtless the same which endeared Tam O'Shanter to the souter: —

"They had been fou for weeks thegither."

He took for his text the first seven verses of the concluding chapter of Ecclesiastes, furnishing in himself its fitting illustration. The evil days had come; the keepers of the house trembled; the windows of life were darkened. A few months later the silver cord was loosened, the golden bowl was broken, and between the poor old man and the temptations which beset him fell the thick curtains of the grave.

One day we had a call from a "pawky auld carle" of a wandering Scotchman. To him I owe my first introduction to the songs of Burns. After eating his bread and cheese and drinking his mug of cider he gave us Bonnie Doon, Highland Mary, and Auld Lang Syne. He had a rich, full voice, and entered heartily into the spirit of his lyrics. I have since listened to the same melodies from the lips of Dempster (than whom the Scottish bard has had no sweeter or truer interpreter); but the skilful performance of the artist lacked the novel charm of the gaberlunzie's

1*

singing in the old farm-house kitchen. Another wanderer made us acquainted with the humorous old ballad of "Our gude man cam hame at e'en." He applied for supper and lodging, and the next morning was set at work splitting stones in the pasture. While thus engaged the village doctor came riding along the highway on his fine, spirited horse, and stopped to talk with my father. The fellow eyed the animal attentively, as if familiar with all his good points, and hummed over a stanza of the old poem: —

> "Our gude man cam hame at e'en,
> And hame cam he;
> And there he saw a saddle horse
> Where nae horse should be.
> 'How cam this horse here?
> How can it be?
> How cam this horse here
> Without the leave of me?'
> 'A horse?' quo she.
> 'Ay, a horse,' quo he.
> 'Ye auld fool, ye blind fool, —
> And blinder might ye be, —
> 'T is naething but a milking cow
> My mamma sent to me.'
> A milch cow?' quo he.
> Ay, a milch cow,' quo she.
> Weel, far hae I ridden,
> And muckle hae I seen;
> But milking cows wi' saddles on
> Saw I never nane.'"

That very night the rascal decamped, taking with him the doctor's horse, and was never after heard of.

Often, in the gray of the morning, we used to see one or more "gaberlunzie men," pack on shoulder and staff in hand, emerging from the barn or other out-building where they had passed the night. I was once sent to the barn to fodder the cattle late in the evening, and, climbing into the mow to pitch down hay for that purpose, I was startled by the sudden apparition of a man rising up before me, just discernible in the dim moonlight streaming through the seams of the boards. I made a rapid retreat down the ladder; and was only reassured by hearing the object of my terror calling after me, and recognizing his voice as that of a harmless old pilgrim whom I had known before. Our farm-house was situated in a lonely valley, half surrounded with woods, with no neighbors in sight. One dark, cloudy night, when our parents chanced to be absent, we were sitting with our aged grandmother in the fading light of the kitchen fire, working ourselves into a very satisfactory state of excitement and terror by recounting to each other all the dismal stories we could remember of ghosts, witches, haunted houses, and robbers, when we were suddenly startled by a loud rap at the door. A stripling of fourteen, I was very naturally regarded as the head of the household; so, with many misgivings, I advanced to the door, which I slowly opened, holding the candle tremulously above my head and peering out into the darkness. The feeble glimmer played upon the apparition of a gigantic horseman, mounted on a steed of a size worthy of such a rider — colossal, motionless, like images cut out of the solid night. The strange visitant gruffly saluted me; and, after making several ineffectual efforts to urge his horse in at the door, dismounted and followed me into the room, evidently enjoying the terror which his huge presence excited. Announcing himself as the great Indian doctor, he drew himself up before the fire, stretched his arms, clinched his fists, struck his broad chest, and invited our attention to what he called his "mortal frame." He demanded in succession all kinds of intoxicating liquors; and, on being assured that we had none to give him, he grew angry, threatened to swallow my younger brother alive, and, seizing me by the hair of my head as the angel did the prophet at Babylon, led me about from room to room. After an ineffectual search, in the course of which he mistook a jug of oil for one of brandy, and, contrary to my explanations and remonstrances, insisted upon swallowing a portion of its contents, he released me, fell to crying and sobbing, and confessed that he was so drunk already that his horse was ashamed of him. After bemoaning and pitying himself to his satisfaction he wiped his eyes, and sat down by the side of my grandmother, giving her to understand that he was very much pleased with her appearance; adding, that, if agreeable to her, he should like the privilege of paying his addresses to her. While vainly endeavoring to make the excellent old lady comprehend his very flattering proposition he was interrupted by the return of my father, who, at once understanding the matter, turned him out of doors without ceremony.

On one occasion, a few years ago, on my return from the field at evening, I was told that a foreigner had asked for lodgings during the night, but that, influenced by his dark, repulsive appearance, my mother had very reluctantly refused his request. I found her by no means satisfied with her decision. "What if a son of mine was in a strange land?" she inquired, self-reproachfully. Greatly to her relief, I volunteered to go in pursuit of the wanderer, and, taking a crosspath over the fields, soon overtook him. He had just been rejected at the house of our nearest neighbor, and was standing in a state of dubious perplexity in the street. His looks quite justified my mother's suspicions. He was an olive-complexioned, black-bearded Italian, with an eye like a live coal, such a face as perchance looks out on the traveller in the passes of the Abruzzi, — one of those bandit visages which Salvator has painted. With some difficulty I gave him to understand my errand, when he overwhelmed me with thanks and joyfully followed me back. He took his seat with us at the supper-table; and, when we were all gathered around the hearth that cold autumnal evening, he told us, partly by words and partly by gestures, the story of his life and misfortunes, amused us with descriptions of the grape-gatherings and festivals of his sunny clime, edified my mother with a recipe for making bread of chestnuts; and in the morning, when, after breakfast, his dark, sullen face lighted up and his fierce eye moistened with grateful emotion as in his own silvery Tuscan accent he poured out his thanks, we marvelled at the fears which had so nearly closed our door against him; and, as he departed, we all felt that he had left with us the blessing of the poor.

It was not often that, as in the above instance, my mother's prudence got the better of her charity. The regular "old stragglers" regarded her as an unfailing friend; and the sight of her plain cap was to them an assurance of forthcoming creature comforts. There was indeed a tribe of lazy strollers, having their place of rendezvous in the town of Barrington, New Hampshire, whose low vices had placed them beyond even the pale of her benevolence. They were not unconscious of their evil reputation; and experience had taught them the necessity of concealing, under well-contrived disguises, their true character. They came to us in all shapes and with all appearances save the true one, with most miserable stories of mishap and sickness and all "the ills which flesh is heir to." It was particularly vexatious to discover, when too late, that our sympathies and charities had been expended upon such graceless vagabonds as the "Barrington beggars." An old withered hag, known by the appellation of Hopping Pat, — the wise woman of her tribe, — was in the habit of visiting us, with her hopeful grandson, who had "a gift for preaching" as well as for many other things not exactly compatible with holy orders. He sometimes brought with him a tame crow, a shrewd, knavish-looking bird, who, when in the humor for it, could talk like Barnaby Rudge's raven. He used to say he could "do nothin' at exhortin' without a white handkercher on his neck and money in his pocket " — a fact going far to confirm the opinions of the Bishop of Exeter and the Puseyites generally, that there can be no priest without tithes and surplice.

These people have for several generations lived distinct from the great mass of the community, like the gypsies of Europe, whom in many respects they closely resemble. They have the same settled aversion to labor and the same disposition to avail themselves of the fruits of the industry of others. They love a wild, out-of-door life, sing songs, tell fortunes, and have an instinctive hatred of " missionaries and cold water." It has been said — I know not upon what grounds — that their ancestors were indeed a veritable importation of English gypsyhood; but if so, they have undoubtedly lost a good deal of the picturesque charm of its unhoused and free condition. I very much fear that my friend Mary Russell Mitford, — sweetest of England's rural painters, — who has a poet's eye for the fine points in gypsy character, would scarcely allow their claims to fraternity with her own vagrant friends, whose camp-fires welcomed her to her new home at Swallowfield.

"The proper study of mankind is man"; and, according to my view, no phase of our common humanity is altogether unworthy of investigation. Acting upon this belief two or three summers ago, when making, in company with my sister, a little excursion into the hill country of New Hampshire, I turned my horse's head towards Barrington for the purpose of seeing these semi-civilized strollers in their own home, and returning, once for all, their numerous visits. Taking leave of our hospitable cousins in old Lee with about as much solemnity as we may suppose Major Laing parted with his friends when he set out in search of desert-girdled Timbuctoo, we drove several miles over a rough road, passed the Devil's Den unmolested, crossed a fretful little streamlet noisily working its way into a valley, where it turned a lonely, half-ruinous mill, and climbing a steep hill beyond, saw before us a wide sandy level, skirted on the west and north by low, scraggy hills, and dotted here and there with dwarf pitch pines. In the centre of this desolate region were some twenty or thirty small dwellings, grouped together as irregularly as a Hottentot kraal. Unfenced, unguarded, open to all comers and goers, stood that city of the beggars — no wall or paling between the ragged cabins to remind one of the jealous distinctions of property. The great idea of its founders seemed visible in its unappropriated freedom. Was not the whole round world their own? and should they haggle about boundaries and title deeds? For them, on distant plains, ripened golden harvests; for them, in far-off workshops, busy hands were toiling; for them, if they had but the grace to note it, the broad earth put on her garniture of beauty, and over them hung the silent mystery of heaven and its stars. That comfortable philosophy which modern transcendentalism has but dimly shadowed forth — that poetic agrarianism, which gives all to each and each to all — is the real life of this city of unwork. To each of its dingy dwellers might be not unaptly applied the language of one who, I trust, will pardon me for quoting her beautiful poem in this connection: —

> "Other hands may grasp the field or forest,
> Proud proprietors in pomp may shine;
> Thou art wealthier — all the world is thine."

But look! the clouds are breaking. "Fair weather cometh out of the north." The wind has blown away the mists; on the gilded spire of John Street glimmers a beam of sunshine; and there is the sky again, hard, blue, and cold in its eternal purity, not a whit the worse for the storm. In the beautiful present the past is no longer needed. Reverently and gratefully let its volume be laid aside; and when again the shadows of the outward world fall upon the spirit, may I not lack a good angel to remind me of its solace, even if he comes in the shape of a Barrington beggar.

DARA.

By JAMES RUSSELL LOWELL

WHEN Persia's sceptre trembled in a hand
    Wilted with harem-heats, and all the land
Was hovered over by those vulture ills
That snuff decaying empire from afar,
Then, with a nature balanced as a star,
Dara arose, a shepherd of the hills.

He who had governed fleecy subjects well,
Made his own village by the self-same spell
Secure and quiet as a guarded fold;
Then, gathering strength by slow and wise degrees,
Under his sway, to neighbor villages
Order returned, and faith, and justice old.

Now when it fortuned that a king more wise
Endued the realm with brain, and hands, and eyes,
He sought on every side men brave and just;
And having heard our mountain shepherd's praise,
How he refilled the mould of elder days,
To Dara gave a satrapy in trust.

So Dara shepherded a province wide,
Nor in his viceroy's sceptre took more pride
Than in his crook before; but envy finds

More food in cities than on mountains bare;
And the frank sun of spirits clear and rare
Breeds poisonous fogs in low and marish minds.

Soon it was whispered at the royal ear
That, though wise Dara's province, year by year,
Like a great sponge, sucked wealth and plenty up,
Yet, when he squeezed it at the king's behest,
Some yellow drops more rich than all the rest
Went to the filling of his private cup.

For proof, they said that, wheresoe'er he went,
A chest, beneath whose weight the camel bent,
Went with him; and no mortal eye had seen
What was therein, save only Dara's own.
But, when 't was opened, all his tent was known
To glow and lighten with heaped jewels' sheen.

The king set forth for Dara's province straight,
Where, as was fit, outside the city's gate,
The viceroy met him with a stately train,
And there, with archers circled, close at hand,
A camel with the chest was seen to stand.
The king's brow reddened, for the guilt was plain.

"Open me here," he cried, "this treasure chest."
'T was done, and only a worn shepherd's vest
Was found within. Some blushed and hung the head;
Not Dara; open as the sky's blue roof
He stood, and "O my lord, behold the proof
That I was faithful to my trust," he said.

"To govern men, lo, all the spell I had!
My soul in these rude vestments ever clad
Still to the unstained past kept true and leal,

Still on these plains could breathe her mountain air,
And fortune's heaviest gifts serenely bear,
Which bend men from their truth and make them reel.

"For ruling wisely I should have small skill,
Were I not lord of simple Dara still:
That sceptre kept, I could not lose my way."
Strange dew in royal eyes grew round and bright,
And strained the throbbing lids; before 'twas night,
Two added provinces blest Dara's sway.

CROMWELL.

By THOMAS CARLYLE.

CROMWELL'S BIRTHPLACE.

HUNTINGDON itself lies pleasantly along the left bank of the Ouse, sloping pleasantly upwards from Ouse Bridge, which connects it with the old village of Godmanchester; the Town itself consisting mainly of one fair street, which towards the north end of it opens into a kind of irregular market-place, and then contracting again soon terminates. The two churches of All-Saints' and St. John's, as you walk up northward from the Bridge, appear successively on your left; the church-yards flanked with shops or other houses. The Ouse, which is of very circular course in this quarter, winding as if reluctant to enter the Fen-country, — says one topographer, has still a respectable drab-color gathered from the clays of Bedfordshire, has not yet the Stygian black which in a few miles further it assumes for good. Huntingdon, as it were, looks over into the Fens; Godmanchester, just across the river, already stands on black bog. The country to the East is all Fen (mostly unreclaimed in Oliver's time, and still of a very dropsical character); to the West it is hard green ground, agreeably broken into little heights, duly fringed with wood, and bearing marks of comfortable long-continued cultivation. Here, on the edge of the firm green land, and looking over into the black marshes with their alder-trees and willow-trees, did Oliver Cromwell pass his young years.

COINCIDENCES.

WHILE Oliver Cromwell was entering himself of Sidney-Sussex College, William Shakespeare was taking his farewell of this world. Oliver's Father had, most likely, come with him; it is but some fifteen miles from Huntingdon; you can go and come in a day. Oliver's Father saw Oliver write in the Album at Cambridge: at Stratford, Shakespeare's Ann Hathaway was weeping over his bed. The first world-great thing that remains of English History, the Literature of Shakespeare, was ending; the second world-great thing that remains of English History, the armed Appeal of Puritanism to the Invisible God of Heaven against many very visible Devils, on Earth and Elsewhere, was, so to speak, beginning. They have their exits and their entrances. And one People, in its time, plays many parts.

Chevalier Florian, in his "Life of Cervantes," has remarked that Shakespeare's death-day, 23d April, 1616, was likewise that of Cervantes at Madrid. "Twenty-third of April" is, sure enough, the authentic Spanish date: but Chevalier Florian has omitted to notice that the English twenty-third is of *Old Style.* The brave Miguel died ten days before Shakespeare; and already lay buried, smoothed right nobly into his long rest. The Historical Student can meditate on these things.

HIS CONVERSION.

IN those years it must be that Dr. Simcott, Physician in Huntingdon, had to do with Oliver's hypochondriac maladies. He told Sir Philip Warwick, unluckily specifying no date, or none that has survived, " he had often been sent for at midnight:" Mr. Cromwell for many years was very "splenetic" (spleen-struck), often thought he was just about to die, and also "had fancies about the Town Cross." Brief intimation, of which the reflecting reader may make a great deal. Samuel Johnson, too, had hypochondrias; all great souls are apt to have, — and to be in thick darkness generally, till the eternal ways and the celestial guiding-stars disclose themselves, and the vague Abyss of Life knit itself up into Firmaments for them. Temptations in the wilderness, Choices of Hercules, and the like, in succinct or loose form, are appointed for every man that will assert a soul in himself and be a man. Let Oliver take comfort in his dark sorrows and melancholies. The quantity of sorrow he has, does it not mean withal the quantity of *sympathy* he has, the quantity of faculty and victory he shall yet have? Our sorrow is the inverted image of our nobleness. The depth of our despair measures what capability and height of claim we have to hope. Black smoke as of Tophet filling all your universe, it can yet by true heart-energy become *flame*, and brilliancy of Heaven. Courage!

It is therefore in these years, undated by History, that we must place Oliver's clear recognition of Calvinistic Christianity; what he, with unspeakable joy, would name his Conversion, — his deliverance from the jaws of Eternal Death. Certainly a grand epoch for a man: properly the one epoch; the turning-point which guides upwards, or guides downwards, him and his activity for evermore. Wilt thou join with the dragons; wilt thou join with the Gods? Of thee, too, the question is asked; — whether by a man in Geneva gown, by a man in " Four surplices at Allhallowtide," with words very imperfect; or by no man and no words, but only by the Silences, by the Eternities, by the Life everlasting and the Death everlasting. That the " Sense of difference between Right and Wrong" had filled all Time and all Space for man, and bodied itself forth into a Heaven and Hell for him; this constitutes the grand feature of those Puritan, Old-Christian Ages;—this is the element which stamps them as Heroic, and has rendered their works great, manlike, fruitful to all generations. It is by far the memorablest achievement of our Species; without that element in some form or other, nothing of Heroic had ever been among us.

For many centuries Catholic Christianity—a fit embodiment of that divine Sense—had been current more or less, making the generations noble: and here in England, in the Century called the Seventeenth, we see the last aspect of it hitherto,—not the last of all, it is to be hoped. Oliver was henceforth a Christian man; believed in God, not on Sundays only, but on all days, in all places, and in all cases.

CHARLES AND THE PARLIAMENT.

SIR OLIVER CROMWELL has faded from the Parliamentary scene into the deep Fen-country, but Oliver Cromwell, Esq. appears there as Member for Huntingdon, at Westminster "on Monday, the 17th of March," 1627-8. This was the Third Parliament of Charles; by much the most notable of all Parliaments till Charles's Long Parliament met, which proved his last.

Having sharply, with swift impetuosity and indignation, dismissed two Parliaments because they would not "supply" him without taking "grievances" along with them; and, meanwhile and afterwards, having failed in every operation foreign and domestic, at Cadiz, at Rhé, at Rochelle; and having failed, too, in getting supplies by unparliamentary methods, Charles "consulted with Sir Robert Cotton what was to be done;" who answered, Summon a Parliament again. So this celebrated Parliament was summoned. It met, as we said, in March, 1628, and continued with one prorogation till March, 1629. The two former Parliaments had sat but a few weeks each, till they were indignantly hurled asunder again; this one continued nearly a year. Wentworth (Strafford) was of this Parliament; Hampden, too, Selden, Pym, Holles, and others known to us; all these had been of former Parliaments as well; Oliver Cromwell, Member for Huntingdon, sat there for the first time.

It is very evident, King Charles, baffled in all his enterprises, and reduced really to a kind of crisis, wished much this Parliament should succeed; and took what he must have thought incredible pains for that end. The poor King strives visibly throughout to control himself, to be soft and patient; inwardly writhing and rustling with royal rage. Unfortunate King, we see him chafing, stamping, — a very fiery steed, but bridled, check-bitted, by innumerable straps and considerations; struggling much to be composed. Alas! it would not do. This Parliament was more Puritanic, more intent on rigorous Law and divine Gospel, than any other had ever been. As indeed all these Parliaments grow strangely in Puritianism; more and ever more earnest rises from the hearts of them all, " O Sacred Majesty, lead us not to Antichrist, to Illegality, to temporal and eternal Perdition!" The Nobility and Gentry of England were then a very strange body of men. The English Squire of the Seventeenth Century clearly appears to have believed in God, not as a figure of speech, but as a very fact, very awful to the heart of the English Squire. " He wore his Bible doctrine round him," says one, "as our Squire wears his shotbelt; went abroad with it, nothing doubting." King Charles was going on his father's course, only with frightful acceleration: he and his respectable Traditions and Notions, clothed in old sheepskin and respectable Church-tippets, were all pulling one way; England and the Eternal Laws pulling another; the rent fast widening till no man could heal it.

This was the celebrated Parliament which framed the Petition of Right, and set London all astir with "bells and bonfires" at the passing thereof; and did other feats not to be particularized here. Across the murkiest element in which any great Entity was ever shown to human creatures, it still rises, after much consideration, to the modern man, in a dim but undeniable manner, as a most brave and noble Parliament. The like of which were worth its weight in diamonds even now; but has grown very unattainable now, next door to incredible now. We have to say that this Parliament chastised sycophant Priests, Mainwaring, Sibthorp, and other Arminian sycophants, a disgrace to God's Church; that it had an eye to other still more elevated Church-sycophants, as the mainspring of all; but was cautious to give offence by naming them. That it carefully "abstained from naming the Duke of Buckingham." That it decided on giving ample subsidies, but not till there were reasonable discussion of grievances. That in manner it was most gentle, soft-spoken, cautious, reverential; and in substance most resolute and valiant. Truly with valiant, patient energy, in a slow, steadfast English manner, it carried, across infinite confused opposition and discouragement, its Petition of Right, and what else it had to carry. Four hundred brave men, — brave men and true, after their sort! One laments to find such a Parliament smothered under Dryasdust's shot-rubbish. The memory of it, could any real memory of it rise upon honorable gentlemen and us, might be admonitory, — would be astonishing at least.

A GENTLEMAN FARMER.

In or soon after 1631, as we laboriously infer from the imbroglio records of poor Noble, Oliver decided on an enlarged sphere of action as a Farmer; sold his properties in Huntingdon, all or some of them; rented certain grazing-lands at St. Ives, five miles down the River, eastward of his native place, and removed thither. The Deed of Sale is dated 7th May, 1631; the properties are specified as in the possession of himself or his Mother; the sum they yielded was £1800. With this sum Oliver stocked his Grazing-Farm at St. Ives. The Mother, we infer, continued to reside at Huntingdon, but withdrawn now from active occupation, in the retirement befitting a widow up in years. There is even some gleam of evidence to that effect: her properties are sold; but Oliver's children born to him at St. Ives are still christened at Huntingdon, in the Church he was used to; which may mean also that their good Grandmother was still there.

Properly this was no change in Oliver's old activities; it was an enlargement of the sphere of them. His Mother still at Huntingdon, within few miles of him, he could still superintend and protect her existence there, while managing his new operations at St. Ives. He continued here till the summer or spring of 1636. A studious imagination may sufficiently construct the figure of his equable life in those years. Diligent grass-farming; mowing, milking, cattle-marketing: add "hypocondria," fits of the blackness of darkness, with glances of the brightness of very Heaven; prayer, religious reading and meditation; household epochs, joys, and cares:— we have a solid, substantial, inoffensive Farmer of St. Ives, hoping to walk with integrity and humble devout diligence through this world; and, by his Maker's infinite mercy, to escape destruction, and find eternal salvation in wider Divine Worlds. This latter, this is the grand clause in his Life, which dwarfs all other clauses. Much wider destinies than he anticipated were appointed him on Earth; but that, in comparison to the alternative of Heaven or Hell to all Eternity, was a mighty small matter.

VESTIGES.

OLIVER, as we observed, has left hardly any memorial of himself at St. Ives. The ground he farmed is still partly capable of being specified, certain records or leases being still in existence. It lies at the lower or South-east end of the Town; a stagnant flat tract of land, extending between the houses or rather kitchen-gardens of St. Ives in that quarter, and the banks of the River, which, very tortuous always, has made a new bend here. If well drained, this land looks as if it would produce abundant grass, but naturally it must be little other than a bog. Tall bushy ranges of willow-trees and the like, at present, divide it into fields; the River, not visible till you are close on it, bounding them all to the South. At the top of the fields next to the Town is an ancient massive Barn, still used as such; the people call it "Cromwell's Barn;" — and nobody can prove that it was not his! It was evidently some ancient man's or series of ancient men's.

Quitting St. Ives Fen-ward or Eastward, the last house of all, which stands on your right hand among gardens, seemingly the best house in the place, and called Slepe Hall, is confidently pointed out as "Oliver's House." It is indisputably Slepe-Hall House, and Oliver's Farm was rented from the estate of Slepe Hall. It is at present used for a Boarding-school: the worthy inhabitants believe it to be Oliver's; and even point out his "Chapel" or secret Puritan Sermon-room in the lower story of the house: no Sermon-room, as you may well discern, but to appearance some sort of scullery or wash-house or bake-house. "It was here he used to preach," say they. Courtesy forbids you to answer, "Never!" But in fact there is no likelihood that this was Oliver's House at all: in its present state it does not seem to be a century old; and originally, as is like, it must have served as residence to the Proprietors of Slepe-Hall estate, not to the Farmer of a part thereof. Tradition makes a sad blur of Oliver's memory in his native country! We know, and shall know, only this, for certain here, that Oliver farmed part or whole of these Slepe-Hall Lands, over which the human feet can still walk with assurance; past which the River Ouse still slumberously rolls towards Earith Bulwark and the Fen-country. Here of a certainty Oliver did walk and look about him habitually during those five years from 1631 to 1636; a man studious of many temporal and many eternal things. His cattle grazed here, his ploughs tilled here, the heavenly skies and infernal abysses overarched and underarched him here. . . . .

How he lived at St. Ives: how he saluted men on the streets; read Bibles; sold cattle; and walked, with heavy footfall and many thoughts, through the Market Green or old narrow lanes in St. Ives, by the shore of the black Ouse River, — shall be left to the reader's imagination. There is in this man talent for farming; there are thoughts enough, thoughts bounded by the Ouse River, thoughts that go beyond Eternity, — and a great black sea of things that he has never yet been able to *think*.

SHIPMONEY.

On the very day while Oliver Cromwell was writing this Letter at St. Ives, two obscure individuals, " Peter Aldridge and Thomas Lane, Assessors of Shipmoney," over in Buckinghamshire, had assembled a Parish Meeting in the Church of Great Kimble, to assess, and rate the Shipmoney of the said Parish: there, in the cold weather, at the foot of the Chiltern Hills, " 11 January, 1635," the Parish did attend, " John Hampden, Esquire," at the head of them, and by a

Return still extant, refused to pay the same or any portion thereof, — witness the above "Assessors," witness also two "Parish Constables" whom we remit from such unexpected celebrity. John Hampden's share for this Parish is thirty-one shillings and sixpence: for another Parish it is twenty shillings; on which latter sum, not on the former, John Hampden was tried.

THE SHIPMONEY TRIAL.

In the end of that same year [1637] there had risen all over England huge rumors concerning the Shipmoney Trial at London. On the 6th of November, 1637, this important Process of Mr. Hampden's began. Learned Mr. St. John, a dark tough man, of the toughness of leather, spake with irrefragable law-eloquence, law-logic, for three days running, on Mr. Hampden's side; and learned Mr. Holborn for three other days; — preserved yet by Rushworth in acres of typography, unreadable now to all mortals. For other learned gentlemen, tough as leather, spoke on the opposite side; and learned judges animadverted, at endless length, amid the expectancy of men. With brief pauses, the Trial lasted for three weeks and three days. Mr. Hampden became the most famous man in England, — by accident partly. The sentence was not delivered till April, 1638; and then it went against Mr. Hampden: judgment in Exchequer ran to this effect, " *Consideratum est per eosdem Barones quod prædictus Johannes Hampden de iisdem viginti solidis oneretur,*" — He must pay the Twenty shillings, — "*et inde satisfaciat.*" No hope in Law-Courts, then; Petition of Right and *Tallagio non concedendo* have become an old song.

BATTLE OF NASEBY.

THE old Hamlet of Naseby stands yet, on its old hill-top, very much as it did in Saxon days, on the Northwestern border of Northamptonshire, some seven or eight miles from Market-Harborough in Leicestershire, nearly on a line, and nearly midway, between that Town and Daventry. A peaceable old Hamlet, of some eight hundred souls; clay cottages for laborers, but neatly thatched and swept; smith's shop, saddler's shop, beer shop, all in order; forming a kind of square, which leads off Southwards into two long streets: the old Church, with its graves, stands in the centre, the truncated spire finishing itself with a strange old Ball, held up by rods; a "hollow copper Ball, which came from Boulogne in Henry the Eighth's time," — which has, like Hudibras's breeches, "been at the Siege of Bullen." The ground is upland, moorland, though now growing corn; was not enclosed till the last generation, and is still somewhat bare of wood. It stands nearly in the heart of England: gentle Dulness, taking a turn at etymology, sometimes derives it from *Navel;* "Navesby, quasi *Navelsby,* from being," &c.: Avon Well, the distinct source of Shakespeare's Avon, is on the Western slope of the high grounds; Nen and Welland, streams leading towards Cromwell's Fen-country, begin to gather themselves from boggy places on the Eastern side. The grounds, as we say, lie high; and are still, in their new subdivisions, known by the name of "Hills," "Rutput Hill," "Mill Hill," "Dust Hill," and the like, precisely as in Rushworth's time: but they are not properly hills at all; they are broad blunt clayey masses, swelling towards and from each other, like indolent waves of a sea, sometimes of miles in extent.

It was on this high moor-ground, in the centre of England, that King Charles, on the 14th of June, 1645, fought his last Battle; dashed fiercely against the New-Model Army, which he had despised till then; and saw himself shivered utterly to ruin thereby. "Prince Rupert, on the King's right wing, charged *up* the hill, and carried all before him;" but Lieutenant-General Cromwell charged down hill on the other wing, likewise carrying all before him,— and did *not* gallop off the field to plunder. He, Cromwell, ordered thither by the Parliament, had arrived from the Association two days before, "amid shouts from the whole Army:" he had the ordering of the Horse this morning. Prince Rupert, on returning from his plunder, finds the King's Infantry a ruin; prepares to charge again with the rallied Cavalry; but the Cavalry, too, when it came to the point, "broke all asunder," never to reassemble more. The chase went through Harborough, where the King had already been that morning, when in an evil hour he turned back, to revenge some "surprise of an outpost at Naseby the night before," and give the Roundheads battle.

Ample details of this Battle, and of the movements prior and posterior to it, are to be found in Sprigge, or copied with some abridgment into Rushworth; who has also copied a strange old Plan of the Battle; half-plan, half-picture, which the Sale-Catalogues are very chary of, in the case of Sprigge. By assiduous attention, aided by this Plan, as the old names yet stick to their localities, the narrative can still be, and has lately been, pretty accurately verified, and the Figure of the old Battle dimly brought back again. The reader shall imagine it, for the present. On the crown of Naseby Height stands a modern Battle-monument; but, by an unlucky oversight, it is above a mile to the east of where the Battle really was. There are, likewise, two modern Books about Naseby and its Battle, both of them without value.

The Parliamentary Army stood ranged on the height still partly called "Mill Hill," as, in Rushworth's time, a mile and half from Naseby; the King's Army, on a parallel "Hill," its back to Harborough, with the wide table of upland now named *Broad Moor* between them, where indeed the main brunt of the action still clearly enough shows itself to have been. There are hollow spots, of a rank vegetation, scattered over that Broad Moor, which are understood to have once been burial *mounds*, some of which, one to my knowledge, have been, with more or less of sacrilege, verified as such. A friend of mine has in his cabinet two ancient grinder-teeth, dug lately from that ground, and waits for an opportunity to rebury them there. — Sound, effectual grinders, one of them very large; which ate their breakfast on the fourteenth morning of June, two hundred years ago, and, except to be clinched once in grim battle, had never work to do more in this world! "A stack of dead bodies, perhaps about a hundred, had been buried in this Trench, piled, as in a wall, a man's length thick; the skeletons lay in courses, the heads of one course to the heels of the next; one figure, by the strange position of the bones, gave us the hideous notion of its having been thrown in *before* death. We did not proceed far;—perhaps some half-dozen skeletons. The bones were treated with all piety, watched rigorously over Sunday, till they could be covered in again." Sweet friends, for Jesus' sake forbear!

At this Battle, Mr. John Rushworth, our Historical Rushworth, had, unexpectedly, for some instants, sight of a very famous person. Mr. John is Secretary to Fairfax, and they have placed him to-day among the Baggage-wagons, near Naseby Hamlet, above a mile from the fighting, where he waits in an anxious manner. It is known how Prince Rupert broke our left wing while Cromwell was breaking their left. "A gentleman of public employment, in the late service near Naseby," writes next day, "Harborough, 15th June, 2 in the morning," a rough graphic Letter in the Newspapers, wherein is this sentence: —

* * * "A party of theirs that broke through the left wing of horse, came quite behind the rear to our Train, the Leader of them being a person somewhat in habit like the General, in a red montero, as the Genèral had. He came as a friend; our commander of the guard of the Train went with his hat in his hand, and asked him, How the day went? thinking it had been the General: the Cavalier, who we since heard was Rupert, asked him and the rest, If they would have quarter? They cried No; gave fire, and instantly beat them off. It was a happy deliverance,"— without doubt.

There were taken here a good few "ladies of quality in carriages," — and above a hundred Irish ladies not of quality, tattery camp-followers, " with long skean-knives about a foot in length," which they well knew how to use, upon whom, I fear, the Ordinance against Papists pressed hard this day. The King's Carriage was also taken, with a Cabinet and many Royal Autographs in it, which, when printed, made a sad impression against his Majesty, — gave, in fact, a most melancholy view of the veracity of his Majesty. " On the word of a King," all was lost!

———◆———

BRIDGET CROMWELL'S WEDDING

AND now, dated on the Monday before, at Holton, a country Parish in those parts, there is this still legible in the old Church Register, — intimately interesting to some friends of ours! " HENRY IRETON, Commissary-General to Sir Thomas Fairfax, and BRIDGET, Daughter to Oliver Cromwell, Lieutenant-General of the Horse, to the said Sir Thomas Fairfax, were married, by Mr. Dell, in the Lady Whorwood her house in Holton, June 15th, 1646.— ALBAN EALES, Rector."

Ireton, we are to remark, was one of Fairfax's Commissioners on the Treaty for surrendering Oxford, and busy under the walls there at present. Holton is some five miles east of the City; Holton House, we guess, by various indications, to have been Fairfax's own quarter. Dell, already and afterwards well known, was the General's Chaplain at this date. Of "the Lady Whorwood" I have traces, rather in the Royalist direction; her strong moated House, very useful to Fairfax in those weeks, still stands conspicuous in that region, though now under new figure and ownership; drawbridge become *fixed*, deep ditch now dry, moated island changed into a flower-garden; — "rebuilt in 1807." Fairfax's lines, we observe, extended "from Headington Hill to Marston," several miles in advance of Holton House, then "from Marston," across the Cherwell, and over from that to the Isis on the North side of the City"; southward, and elsewhere, the besieged, "by a dam at St. Clement's Bridge, had laid the country all under water": in such scenes, with the treaty just ending, and general peace like to follow, did Ireton welcome his bride, — a brave young damsel of twenty-one, escorted, doubtless, by her Father, among others, to the Lord General's house, and there, by Rev. Mr. Dell, solemnly handed over to new destinies!

DEATH WARRANT.

THE Trial of Charles Stuart falls not to be described in this place: the deep meanings that lie in it cannot be so much as glanced at here. Oliver Cromwell attends in the High Court of Justice at every session except one; Fairfax sits only in the first. Ludlow, Whalley, Walton, names known to us, are also constant attendants in that High Court, during that long-memorable Month of January, 1649.

The King is thrice brought to the Bar; refuses to plead, comports himself with royal dignity, with royal haughtiness, strong in his divine right; "smiles" contemptuously, "looks with an austere countenance;" does not seem, till the very last, to have fairly believed that they would dare to sentence him. But they were men sufficiently provided with daring; men, we are bound to see, who sat there as in the Presence of the Maker of all men, as executing the judgments of Heaven above, and had not the fear of any man or thing on the Earth below. Bradshaw said to the King, "Sir, you are not permitted to issue out in these discoursings. This Court is satisfied of its authority. No Court will bear to hear its authority questioned in that manner."— "Clerk, read the Sentence!"

And so, under date, Monday 29th January, 1648-9, there is this stern Document to be introduced; not specifically of Oliver's composition; but expressing in every letter of it the conviction of Oliver's heart, in this, one of his most important appearances on the stage of earthly life.

To Colonel Francis Hacker, Colonel Huncks, and Lieutenant-Colonel Phayr, and to every one of them.

At the High Court of Justice for the Trying and Judging of Charles Stuart, King of England, 29th January, 1648.

WHEREAS Charles Stuart, King of England, is and standeth convicted, attainted and condemned of High Treason and other high Crimes; and Sentence upon Saturday last was pronounced against him by this Court, To be put to death by the severing of his head from his body; of which Sentence execution yet remaineth to be done:

These are therefore to will and require you to see the said Sentence executed, in the open street before Whitehall, upon the morrow, being the Thirtieth day of this instant month of January, between the hours of Ten in the morning and Five in the afternoon, with full effect. And for so doing, this shall be your warrant.

And these are to require all Officers and Soldiers, and others the good People of this Nation of England, to be assisting unto you in this service.

Given under our hands and seals.
JOHN BRADSHAW,
THOMAS GREY, " Lord Groby,"
OLIVER CROMWELL.
(" And Fifty-six others.")

" *Tetræ belluæ, ac molossis suis ferociores.* Hideous monsters, more ferocious than their own mastiffs!" shrieks Saumaise; shrieks all the world, in unmelodious soul-confusing diapason of distraction, — happily at length grown very faint in our day. The truth is, no modern reader can conceive the then atrocity, ferocity, unspeakability of this fact. First, after long reading in the old dead Pamphlets does one see the magnitude of it. To be equalled, nay to be preferred think some, in point of horror, to " the Crucifixion of Christ." Alas, in these irreverent times of ours, if all the Kings of Europe were cut in pieces at one swoop, and flung in heaps in St. Margaret's Churchyard on the same day, the emotion would, in strict arithmetical truth, be small in comparison! We know it not, this atrocity of the English Regicides; shall never know it. I reckon it perhaps the most daring action any Body of Men to be met with in History ever, with clear consciousness, deliberately set themselves to do. Dread Phantoms, glaring supernal on you, — when once they are quelled and their light snuffed out, none knows the terror of the Phantom! The Phantom is a poor paper-lantern with a candle-end in it, which any whipster dare now beard.

A certain Queen in some South-Sea Island, I have read in Missionary Books, had been converted to Christianity did not any longer believe in the old gods. She assembled her people; said to them, "My faithful People, the gods do *not* dwell in that burning mountain in the centre of our Isle. That is not God; no, that is a common burning-mountain, — mere culinary fire burning under peculiar circumstances. See, I will walk before you to that burning-mountain; will empty my wash-bowl into it, cast my slipper over it, defy it to the uttermost; and stand the consequences!" She walked accordingly, this South-Sea Heroine, nerved to the sticking-place; her people following in pale horror and expectancy: she did her experiment; — and, I am told, they have truer notions of the gods in that Island ever since! Experiment which it is now very easy to *repeat*, and very needless. Honor to the Brave who deliver us from Phantom-dynasties, in South-Sea Islands and in North!

This action of the English Regicides did in effect strike a damp like death through the heart of Flunkeyism universally in this world. Whereof Flunkeyism, Cant, Cloth-worship, or whatever ugly name it have, has gone about incurably sick ever since; and is now at length, in these generations, very rapidly dying. The like of which action will not be needed for a thousand years again. Needed, alas — not till a new genuine Hero-worship has arisen, has perfected itself; and had time to generate into a Flunkeyism and Cloth-worship again! Which I take to be a very long date indeed.

MR. MILTON.

ON which same evening, [March 13, 1468,] furthermore, one discerns in a faint but an authentic manner, certain dim gentlemen of the highest authority, young Sir Harry Vane to appearance one of them, repairing to the lodging of one

Mr. Milton, "a small house in Holborn, which opens backwards into Lincoln's Inn Fields; to put an official question to him there." Not a doubt of it they saw Mr. John this evening. In the official Book this yet stands legible:
"*Die Martis*, 13° *Martii*, 1648." " That it is referred to the same Committee," Whitlocke, Vane, Lord Lisle, Earl of Denbigh, Harry Marten, Mr. Lisle, " or any two of them, to speak with Mr. Milton, to know, Whether he will be employed as Secretary for the Foreign Languages? and to report to the Council." I have authority to say that Mr. Milton, thus unexpectedly applied to, consents; is formally appointed on Thursday next; makes his proof-shot, " to the Senate of Hamburgh," about a week hence; — and gives, and continues to give, great satisfaction to that Council, to me, and to the whole Nation now, and to all Nations! Such romance lies in the State-Paper Office.

―――――♦―――――

THE LEVELLERS — ENGLISH SANSCULOTTISM.

WHILE Miss Dorothy Mayor is choosing her wedding-dresses, and Richard Cromwell is looking forward to a life of Arcadian felicity now near at hand, there has turned up for Richard's Father and other parties interested, on the public side of things, a matter of very different complexion, requiring to be instantly dealt with in the interim. The matter of the class called Levellers; concerning which we must now say a few words.

In 1647 there were Army Adjutators; and among some of them wild notions afloat, as to the swift attainability of Perfect Freedom, civil and religious, and a practical Millennium on this Earth; notions which required, in the Rendezvous at Corkbushfield, " Rendezvous of Ware," as they oftenest call it, to be very resolutely trodden out. Eleven chief mutineers were ordered from the ranks in that Rendezvous; were condemned by swift Court-Martial to die; and Trooper Arnald, one of them, was accordingly shot there and then; which extinguished the mutiny for that time. War since, and Justice on Delinquents, England made a Free Commonwealth, and such like, have kept the Army busy; but a deep republican leaven, working all along among these men, breaks now again into very formidable development. As the following brief glimpses and excerpts may satisfy an attentive reader who will spread them out, to the due expansion, in his mind. Take first this glimpse into the civil province; and discern with amazement, a whole submarine world of Calvinistic Sansculottism, Five-point Charter, and the Rights of Man, threatening to emerge almost two centuries before its time.

"The Council of State," says Whitlocke, just while Mr. Barton is boggling about the Hursley Marriage-settlements, "has intelligence of certain *Levellers* appearing at St. Margaret's Hill, near Cobham in Surrey, and at St. George's Hill," in the same quarter: "that they were digging the ground, and sowing it with roots and beans. One Everard, once of the Army, who terms himself a Prophet, is the chief of them:" one Winstanley is another chief. They were Thirty men, and said that they should be shortly Four-thousand. They invited all to come in and help them; and promised them meat, drink, and clothes. They threatened to pull down Park-pales, and to lay all open; and threaten the neighbors that they will shortly make them all come up to the hills and work." These infatuated persons, beginning a new era in this headlong manner on the chalk hills of Surrey, are laid hold of by certain Justices, "by the country people," and also by "two troops of horse;" and complain loudly of such treatment; appealing to all men whether it be fair. This is the account they give of themselves when brought before the General some days afterwards:

"*April* 20th, 1649. Everard and Winstanley, the chief of those that digged at St. George's Hill in Surrey, came to the General and made a large declaration, to justify their proceedings. Everard said, He was of the race of the Jews," as most men called Saxon, and other, properly are; " That all the Liberties of the People were lost by the coming in of William the Conquerer; and that, ever since, the People of God had lived under tyranny and oppression worse than that of our Forefathers under the Egyptians. But now the time of deliverance was at hand; and God would bring His People out of this slavery, and restore them to their freedom in enjoying the fruits and benefits of the Earth. And that there had lately appeared to him, Everard, a vision; which bade him, Arise and dig and plough the Earth, and receive the fruits thereof. That their intent is to restore the Creation to its former condition. That as God had promised to make the barren land fruitful, so now what they did, was to restore the ancient Community of enjoying the Fruits of the Earth, and to distribute the benefit thereof to the poor and needy, and to feed the hungry and clothe the naked. That they intend not to meddle with any man's property, nor to break down any pales or enclosures," in spite of reports to the contrary; " but only to meddle with what is common and untilled, and to make it fruitful for the use of man. That the time will suddenly be, when all men shall willingly come in and give up their lands and estates, and submit to this Community of Goods."

These are the principles of Everard, Winstanley, and the poor Brotherhood, seemingly Saxon, but properly of the race of the Jews, who were found dibbling beans on St. George's Hill, under the clear April skies in 1649, and hastily bringing in a new era in that manner. " And for all such as will come in and work with them, they shall have meat, drink, and clothes, which is all that is necessary to the life of man: and as for money, there is not any need of it; nor of clothes more than to cover nakedness." For the rest, "That they will not defend themselves by arms, but will submit unto authority, and wait till the promised opportunity be offered, which they conceive to be at hand. And that as their forefathers lived in tents, so it would be suitable to their condition, now to live in the same.

"While they were before the General, they stood with their hats on; and being demanded the reason thereof, they said, Because he was but their fellow-creature. Being asked the meaning of that phrase, Give honor to whom honor is due, — they said, Your mouths shall be stopped that ask such a question."

Dull Bulstrode hath "set down this the more largely because it was the beginning of the appearance" of an extensive levelling doctrine, much to be "avoided" by judicious persons, seeing it is "a weak persuasion." The germ of Quakerism, and much else, is curiously visible here. But let us look now at the military phasis of the matter; where "a weak persuasion," mounted on cavalry horses, with sabres and fire-arms in its hand, may become a very perilous one.

Friday, 20th *April*, 1649. The Lieutenant-General has consented to go to Ireland; the City also will lend money; and now this Friday the Council of the Army meets at Whitehall to decide what regiments shall go on that service. "After a solemn seeking of God by prayer," they agree that it shall be by lot: tickets are put into a hat, a child draws them: the regiments, fourteen of foot and fourteen of horse, are decided on in this manner. "The officers on whom the lot fell, in all the twenty-eight regiments, expressed much cheerfulness at the decision." The officers did: — but the common men are by no means all of that humor. The common men, blown upon by Lilburn, and his five small Beagles, have notions about Engand's *new*

Chains, about the Hunting of Foxes from Triploe Heath, and in fact ideas concerning the capability that lies in man, and in a free Commonwealth, which are of the most alarming description.

Thursday, 26th *April.* This night at the Bull in Bishopsgate there has an alarming mutiny broken out in a troop of Whalley's regiment there. Whalley's men are not allotted for Ireland: but they refuse to quit London, as they are ordered; they want this and that first; they seize their colors from the Cornet, who is lodged at the Bull there: — the General and the Lieutenant-General have to hasten thither; quell them, pack them forth on their march; seizing fifteen of them first, to be tried by Court-Martial. Tried by instant Court-Martial, five of them are found guilty, doomed to die, but pardoned; and one of them, Trooper Lockyer, is doomed and not pardoned. Trooper Lockyer is shot, in Paul's Churchyard, on the morrow. A very brave young man, they say; though but three-and-twenty, " he has served seven years in these Wars," ever since the Wars began. " Religious," too, " of excellent parts and much beloved;" — but with hot notions as to human Freedom, and the rate at which the millenniums are attainable, poor Lockyer! He falls shot in Paul's Churchyard on Friday, amid the tears of men and women. Paul's Cathedral, we remark, is now a Horseguard; horses stamp in the Canons' stalls there: and Paul's Cross itself, as smacking of Popery, where in fact Alablaster once preached flat Popery, is swept altogether away, and its leaden roof melted into bullets, or mixed with tin for culinary pewter. Lockyer's corpse is watched and wept over, not without prayer, in the eastern regions of the City, till a new week come; and on Monday, this is what we see advancing westward by way of funeral to him.

" About one hundred went before the Corpse, five or six in a file; the Corpse was then brought, with six trumpets sounding a soldier's knell; then the Trooper's Horse came, clothed all over in mourning, and led by a footman. The Corpse was adorned with bundles of Rosemary, one half stained in blood; and the Sword of the deceased along with them. Some thousands followed in rank and file: all had sea-green-and-black ribbons tied on their hats, and to their breasts: and the women brought up the rear. At the new Churchyard in Westminster, some thousands more of the better sort met them, who thought not fit to march through the City. Many looked upon this funeral as an affront to the Parliament and Army; others called these people 'Levellers;' but they took no notice of any one's sayings."

That was the end of Trooper Lockyer: six trumpets wailing stern music through London streets; Rosemaries and Sword half-dipped in blood; funeral of many thousands in seagreen Ribbons and black: — testimony of a weak persuasion, now looking somewhat perilous. Lieutenant-Colonel Lilburn, and his five small Beagles, now in a kind of loose arrest under the Lieutenant of the Tower, make haste to profit by the general emotion; publish on the 1st of May *their* " Agreement of the People," — their Bentham-Sieyes Constitution:- Annual very exquisite Parliament, and other Lilburn apparatus; whereby the Perfection of Human Nature will with a maximum of rapidity be secured, and a millennium straightway arrive, sings the Lilburn Oracle.

May 9th. Richard Cromwell is safe wedded; Richard's Father is reviewing troops in Hyde Park, "seagreen colors in some of their hats." The Lieutenant-General speaks earnestly to them. Has not the Parliament been diligent, doing its best? It has punished Delinquents; it has voted, in these very days, resolutions for dissolving itself and assembling future Parliaments. It has protected trade; got a good Navy afloat. You soldiers, there is exact payment provided for you. Martial Law? Death, or other punishment of mutineers? Well! Whoever cannot stand Martial Law is not fit to be a soldier: *his* best plan will be to lay down his arms; he shall have his ticket, and get his arrears as we others do, — we that still mean to fight against the enemies of England and this Cause. — One trooper showed signs of insolence; the Lieutenant-General suppressed him by rigor and by clemency: the seagreen ribbons were torn from such hats as had them. The humor of the men is not the most perfect. This Review was on Wednesday: Lilburn and his five small Beagles are, on Saturday, committed close Prisoners to the Tower, each rigorously to a cell of his own.

It is high time. For now the flame has caught the ranks of the Army itself, in Oxfordshire, in Gloucestershire, at Salisbury, where head-quarters are; and rapidly there is, on all hands, a dangerous conflagration blazing out. In Oxfordshire, one Captain Thompson, not known to us before, has burst from his quarters at Banbury, with a Party of Two-Hundred, in these same days; has sent forth his *England's Standard Advanced;* insisting passionately on the *New Chains* we are fettered with; indignantly demanding swift perfection of Human Freedom, justice on the murderers of Lockyer and Arnald; — threatening that if a hair of Lilburn and the five small Beagles be hurt, he will avenge it "seventy-and-seven fold." This Thompson's Party, swiftly attacked by his Colonel, is broken within the week; he himself escapes with a few, and still roves up and down. To join whom, or to communicate with Gloucestershire where help lies, there has, in the interim, open mutiny, "above a Thousand strong," with subalterns, with a Cornet Thompson brother of the Captain, but without any leader of mark, broken out at Salisbury: the General and Lieutenant-General, with what force can be raised, are hastening thitherward in all speed. Now were the time for Lieutenant-Colonel Lilburn; now or never might noisy John do some considerable injury to the Cause he has at heart: but he sits, in these critical hours, fast within stone walls!

Monday, 14th May. All Sunday the General and Lieutenant-General marched in full speed, by Alton, by Andover, towards Salisbury; the mutineers, hearing of them, start northward for Buckinghamshire, then for Berkshire; the General and Lieutenant-General turning also northward after them in hot chase. The mutineers arrive at Wantage; make for Oxfordshire by Newbridge; find the Bridge already seized; cross higher up by swimming; get to Burford, very weary, and "turn out their horses to grass; Fairfax and Cromwell still following in hot speed, a march of near fifty miles that Monday. What boots it, there is no leader, noisy John is sitting fast within stone walls! The mutineers lie asleep in Burford, their horses out at grass; the Lieutenant-General, having rested at a safe distance since dark, bursts into Burford as the clocks are striking midnight. He has beset some hundreds of the mutineers, " who could only fire some shots out of windows;"— has dissipated the mutiny, trodden down the Levelling Principle out of English affairs once more. Here is the last scene of the business; the rigorous Court-Martial having now sat; the decimated doomed Mutineers being placed on the leads of the Church to see.

Thursday, 17th May. — " This day in Burford Churchyard, Cornet Thompson, brother to Thompson the chief leader, was brought to the place of execution; and expressed himself to this purpose, That it was just what did befall him; that God did not own the ways he went; that he had offended the General: he desired the prayers of the people; and told the soldiers who were appointed to shoot him, that when he held out his hands, they should do their duty. And accordingly he was immediately, after the sign given, shot to death. Next after him was a corporal, brought to the same place of execution; where, looking upon his fellow-mutineers, he set his back against the wall; and bade them who were appointed to shoot, 'Shoot!' and died desperately. The third, being also a corporal, was brought to the same place; and without the least acknowledgment of error, or show of fear, he pulled off his doublet, standing a pretty distance from the wall; and bade the soldiers do their duty; looking them in the face till they gave fire, not showing the least kind of terror or fearfulness of spirit." So die the Leveller Corporals; strong they, after their sort, for the Liberties of England; resolute to the very death. Misguided Corporals! But History, which has wept for a misguided Charles Stuart, and blubbered, in the most copious helpless manner, near two centuries now, whole floods of brine, enough to salt the Herring fishery, — will not refuse these poor Corporals also her tributary sigh. With Arnald of the Rendezvous at Ware, with Lockyer of the Bull in Bishopsgate, and other misguided martyrs to the Liberties of England then and since, may they sleep well!

Cornet Dean who now came forward, as the next to be shot, expressed penitence; got pardon from the General: and there was no more shooting. Lieutenant-General Cromwell went into the Church, called down the Decimated of the Mutineers; rebuked, admonished; said, the General in his mercy had forgiven them. Misguided men, would you ruin this Cause, which marvellous Providences have so confirmed to us to be the Cause of God? Go, repent, and rebel no more lest a worse thing befall you! "They wept," says the old Newspaper; they retired to the Devizes for a time; were then restored to their regiments, and marched cheerfully for Ireland. Captain Thompson, the Cornet's brother, the first of all the Mutineers, he too, a few days afterwards, was fallen in with in Northamptonshire, still mutinous; his men took quarter; he himself "fled to a wood," fired and fenced there, and again desperately fired, declared he would never yield alive; — whereupon "a Corporal with seven bullets in his carbine" ended Captain Thompson too; and this formidable conflagration, to the last glimmer of it, was extinct.

Sansculottism, as we said above, has to lie submerged for almost two centuries yet. Levelling, in the practical civil or military provinces of English things, is forbidden to be. In the spiritual provinces it cannot be forbidden; for there it everywhere already is. It ceases dibbling beans on St. George's Hill near Cobham; ceases galloping in mutiny across the Isis to Burford; takes into Quakerisms, and kingdoms which are not of this world. My poor friend Dryasdust lamentably tears his hair over the intolerance of that old Time to Quakerism and such like; if Dryasdust had seen the dibbling on St. George's Hill, the threatened fall of "Park-pales," and the gallop to Burford, he would reflect that conviction in an earnest age means, not lengthy Spouting in Exeter-hall, but rapid silent Practice on the face of the Earth; and would perhaps leave his poor hair alone.

SCOTCH PURITANISM.

THE faults or misfortunes of the Scotch People, in their Puritan business, are many; but, properly their grand fault is this, That they have produced for it no sufficiently heroic man among them. No man that has an eye to see beyond the letter and the rubric; to discern, across many consecrated rubrics of the Past, the inarticulate divineness too of the Present and the Future, and dare all perils in the faith of that! With Oliver Cromwell born a Scotchman, with a Hero King and a unanimous Hero Nation at his back, it might have been far otherwise. With Oliver born Scotch, one sees not but the whole world might have become Puritan; might have struggled, yet a long while, to fashion itself according to that divine Hebrew Gospel, — to the exclusion of other Gospels not Hebrew, which also are divine, and will have their share of fulfilment here! — But of such issue there is no danger. Instead of inspired Olivers, glowing with direct insight and noble daring, we have Argyles, Loudons, and narrow, more or less opaque persons of the Pedant species. Committees of Estates, Committees of Kirks, much tied-up in formulas, both of them: a bigoted Theocracy *without* the Inspiration; which is a very hopeless phenomenon indeed. The Scotch People are all willing, eager of heart; asking, Whitherward? But the Leaders stand aghast at the new forms of danger, and in a vehement discrepant manner some calling, Halt! others calling, Backward! others, Forward! — huge confusion ensues. Confusion which will need an Oliver to repress it; to bind it up in tight manacles, if not otherwise; and say, "There, sit there and consider thyself a little!"

The meaning of the Scotch Covenant was, That God's divine Law of the Bible should be put in practice in these Nations; verily *it*, and not the Four Surplices at Allhallowtide, or any Formula of cloth or sheepskin here or elsewhere which merely pretended to be it: but then the Covenant says expressly, there is to be a Stuart King in the business: we cannot do without our Stuart King! Given a divine Law of the Bible on one hand, and a Stuart King, Charles First or Charles Second, on the other: alas, did History ever present a more irreducible case of equations in this world? I pity the poor Scotch Pedant Governors, still more the poor Scotch People, who had no other to follow! Nay, as for that, the People did get through in the end, such was their indomitable pious constancy, and other worth and fortune: and Presbytery became a Fact among them, to the whole length possible for it; not without endless results. But for the poor Governors this irreducible case proved, as it were, fatal! They have never since, if we will look narrowly at it, governed Scotland, or even well known that they were there to attempt governing it. Once they lay on Dunse Hill, "each Earl with his Regiment of Tenants round him," *For Christ's Crown and Covenant;* and never since had they any noble National act, which it was given them to do. Growing desperate of Christ's Crown and Covenant, they, in the next generation, when our *Annus Mirabilis* arrived, hurried up to Court, looking out for other Crowns and Covenants; deserted Scotland and her Cause, somewhat basely; took to *booing* and *booing* for Causes of their own, unhappy mortals;—and Scotland and all Causes that were Scotland's have had to go on very much without *them* ever since!

THE BATTLE OF DUNBAR.

THE small Town of Dunbar stands, high and windy, looking down over its herring-boats, over its grim old Castle now much honeycombed,—on one of those projecting rock promontories with which that shore of the Frith of Forth is niched and vandyked, as far as the eye can reach. A beautiful sea; good land too, now that the plougher understands his trade; a grim niched barrier of whinstone sheltering it from the chafings and tumblings of the big blue German Ocean. Seaward, St. Abb's Head, of whinstone, bounds your horizon to the east, not very far off; west, close by, is the deep bay, and fishy little village of Belhaven: the gloomy Bass and other rock-islets, and farther the Hills of Fife, and foreshadows of the Highlands, are visible as you look seaward. From the bottom of Belhaven Bay to that of the next sea-bight, St. Abb's ward, the Town and its environs form a peninsula. Along the base of which peninsula, "not much above a mile and a half from sea to sea," Oliver Cromwell's Army, on Monday, the 2d of September, 1650, stands ranked, with its tents and Town behind it, — in very forlorn circumstances. This now is all the ground that Oliver is lord of in Scotland. His Ships lie in the offing, with biscuit and transport for him; but visible elsewhere in the Earth no help.

Landward, as you look from the Town of Dunbar there rises, some short mile off, a dusky continent of barren heath Hills; the Lammermoor, where only mountain-sheep can be at home. The crossing of *which*, by any of its boggy passes, and brawling stream-courses, no Army, hardly a solitary Scotch Packman could attempt, in such weather. To the edge of these Lammermoor Heights, David Lesley has betaken himself; lies now along the outmost spur of them, — a long Hill of considerable height, which the Dunbar people call the Dun, Doon, or sometimes for fashion's sake the Down, adding to it the Teutonic *hill* likewise, though *Dun* itself in old Celtic signifies Hill. On this Doon Hill lies David Lesley, with the victorious Scotch Army, upwards of Twenty thousand strong; with the Committees of Kirk and Estates, the chief Dignitaries of the Country, and in fact the flower of what the pure Covenant in this the Twelfth year of its existence can still bring forth. There lies he, since Sunday night, on the top and slope of this Doon Hill, with the impassable heath continents behind him: embraces, as within outspread tiger-claws, the base-line of Oliver's Dunbar Peninsula; waiting what Oliver will do. Cockburnspath with its ravines has been seized on Oliver's left, and made impassable; behind Oliver is the sea; in front of him Lesley, Doon Hill, and the heath-continent of Lammermoor. Lesley's force is of Three-and-twenty thousand, in spirits as of men chasing: Oliver's about half as many, in spirits as of men chased. What is to become of Oliver? . . . .

The base of Oliver's Dunbar Peninsula, as we have called it (or Dunbar Pinfold, where he is now hemmed in, upon "an entanglement very difficult"), extends from Belhaven Bay on his right, to Brocksmouth House on his left; "about a mile and a half from sea to sea:" Brocksmouth House, the Earl (now Duke) of Roxburgh's mansion, which still stands there, his soldiers now occupy as their extreme post on the left. As its name iudicates, it is the *mouth* or issue of a small Rivulet, or *Burn* called *Brock*, *Brocksburn;* which, springing from the Lammermoor, and skirting David Lesley's Doon Hill, finds its egress here, into the sea. The reader who would form an image to himself of the great Tuesday, 3d of September, 1650, at Dunbar, must note well this little *Burn*. It runs in a deep grassy glen, which the South-country Officers in those old Pamphlets describe as a "deep *ditch,* forty feet in depth, and about as many in width," — ditch dug out by the little Brook itself, and carpeted with greensward, in the course of long thousands of years. It runs pretty close by the foot of Doon Hill; forms, from this point to the sea, the boundary of Oliver's position: his force is arranged in battle-order along the left bank of this Brocksburn, and its grassy glen; he is busied all Monday, he and his Officers, in ranking them there. "Before sunrise on Monday" Lesley sent down his horse from the Hill-top, to occupy the other side of this Brook; "about four in the afternoon," his train came down, his whole Army gradually came down; and they now are ranking themselves on the opposite side of Brocksburn, — on rather narrow ground; cornfields, but swiftly sloping upwards to the steep of Doon Hill. This goes on, in the wild showers and winds of Monday, 2nd September, 1650, on both sides of the Rivulet of Brock. Whoever will begin the attack, must get across this Brook and its glen first; a thing of much disadvantage.

Behind Oliver's ranks, between him and Dunbar, stand

his tents; sprinkled up and down, by battalions, over the face of this "Peninsula"; which is a low though very uneven tract of ground; now in our time all yellow with wheat and barley in the autumn season, but at that date only partially tilled, — describable by Yorkshire Hodgson as a place of plashes and rough bent-grass; terribly beaten by showery winds that day, so that your tent will hardly stand. There was then but one Farm-house on this tract, where now are not a few: thither were Oliver's Cannon sent this morning; they had at first been lodged "in the Church," an edifice standing then as now somewhat apart, at the south end of Dunbar. . . . .

And now farther, on the great scale, we are to remark very specially that there is just one other "pass" across the Brocksburn; and this is precisely where the London road now crosses it; about a mile east from the former pass, and perhaps two gunshots west from Brocksmouth House. There the great road then as now crosses the Burn of Brock; the steep grassy glen, or "broad ditch forty feet deep," flattening itself out here once more into a passable slope: passable, but still steep on the southern or Lesley side, still mounting up there, with considerable acclivity, into a high table-ground, out of which the Doon Hill, as outskirt of the Lammermoor, a short mile to your right, gradually gathers itself. There, at this "pass," on and above the present London road, as you discover after long dreary dim examining, took place the brunt or essential agony of the Battle of Dunbar long ago. Read in the extinct old Pamphlets, and ever again obstinately read, till some light arise in them, look even with unmilitary eyes at the ground as it now is, you do at least obtain small glimmerings of distinct features here and there, — which gradually coalesce into a kind of image for you; and some spectrum of the Fact becomes visible; rises veritable, face to face on you, grim and sad in the depths of the old dead Time. Yes, my travelling friends, vehiculating in gigs or otherwise over that piece of London road, you may say to yourselves, Here without monument is the grave of a valiant thing which was done under the Sun; the footprint of a Hero, not yet quite undistinguishable, is here!

"The Lord General about four o'clock," say the old Pamphlets, "went into the Town to take some refreshment," a hasty late dinner, or early supper, whichever we may call it; "and very soon returned back,"— having written Sir Arthur's Letter, I think, in the interim. Coursing about the field, with enough of things to order; walking at last with Lambert in the Park or Garden of Brocksmouth House, he discerns that Lesley is astir on the Hillside; altering his position somewhat. That Lesley in fact is coming wholly down to the basis of the Hill, where his horse had been since sunrise: coming wholly down to the edge of the Brook and glen, among the sloping harvest-fields there; and also is bringing up his left wing of horse, most part of it, towards his right; edging himself, "shogging," as Oliver calls it, his whole line more and more to the right! His meaning is, to get hold of Brocksmouth House and the pass of the Brook there; after which it will be free to him to attack us when he will! Lesley in fact considered, or at least the Committee of Estates and Kirk consider, that Oliver is lost; that, on the whole, he must not be left to retreat, but must be attacked and annihilated here. A vague story, due to Bishop Burnet, the watery source of many such, still circulates about the world, That it was the Kirk Committee who forced Lesley down against his will; that Oliver, at sight of it, exclaimed, "The Lord hath delivered," &c.: which nobody is in the least bound to believe. It appears, from other quarters, that Lesley *was* advised or sanctioned in this attempt by the Committee of Estates and Kirk, but also that he was by no means hard to advise; that, in fact, lying on the top of Doon Hill, shelterless in such weather, was no operation to spin out beyond necessity; and that if anybody pressed too much upon him with advice to come down and fight, it was likeliest to be Royalist Civil Dignitaries, who had plagued him with their cavillings at his cunctations, at his "secret fellow-feeling for the Sectarians and Regicides." ever since this War began. The poor Scotch Clergy have enough of their own to answer for in this business; let every back bear the burden that belongs to it. In a word, Lesley descends, has been descending all day, and "shogs" himself to the right, urged I believe, by manifold counsel, and by the nature of the case; and, what is equally important for us, Oliver sees him, and sees through him, in this movement of his.

At sight of this movement, Oliver suggests to Lambert standing by him, Does it not give *us* an advantage, if we, instead of him, like to begin the attack? Here is the Enemy's right wing coming out to the open space, free to be attacked on any side; and the main-battle hampered in narrow sloping ground, between Doon Hill and the Brook, has no room to manœuvre or assist: beat this right wing where it now stands; take it in flank and front with an overpowering force,—it is driven upon its own main-battle, the whole Army is beaten? Lambert eagerly assents "had meant to say the same thing." Monk, who comes up at the moment, likewise assents; as the other Officers do, when the case is set before them. It is the plan resolved upon for battle. The attack shall begin to-morrow before dawn.

And so the soldiers stand to their arms, or lie within instant reach of their arms, all night; being upon an engagement very difficult indeed. The night is wild and wet;— 2d of September means 12th by our calendar: the Harvest Moon wades deep among clouds of sleet and hail. Whoever has a heart for prayer, let him pray now, for the wrestle of death is at hand. Pray,—and withal keep his powder dry! And be ready for extremities, and quit himself like a man! Thus they pass the night; making that Dunbar Peninsula and Brock Rivulet long memorable to me. We English have some tents; the Scots have none. The hoarse sea moans bodeful, swinging low and heavy against these whinstone bays; the sea and the tempests are abroad, all else asleep but we, — and there is One that rides on the wings of the wind.

Towards three in the morning, the Scotch foot, by order of a Major-General, say some, extinguish their matches, all but two in a company; cower under the corn-shocks, seeking some imperfect shelter and sleep. Be wakeful, ye English; watch, and pray, and keep your powder dry. About four o'clock comes order to my pudding-headed Yorkshire friend, that his regiment must mount and march straightway; his and various other regiments march, pouring swiftly to the left to Brocksmouth House, to the Pass over the Brock. With overpowering force let us storm the Scots right wing there; beat that, and all is beaten. Major Hodgson, riding along, heard, he says, "a Cornet praying in the night"; a company of poor men, I think, making worship there, under the void Heaven, before battle joined: Major Hodgson, giving his charge to a brother Officer, turned aside to listen for a minute, and worship and pray along with them; haply his last prayer on this Earth, as it might prove to be. But no; this Cornet prayed with such effusion as was wonderful; and imparted strength to my Yorkshire friend, who strengthened his men by telling them of it. And the Heavens, in their mercy, I think, have opened us a way of deliverance! — The Moon gleams out, hard and blue, riding among hail-clouds; and over St. Abb's Head a streak of dawn is rising.

And now is the hour when the attack should be, and no Lambert is yet here, he is ordering the line far to the right yet; and Oliver occasionally, in Hodgson's hearing, is impatient for him. The Scots too, on this wing, are awake; thinking to surprise us; there is their trumpet sounding, we heard it once; and Lambert, who was to lead the attack, is not here. The Lord General is impatient; — behold Lambert at last! The trumpets peal, shattering with fierce clangor Night's silence; the cannons awaken along all the line: "The Lord of Hosts! The Lord of Hosts!" On, my brave ones, on!

The dispute "on this right wing, was hot and stiff for three quarters of an hour." Plenty of fire, from field-pieces, snaphances, matchlocks, entertained the Scotch main-battle across the Brock; — poor stiffened men, roused from the corn-shocks with their matches all out! But here on the right, their horse "with lancers in the front rank," charge desperately; drive us back across the hollow of the Rivulet; back a little; but the Lord gives us courage, and we storm home again, horse and foot, upon them, with a shock like tornado tempests; break them, beat them, drive them all adrift. "Some fled towards Copperspath, but most across their own foot." Their own poor foot, whose matches were hardly well alight yet! Poor men, it was a terrible awakening for them: field-pieces and charge of foot across the Brocksburn: and now here is their own horse in mad panic, trampling them to death. Above Three-thousand killed upon the place: "I never saw such a charge of foot and horse," says one; nor did I. Oliver was still near to Yorkshire Hodgson, when the shock succeeded. Hodgson heard him say: "They run! I profess they run!" And over St. Abb's Head, and the German Ocean, just then, burst the first gleam of the level sun upon us, " and I heard Nol say, in the words of the Psalmist, 'Let God arise, let His enemies be scattered,'" — or in Rous's metre,

    Let God arise, and scattered
      Let all his enemies be;
    And let all those that do him hate
      Before his presence flee!

Even so. The Scotch Army is shivered to utter ruin; rushes in tumultuous wreck, hither, thither; to Belhaven, or, in their distraction, even to Dunbar; the chase goes as far as Haddington; led by Hacker. "The Lord General made a halt," says Hodgson, "and sang the Hundred-and-seventeenth Psalm," till our horse could gather for the chase. Hundred-and-seventeenth Psalm, at the foot of the Doon Hill; there we uplift it, to the tune of Bangor, or some still higher score, and roll it strong and great against the sky:

>O give ye praise unto the Lord,
>   All nati-ons that be;
>Likewise ye people all accord
>   His name to magnify!
>
>For great to-us-ward ever are
>   His loving kindnesses;
>His truth endures for evermore:
>   The Lord, O do ye bless!

And now to the chase again.

The prisoners are Ten-thousand, — all the foot in a mass. * * * Such is Dunbar Battle; which might almost be called Dunbar Drove, for it was a frightful rout. Brought on by miscalculation; misunderstanding of the difference between substances and semblances; — by mismanagement and the chance of war.

DISMISSAL OF THE RUMP.

Wednesday, 20th April, 1653. — My Lord General is in his reception-room this morning, in plain black clothes and gray worsted stockings; he, with many Officers: but few Members have yet come, though punctual Bulstrode and certain others are there. Some waiting there is; some impatience that the Members would come. The Members do not come: instead of Members, comes a notice that they are busy getting on with their Bill [for Parliamentary Reform] in the House, hurrying it double quick through all the stages. Possible, New message that it will be Law in a little while, if no interposition take place! Bulstrode hastens off to the House: my Lord General, at first incredulous, does now also hasten off,—nay orders that a company of Musketeers of his own regiment attend him. Hastens off, with a very high expression of countenance, I think; saying or feeling: Who would have believed it of them? "It is not honest; yea it is contrary to common honesty!"— My Lord General, the big hour is come!

Young Colonel Sidney, the celebrated Algernon, sat in the House this morning: a House of some Fifty-three. Algernon has left distinct note of the affair; less distinct we have from Bulstrode, who was also there, who seems in some points to be even wilfully wrong. Solid Ludlow was far off in Ireland, but gathered many details in after-years; and faithfully wrote them down, in the unappeasable indignation of his heart. Combining these three originals, we have, after various perusals and collations and considerations, obtained the following authentic, moderately conceivable account.

"The Parliament sitting as usual, and being in debate upon the Bill, with the amendments, which it was thought would have been passed that day, the Lord General Cromwell came into the House, clad in plain black clothes and gray worsted-stockings, and sat down, as he used to do, in an ordinary place." For some time he listens to this interesting debate on the Bill; beckoning once to Harrison, who came over to him, and answered dubitatingly. Whereupon the Lord General sat still, for about a quarter of an hour longer. But now the question being to be put, That this Bill do now pass, he beckons again to Harrison, says,

"This is the time I must do it!"—and so "rose up, put off his hat, and spake. At the first, and for a good while, he spake to the commendation of the Parliament for their pains and care of the public good; but afterwards he changed his style, told them of their injustice, delays of justice, self-interest, and other faults,"—rising higher and higher, into a very aggravated style indeed. An honorable Member, Sir Peter Wentworth by name, not known to my readers, and by me better known than trusted, rises to order, as we phrase it; says, "It is a strange language this; unusual within the walls of Parliament this! And from a trusted servant too; and one whom we have so highly honored; and one—" "Come, come!" exclaims my Lord General, in a very high key. "We have had enough of this,"— and in fact my Lord'General, now blazing all up into clear conflagration, exclaims, "I will put an end to your prating," and steps forth into the floor of the House, and "clapping on his hat," and occasionally "stamping the floor with his feet," begins a discourse which no man can report! He says—Heavens! he is heard saying: "It is not fit that you should sit here any longer! You have sat too long here for any good you have been doing lately. You shall now give place to better men!—Call them in!" adds he briefly, to Harrison, in word of command: "and some twenty or thirty" grim musketeers enter, with bullets in their snap-hances; grimly prompt for orders; and stand in some attitude of Carry-arms there. Veteran men: men of might and men of war, their faces are as the faces of lions, and their feet are swift as the roes upon the mountains:—not beautiful to honorable gentlemen at this moment.

"You call yourselves a Parliament," continues my Lord General, in clear blaze of conflagration: "you are no Parliament; I say, you are no Parliament! some of you are drunkards,"—and his eye flashes on poor Mr Chaloner, an official man of some value, addicted to the bottle; "some of you are ——," and he glares into Harry Marten, and the poor Sir Peter, who rose to order, lewd livers both; "living in open contempt of God's Commandments. Following your own greedy appetites, and the Devil's Commandments. 'Corrupt, unjust persons.'" "And here, I think, he glanced at Sir Bulstrode Whitlocke, one of the Commissioners of the Great Seal, giving him and others very sharp language, though he named them not": "Corrupt, unjust persons; scandalous to the profession of the Gospel: how can you be a Parliament for God's People? Depart, I say; and let us have done with you. In the name of God,—go!"

The House is of course all on its feet,—uncertain almost whether not on its head: such a scene as was never seen before in any House of Commons. History reports with a shudder that my Lord General, lifting the sacred Mace itself, said, "What shall we do with this bawble? Take it away!"—and gave it to a musketeer. And now, "Fetch him down!" says he to Harrison, flashing on the Speaker. Speaker Lenthall, more an ancient Roman than anything else, declares, He will not come till forced. "Sir," said Harrison, "I will lend you a hand";—on which Speaker Lenthall came down, and gloomily vanished. They all vanished; flooding gloomily, clamorously out, to their ulterior business, and respective places of abode: the Long Parliament is dissolved! "'It's you, that have forced me to this,' exclaims my Lord General: 'I have sought the Lord night and day, that He would rather slay me than put me upon the doing of this work.' At their going out, some say, the Lord General said to young Sir Harry Vane, calling him by his name, that *he* might have prevented this; but that he was a juggler, and had not common honesty. 'O, Sir Harry Vane, thou with thy subtle casuistries, and abstruse hair-splittings, thou art other than a good one, I think! The Lord deliver thee from me, Sir Harry Vane!'

All being gone out, the door of the House was locked, and the Key with the Mace, as I heard, was carried away by Colonel Otley";—and it is all over, and the unspeakable Catastrophe has come, and remains.

THE BAREBONES PARLIAMENT.

CONCERNING this Puritan Convention of the Notables, which in English History is called the *Little Parliament*, and derisively *Barebones's Parliament*, we have not much more to say. They are, if by no means the remarkablest Assembly, yet the Assembly for the remarkablest purpose who have ever met in the Modern World. The business is, No less than introducing of the Christian Religion into real practice in the Social Affairs of this Nation. Christian Religion, Scriptures of the Old and New Testaments: such, for many hundred years, has been the universal solemnly recognized Theory of all men's Affairs; Theory sent down out of Heaven itself; but the question is now that of reducing it to Practice in said Affairs;—a most noble, surely, and most necessary attempt; which should not have been put off so long in this Nation! We have conquered the Enemies of Christ; let us now, in real practical earnest, set about doing the Commandments of Christ, now that there is free room for us! Such was the purpose of this Puritan Assembly of the Notables, which History calls the *Little Parliament*, or derisively *Barebones's Parliament*.

It is well known they failed: to us, alas! it is too evident they could not but fail. Fearful impediments lay against that effort of theirs; the sluggishness, the slavish half-and-halfness, the greediness, the cowardice, and general opacity and falsity of some ten million men against it; alas, the whole world, and what we call the Devil and all his angels, against it! Considerable angels, human and other; most extensive arrangements, investments to be sold off at a tremendous sacrifice; in general the entire set of luggage-traps and very extensive stock of merchant-goods and real and floating property, amassed by that assiduous Entity abovementioned, for a thousand years or more! For these, and also for other obstructions, it could not take effect at that time; and the *Little Parliament* became a *Barebones's Parliament*, and had to go its ways again.

———♦———

CONSPIRACIES.

To see a little what kind of England it was, and what kind of incipient Protectorate it was, take, as usual, the following small and few fractions of Authenticity of various complexion, fished from the doubtful slumber-lakes, and dust vortexes, and hang them out at their places in the void night of things. They are not very luminous; but if they were well let alone, and the positively tenebrific were well forgotten, they might assist our imaginations in some slight measure.

Sunday, 18th December, 1653. A certain loud-tongued, loud-minded Mr. Feak, of Anabaptist-Leveller persuasion, with a Colleague seemingly Welsh, named Powel, have a Preaching-Establishment, this good while past in Blackfriars; a Preaching-Establishment every Sunday, which on Monday evening becomes a National-Charter Convention as we should now call it; there Feak, Powel, and Company are in the habit of vomiting forth from their own inner-man, into other inner-men greedy of such pabulum, a very flamy fuliginous set of doctrines, — such as the human mind, superadding Anabaptistry to Sansculottism, can make some attempt to conceive. Sunday, the 18th, which is two days after the Lord Protector's Installation, this Feak-Powel Meeting was unusually large; the Feak-Powel inner-man unusually charged. Elements of soot and fire really copious: fuliginous flamy in a very high degree! At a time, too, when all Doctrine does not satisfy itself with spouting, but longs to become instant Action. " Go and tell your Protector," said the Anabaptist Prophet, " that he has deceived the Lord's People ; that he is a perjured villain," — " will not reign long," or I am deceived: " will end worse than the last Protector did," Protector Somerset who died on the scaffold, or the tyrant Crooked Richard himself! Say I said it! A very foul chimney indeed, here got on fire. And "Major General Harrison, the most eminent man of the Anabaptist Party, being consulted whether he would own the new Protectoral Government, answered frankly, No "; was thereupon ordered to retire home to Staffordshire, and keep quiet.

Does the reader bethink him of those old Leveller Corporals at Burford, and Diggers at St. George's Hill five years ago; of Quakerisms, Calvinistic Sansculottisms, and one of the strangest Spiritual Developments ever seen in any country? The reader sees here one foul chimney on fire, the Feak-Powel chimney in Blackfriars ; and must consider for himself what masses of combustible materials, noble fuel and base soot and smoky explosive fire-damp, in the general English Household it communicates with! Republicans Proper, of the Long Parliament; Republican Fifth-Monarchists of the Little Parliament; the solid Ludlows, the fervent Harrisons: from Harry Vane down to Christopher Feak, all manner of Republicans find Cromwell unforgivable. To the Harrison-and-Feak species Kingship in every sort, and government of man by man, is carnal, expressly contrary to various Gospel Scriptures. Very horrible for a man to think of governing men ; whether he ought even to govern cattle, and drive them to field and to needful penfold, "except in the way of love and persuasion," seems doubtful to me! But fancy a reign of Christ and his Saints; Christ and his Saints just about to come, — had not Oliver Cromwell stept in and prevented it! The reader discerns combustabilities enough; conflagrations, plots, stubborn disaffections and confusions, on the Republican and Republican-Anabaptist side of things. It is the first Plot-department which my Lord Protector will have to deal with all his life long. This he must wisely damp down, as he may. Wisely: for he knows what is noble in the matter, and what is base in it; and would not sweep the fuel and the soot both out of doors at once.

Tuesday, 14th February, 1653-4. "At the Ship-Tavern in the Old Bailey, kept by Mr. Thomas Amps," we come upon the second life-long Plot-department: Eleven truculent, rather threadbare persons, sitting over small drink there, on the Tuesday night, considering how the Protector might be assassinated. Poor broken Royalist men; payless old Captains, most of them, or such like; with their steeple-hats worn very brown, and jack-boots slit, — and projects that cannot be executed. Mr. Amps knows nothing of them, except that they came to him to drink; nor do we. Probe them with questions; clap them in the Tower for a while; Guilty, poor knaves: but not worth hanging: — disappear again into the general mass of Royalist Plotting, and ferment there.

The Royalists have lain quiet ever since Worcester, waiting what issue matters would take. Dangerous to meddle with a Rump Parliament; or other steadily regimented thing; safer if you can find it fallen out of rank; hopefullest of all when it collects itself into a Single Head. The Royalists judge, with some reason, that if they could kill Oliver Protector, this Commonwealth were much endangered. In these Easter weeks, too, or Whitsun weeks, there comes "from our Court," (Charles Stuart's Court,) "at Paris," great encouragement to all men of spirit in straitened circumstances, A Royal Proclamation "By the King," drawn up, say some, by Secretary Clarendon; setting forth that "Whereas a certain base, mechanic fellow, by name Oliver Cromwell, has usurped our throne," much to our and other people's inconvenience, whosoever will kill the said mechanic fellow "by sword, pistol, or poison," shall have £500 a year settled upon him, with colonelcies in our Army, and other rewards suitable, and be a made man,— "on the word and faith of a Christian King." A Proclamation which cannot be circulated except in secret; but is well worth reading by all loyal men. And so Royalist Plots also succeed one another, thick and threefold through Oliver's whole life;—but cannot take effect. Vain for a Christian King and his cunningest Chancellors to summon all the sinners of the Earth, and whatever of necessitous Truculent-Flunkeyism there may be, and to bid, in the name of Heaven and of another place, for the Head of Oliver Cromwell; once for all, they cannot have it, that Head of Cromwell;—not till *he* has entirely done with it, and can make them welcome to their benefit from it.

JAMES NAYLER AND COMPANY.

"In the month of October, 1655," there was seen a strange sight at Bristol in the West. A Procession of Eight Persons; one, a man on horseback, riding single; the others, men and women, partly riding double, partly on foot, in the muddiest highway, in the wettest weather; singing, all but the single rider, at whose bridle splash and walk two women: "Hosannah! Holy, holy! Lord God of Sabaoth!" and other things, "in a buzzing tone," which the impartial hearer could not make out. The single-rider is a rawboned male figure, "with lank hair reaching below his cheeks;" hat drawn close over his brows; "nose rising slightly in the middle;" of abstruse "down look," and large dangerous jaws strictly closed: he sings not; sits there covered; and is sung to by the others bare. Amid pouring deluges, and mud knee-deep: "so that the rain ran in at their necks, and they vented it at their hose and breeches": a spectacle to the West of England and Posterity! Singing as above; answering no question except in song. From Bedminster to Ratcliffe Gate, along the streets to the High Cross of Bristol: at the High Cross they are laid hold of by the Authorities; — turn out to be James Nayler and Company. James Nayler, "from Andersloe" or Ardsley "in Yorkshire," heretofore a Trooper under Lambert; now a Quaker and something more. Infatuated Nayler and Company; given up to Enthusiam, — to Animal-Magnetism, to Chaos and Bedlam in one shape or other! Who will need to be coerced by the Major-Generals, I think; — to be forwarded to London, and there sifted and cross-questioned. Is not the Spiritualism of England developing itself in strange forms? The Hydra, royalist and sansculottic, has many heads.

THE WEST INDIAN INTEREST.

The Grand Sea-Armament which sailed from Portsmouth at Christmas, 1654, proved unsuccessful. It went westward; opened its sealed Instructions at a certain latitude; found that they were instructions to attack Hispaniola, to attack the Spanish Power in the West Indies; it did attack Hispaniola, and lamentably failed; attacked the Spanish Power in the West Indies, and has hitherto realized almost nothing, — a mere waste Island of Jamacia, to all appearance little worth the keeping at such cost. It is hitherto the unsuccessfulest enterprise Oliver Cromwell ever had concern with. Desborow fitted it out at Portsmouth, while the Lord Protector was busy with his First refractory Pedant Parliament; there are faults imputed to Desborow: but the grand fault the Lord Protector imputes to himself, That he chose, or sanctioned the choice of Generals improper to command it. Sea-General Penn, Land-General Venables, they were unfortunate, they were incompetent; fell into disagreements, into distempers of the bowels; had critical Civil Commissioners with them, too, who did not mend the matter. Venables lay "six weeks in bed," very ill of sad West-India maladies; for the rest, a covetous lazy dog, who cared nothing for the business, but wanted to be home at his Irish Government again. Penn is Father of Penn the Pennsylvanian Quaker; a man somewhat quick of temper "like to break his heart," when affairs went wrong; unfit to right them again. The two Generals came voluntarily home in the end of last August [1655], leaving the wreck of their forces in Jamaica; and were straightway lodged in the Tower for quitting their post.

A great Armament of Thirty, nay of Sixty ships; of Four-thousand soldiers, two regiments of whom were veterans, the rest a somewhat sad miscellany of broken Royalists, unruly Levellers, and the like, who would volunteer, — whom Venables augmented at Barbadoes, with a still more unruly set to Nine-thousand: this great Armament the Lord Protector has strenuously hurled, as a sudden fiery bolt, into the dark Domdaniel of Spanish Iniquity in the far West; and it has exploded there, almost without effect. The Armament saw Hispaniola, and Hispaniola with fear and wonder saw it, on the 14th of April, 1655: but the Armament, a sad miscellany of distempered unruly persons, durst not land "where Drake had landed," and at once take the Town and Island: the Armament hovered hither and thither; and at last agreed to land some sixty miles off;

marched therefrom through thick-tangled woods, under tropical heats, till it was nearly dead with mere marching; was then set upon by ambuscadoes; fought miserably ill, the unruly persons of it, or would not fight at all; fled back to its ships a mass of miserable disorganic ruin; and "dying there at the rate of two-hundred a day," made for Jamaica.

Jamaica, a poor unpopulous Island, was quickly taken, as rich Hispaniola might have been, and the Spaniards were driven away: but to men in biliary humor it seemed hardly worth the taking or the keeping. " Immense droves of wild cattle: cows and horses, run about Jamacia"; dusky Spaniards dwell in *hatos*, in unswept shealings: " 80,000 hogs are killed every year for the sake of their lard, which is sold under the name of *hog's-butter* at Carthagena": but what can we do with all that! The poor Armament continuing to die as if by murrain, and all things looking worse and worse to poor biliary Generals. Sea-General Penn set sail for home, whom Land-General Venables swiftly followed: leaving Vice-Admiral Goodson, "Major-General Fortescue," or almost whosoever liked, to manage in their absence, and their ruined moribund forces to die as they could; — and are now lodged in the Tower, as they deserved to be. The Lord Protector, and virtually England with him, had hoped to see the dark empire of bloody Antichristian Spain a little shaken in the West; some reparation got for its inhuman massacrings, and long continued tyrannies, — massacrings, exterminations of us, "at St. Kitts in 1629, at Tortuga in 1637, at Santa Cruz in 1650": so, in the name of England, had this Lord Protector hoped; and he has now to take his disappointment.

The ulterior history of these Western Affairs, of this new Jamaica under Cromwell, lies far dislocated, drowned deep, in the Slumber-Lakes of *Thurloe* and Company; in a most dark, stupefied, and altogether dismal condition. A history indeed, which, as you painfully fish it up and by degrees reawaken it to life, is in itself sufficiently dismal. Not much to be intermeddled with here. The English left in Jamaica, the English successively sent thither, prosper as ill as need be; still die, soldiers and settlers of them, at a frightful rate per day; languish, for most part, astonished in their sultry strange new element; and cannot be brought to front with right manhood the deadly inextricable jungle of tropical confusions, outer and inner, in which they find themselves. Brave Governors, Fortescue, Sedgwick, Brayne, one after the other, die rapidly, of the climate and of broken heart; their life-fire all spent there, in that dark chaos, and as yet no result visible. It is painful to read what misbehavior there is, what difficulties there are.

Almost the one steady light-point in the business is the Protector's own spirit of determination. If England have now a "West-India Interest," and Jamaica be an Island worth something, it is to this Protector mainly that we owe it. Here too, as in former darknesses, "Hope shines in him, like a pillar of fire, when it has gone out in all the others." Having put his hand to this work, he will not for any discouragement turn back. Jamaica shall yet be a colony; Spain and its dark Domdaniel shall yet be smitten to the heart, — the enemies of God and His Gospel, by the soldiers and servants of God. It must, and it shall. We have failed in the West, but not wholly; in the West and in the East, by sea and by land, as occasion shall be ministered, we will try it again and again. . . . . Reinforcement went on the back of reinforcement, during this Protector's lifetime; "a Thousand Irish Girls" went; not to speak of the rogue-and-vagabond species from Scotland, — "we can help you" at any time "to two or three hundred of these." And so at length a West-India Interest did take root; and bears spices and poisons, and other produce, to this day.

QUARTERMASTER SINDERCOMB THE ASSASSIN.

MILES SINDERCOMB, now a cashiered Quartermaster living about Town, was once a zealous Deptford lad, who enlisted to fight for Liberty, at the beginning of these wars. He fought strongly on the side of Liberty, being an earnest fierce young fellow;—then gradually got astray into Levelling courses, and wandered ever deeper there, till daylight forsook him, and it became quite dark. He was one of the desperate misguided Corporals, or Quartermasters, doomed to be shot at Burford, seven years ago: but he escaped over night, and was not shot there; took service in Scotland; got again to be Quartermaster; was in the Overton Plot, for seizing Monk and marching into England, lately; whereupon Monk cashiered him: and he came to Town; lodged himself here, in a sulky threadbare manner,—in Alsatia or elsewhere. A gloomy man and Ex-Quartermaster; has become one of Sexby's people, " on the faith of a Christian King"; nothing now left of him but the fierceness, groping some path for itself, in the utter *dark*. Henry Toope, one of his Highness's Lifeguard: gives us, or will give us, an inkling of Sindercomb; and we know something of his courses and inventions, which are many. He rode in Hyde Park among his Highness's escort, with Sexby; but the deed could not then be done. Leave me the £1600, said he; and I will find a way to do it. Sexby left it him and went abroad.

Inventive Sindercomb then took a House in Hammersmith; Garden-House, I think, " which had a banqueting-room looking into the road"; road very narrow at that part;—road from Whitehall to Hampton Court on Saturday afternoons. Inventive Sindercomb here set about providing blunderbusses of the due explosive force,—ancient " infernal machines," in fact,—with these he will blow his

Highness's Coach and his Highness's self into small pieces, if it please Heaven. It did not please Heaven,— probably not Henry Toope of his Highness's Lifeguard. This first scheme proved a failure.

Inventive Sindercomb, to justify his £1600, had to try something. He decided to fire Whitehall by night, and have a stroke at his Highness in the tumult. He has "a hundred swift horses, two in a stable, up and down": — set a hundred stout ruffians on the back of these, in the nocturnal fire; and try Thursday, 8th January, 1656–7; that is to be the Night. On the dusk of Thursday, January 8th, he with old-trooper Cecil, his second in the business, attends Public Worship in Whitehall Chapel; is seen loitering there afterwards, "near the Lord Lambert's seat." Nothing more is seen of him: but about half-past eleven at night, the sentinel on guard catches a smell of fire; — finds holed wainscots, picked locks; a basket of the most virulent wildfire, "fit almost to burn through stones," with lit match slowly creeping towards it, computed to reach it in some half-hour hence, about the stroke of midnight! — His Highness is summoned, the Council is summoned; — alas, Toope of the Lifeguard is examined and Sindercomb's lodging is known. Just when the wildfire should have blazed, two Guardsmen wait upon Sindercomb; seize him, not without hard defence on his part, "wherein his nose was nearly cut off"; bring him to his Highness. Toope testifies; Cecil peaches: — inventive Sindercomb has failed for the *last* time. To the Tower with him, to a jury of his country with him! — The emotion in the Parliament and in the Public, next morning, was great. It had been proposed to ring an alarm at the moment of discovery, and summon the Trainbands; but his Highness would not hear of it.

This Parliament, really intent on settling the Nation, could not want for emotions, in regard to such a matter! Parliament adjourns for a week, till the roots of the Plot are investigated somewhat. Parliament, on reassembling, appoints a day of Thanksgiving for the Nation; Friday, come four weeks, which is February 20th, that shall be the general Thanksgiving Day: and in the mean time we decide to go over in a body, and congratulate his Highness. A mark of great respect to him. . . . .

On Monday, 9th February, Sindercomb was tried by a jury in the Upper Bench; and doomed to suffer as a traitor and assassin, on the Saturday following. The night before Saturday his poor Sister, though narrowly watched, smuggled him some poison: he went to bed, saying, "Well, this is the last time I shall go to bed"; the attendants heard him snore heavily, and then cease; they looked, and he lay dead. "He was of that wretched sect called *Soul-Sleepers*, who believe that the soul falls *asleep* at death"; a gloomy, far-misguided man. They buried him on Tower-hill, with due ignominy, and there he rests; with none but frantic Anabaptist Sexby, or Deceptive Presbyterian Titus, to sing his praise.

———•———

INSTALLED AS PROTECTOR.

LAND-GENERAL REYNOLDS has gone to the French Netherlands, with Six-thousand men, to join Turenne in fighting the Spaniards there; and Sea-General Montague, is about hoisting his flag to co-operate with him from the other element. By sea and land are many things passing; — and here in London is the loudest thing of all: not yet to be entirely omitted by us, though now it has fallen very silent in comparison. Inauguration of the Lord Protector; second and more solemn Installation of him, now that he is fully recognized by Parliament itself. He cannot yet, as it proves, be crowned King; but he shall be installed in his Protectorship with all solemnity befitting such an occasion.

Friday, 26th June, 1657. The Parliament and all the

world are busy with this grand affair; the labors of the Session being now complete, the last finish being now given to our new Instrument of Government, to our elaborate Petition and Advice, we will add this topstone to the work, and so amid the shoutings of mankind, disperse for the recess. Friday at two o'clock, "in a place prepared," duly prepared, with all manner of "platforms," "cloths of state," and "seats raised one above the other," "at the upper end of Westminster Hall." Palace Yard, and London generally, is all a-tiptoe, out of doors. Within doors, Speaker Widdrington and the Master of the Ceremonies have done their best: the Judges, the Aldermen, the Parliament, the Council, the foreign Ambassadors, and domestic Dignitaries without end; chairs of state, cloths of state, trumpet-peals, and acclamations of the people — Let the reader conceive it; or read in old pamphlets the "exact relation" of it with all the speeches and phenomena, worthier than such things usually are of being read.

"His Highness standing under the Cloth of State," says Bulstrode, whose fine feelings are evidently touched by it, "the Speaker, in the name of the Parliament, presented to him: First, a *Robe* of purple velvet; which the Speaker, assisted by Whitlocke and others, put upon his Highness. Then he," the Speaker, "delivered to him the Bible richly gilt and bossed," an affecting symbolic Gift: "After that, the Speaker girt the *Sword* about his Highness; and delivered into his hand the Sceptre of massy gold. And then, this done, he made a Speech to him on these several things presented"; eloquent mellifluous Speech, setting forth the high and true significance of these several Symbols, Speech still worth reading; to which his Highness answered in silence by dignified gesture only. "Then Mr. Speaker gave him the Oath"; and so ended really in a solemn manner. "And Mr. Manton, by prayer, recommended his Highness, the Parliament, the Council, the Forces by land

and sea, and the whole Government and People of the Three Nations, to the blessing and protection of God."— And then "the people gave several great shouts"; and "the trumpets sounded; and the Protector sat in his chair of state, holding the Sceptre in his hand"; a remarkable sight to see. "On his right sat the Ambassador of France," on his left some other Ambassador; and all round, standing or sitting, were Dignitaries of the highest quality; "and near the Earl of Warwick, stood the Lord Viscount Lisle, stood General Montague and Whitlocke, each of them having a drawn sword in his hand,"—a sublime sight to some of us!

And so this Solemnity transacts itself;—which, at the moment, was solemn enough; and is not yet, at this or any hollowest moment of Human History, intrinsically altogether other. A really dignified and veritable piece of Symbolism; perhaps the last we hitherto, in these quack-ridden histrionic ages, have been privileged to see on such an occasion.

———◆———

ROYALIST INSURRECTION FAILURE.

His Highness, before this Monday's sun sets [Feb. 4, 1658], has begun to lodge the Anarchic Ringleaders, Royalist, Fifth-Monarchist, in the Tower; his Highness is bent once more with all his faculty, the Talking-Apparatus being gone, to front this Hydra, and trample it down once again. On Saturday he summons his Officers, his Acting-Apparatus, to Whitehall round him; explains to them "in a Speech two hours long" what kind of Hydra it is; asks, Shall it conquer us, involve us in blood and confusion? They answer from their hearts, No, it shall not! "We will stand and fall with your Highness, we will live and die with you!"— It is the last duel this Oliver has with any Hydra fomented into life by a Talking-Apparatus; and he again conquers it, invincibly compresses it, as he has heretofore done.

One day, in the early days of March next, his Highness said to Lord Broghil: An old friend of yours is in Town, the Duke of Ormond, now lodged in Drury Lane, at the Papist Surgeon's there; you had better tell him to be gone! Whereat his Lordship stared; found it a fact however; and his Grace of Ormond did go with exemplary speed, and got again to Bruges and the Sacred Majesty, with report That Cromwell had many enemies, but that the rise of the Royalists was moonshine. And on the 12th of the month his Highness had the Mayor and Common Council with him in a body at Whitehall; and "in a Speech at large" explained to them that his Grace of Ormond was gone only "on Tuesday last"; that there were Spanish Invasions, Royalist Insurrections, and Frantic-Anabaptist Insurrections rapidly ripening; — that it would well beseem the City of London to have its Militia in good order. To which the Mayor and Common Council "being very sensible thereof," made zealous response by speech and by act. In a word, the Talking-Apparatus being gone, and an Oliver Protector now at the head of the Acting-Apparatus, no Insurrection, in the eyes of reasonable persons, had any chance. The leading Royalists shrank close into their privacies again, — considerable numbers of them had to shrink into durance in the Tower. Among which latter class his Highness, justly incensed, and "considering," as Thurloe says, "that it was not fit there should be a Plot of this kind every winter," had determined that a High Court of Justice should take cognizance of some. High Court of Justice is accordingly nominated as the Act of Parliament prescribes: among the parties marked for Trial by it are Sir Henry Slingsby, long since prisoner for Penruddock's business, and the Rev. Dr. Hewit, a man of much forwardness in Royalism. Sir Henry, prisoner in Hull and acquainted with the Chief Officers there, has been treating with them for betrayal of the place to his Majesty; has even, to that end, given one of them a Majesty's Commission; for whose Spanish Invasion such a Haven and Fortress would have been extremely convenient. Reverend Dr. Hewit, preaching by sufferance, according to the old ritual, "in St. Gregory's Church near Paul's," to a select disaffected audience, has farther seen good to distinguish himself very much by secular zeal in this business of the Royalist Insurrection and Spanish Charles-Stuart Invasion; — which has now come to nothing, and left poor Dr. Hewit in a most questionable position. Of these two, and of others, a High Court of Justice shall take cognizance.

The Insurrection having no chance in the eyes of reasonable Royalists, and they in consequence refusing to lead it, the large body of *un*reasonable Royalists now in London City, or gathering thither, decide, with indignation, That they will try it on their own score and lead it themselves. Hands to work, then, ye unreasonable Royalists; pipe, All hands! Saturday the 15th of May, that is the night appointed: To rise that Saturday Night; beat drums for "Royalist Apprentices," "fire houses at the Tower," slay this man, slay that, and bring matters to a good issue. Alas, on the very edge of the appointed hour, as usual, we are all seized; the ringleaders of us are all seized, "at the Mermaid in Cheapside," — for Thurloe and his Highness have long known what we were upon! Barkstead, Governor of the Tower, "marches into the City with five drakes," at the rattle of which every Royalist Apprentice, and party implicated, shakes in his shoes: — and this also has gone to vapor, leaving only for result certain new individuals of the Civic class to give account of it to the High Court of Justice.

Tuesday, 25th May, 1658, the High Court of Justice sat; a formidable Sanhedrim of above a Hundred-and-thirty heads; consisting of "all the Judges," chief Law Officials, and others named in the Writ, according to Act of Parliament; — sat "in Westminster Hall, at nine in the morning, for the Trial of Sir Henry Slingsby, Knight, John Hewit, Doctor of Divinity," and three others whom we may forget. Sat day after day till all were judged. Poor Sir Henry, on the first day, was condemned; he pleaded what he could, poor gentleman, a very constant Royalist all along; but the Hull business was too palpable; he was condemned to die. Reverend Dr. Hewit, whose proceedings also had become very palpable, refused to plead at all; refused even "to take off his hat," says Carrion Heath, "till the officer was coming to do it for him"; had a "Paper of Demurrers prepared by the learned Mr. Prynne," who is now again doing business this way; "conducted himself not very wisely," says Bulstrode. He likewise received sentence of death. The others, by narrow missing, escaped; by good luck, or the Protector's mercy, suffered nothing.

As to Slingsby and Hewit, the Protector was inexorable. Hewit has already taken a very high line: let him persevere in it! Slingsby was the Lord Fauconberg's uncle, married to his Aunt Bellasis; but that could not stead him, — perhaps that was but a new monition to be strict with him. The Commonwealth of England and its Peace are not nothing! These Royalist Plots every winter, deliveries of garrisons to Charles Stuart, and reckless "usherings of us into blood," shall end! Hewit and Slingsby suffered on Tower Hill, on Monday, 8th June; amid the manifold rumor and emotion of men. Of the City insurrectionists six were condemned; three of whom were executed, three pardoned. And so the High Court of Justice dissolved itself; and at this and not at more expense of blood, the huge Insurrectionary movement ended, and lay silent within its caves again.

Whether in any future year it would have tried another rising against such a Lord Protector, one does not know, — one guesses rather in the negative. The Royalist Cause, after so many failures, after such a sort of enterprises "on the word of a Christian King," had naturally sunk very low. Some twelvemonth hence, with a Commonwealth not now under Cromwell, but only under the impulse of Cromwell, a Christian King hastening down to the Treaty of the Pyrenees, where France and Spain were making Peace, found one of the coldest receptions. Cardinal Mazarin "sent his coaches and guards a day's journey to meet Lockhart, the Commonwealth Ambassador"; but refused to meet the Christian King at all; would not even meet Ormond except as if by accident, "on the public road," to say that there was no hope. The Spanish Minister, Don Louis de Haro, was civiller in manner; but as to Spanish Charles-Stuart Invasions or the like, he also decisively shook his head. The Royalist cause was as good as desperate in England; a melancholy Reminiscence, fast fading away into the realm of shadows. Not till Puritanism sank of its own accord, could Royalism rise again. But Puritanism, the King of it once away, fell loose very naturally in every fibre,—fell into *Kinglessness*, what we call Anarchy; crumbled down, ever faster, for Sixteen Months, in mad suicide, and universal clashing and collision; proved, by trial after trial, that there lay not in it either Government or so much as Self-Government any more; that a Government of England by *it* was henceforth an impossibility. Amid the general wreck of things, all Government threatening now to be impossible, the Reminiscence of Royalty rose again, "Let us take refuge in the Past, the Future is not possible!" and Major-General Monk crossed the Tweed at Coldstream, with results which are well known.

. Results which we will not quarrel with, very mournful as they have been! If it please Heaven, these Two Hundred Years of universal Cant in Speech, with so much of Cotton-spinning, Coal-boring, Commercing, and other valuable Sincerity of Work going on the while, shall not be quite lost to us! Our Cant will vanish, our whole baleful cunningly-compacted Universe of Cant, as does a heavy Nightmare Dream. We shall awaken; and find ourselves in a world greatly *widened.* — Why Puritanism could not continue? My friend, Puritanism was *not* the Complete Theory of this immense Universe; no, only a part thereof! To me it seems, in my hours of hope, as if the Destinies meant something grander with England than even Oliver Protector did! We will not quarrel with the Destinies; we will work as we can towards fulfilment of them.

DEATH OF THE PROTECTOR.

OLIVER's look was yet strong; and young for his years, which were Fifty-nine last April [1658]. The "Threescore and ten years," the Psalmist's limit, which probably was often in Oliver's thoughts and in those of others there, might have been anticipated for him: Ten years more of Life; — which, we may compute, would have given another History to all the Centuries of England. But it was not to be so, it was to be otherwise. Oliver's health, as we might observe, was but uncertain in late times; often "indisposed" the spring before last. His course of life had not been favorable to health! "A burden too heavy for man!" as he himself, with a sigh, would sometimes say. Incessant toil; inconceivable labor, of head and heart and hand; toil, peril, and sorrow manifold, continued for near Twenty years now, had done their part: those robust life-energies, it afterward appeared, had been gradually eaten out. Like a Tower strong to the eye, but with its foundations undermined; which has not long to stand; the fall of which, on any shock, may be sudden.

The Manzinis and Ducs de Crequi, with their splendors,

and congratulations about Dunkirk, interesting to the street populations and general public, had not yet withdrawn, when at Hampton Court there had begun a private scene, of much deeper and quite opposite interest there. The Lady Claypole, Oliver's favorite Daughter, a favorite of all the world, had fallen sick we know not when; lay sick now, — to death, as it proved. Her disease was of internal female nature; the painfullest and most harassing to mind and sense, it is understood, that falls to the lot of a human creature. Hampton Court we can fancy once more, in those July days, a house of sorrow; pale Death knocking there, as at the door of the meanest hut. "She had great sufferings, great exercises of spirit!" Yes: — and in the depths of the old Centuries, we see a pale anxious Mother, anxious Husband, anxious weeping Sisters, a poor young Frances weeping anew in her weeds. "For the last fourteen days" his Highness has been by her bedside at Hampton Court, unable to attend to any public business whatever. Be still, my Child; trust thou yet in God: in the waves of the Dark River, there too is He a God of help! — On the 6th day of August she lay dead; at rest forever. My young, my beautiful, my brave! She is taken from me; I am left bereaved of her. The Lord giveth, and the Lord taketh away; blessed be the Name of the Lord! . . . .

In the same dark days occurred George Fox's third and last interview with Oliver. . . . . George dates nothing; and his facts everywhere lie round him like the leather-parings of his old shop: but we judge it may have been about the time when the Manzinis and Ducs de Crequi were parading in their gilt coaches, That George and two Friends "going out of Town," on a summer day, "two of Hacker's men" had met them, — taken them, brought them to the Mews. "Prisoners there a while": — but the Lord's power was over Hacker's men; they had to let us go. Whereupon:

"The same day, taking boat I went down" (*up*) "to Kingston, and from thence to Hampton Court, to speak with the Protector about the Sufferings of Friends. I met him riding into Hampton-Court Park; and before I came to him as he rode at the head of his Lifeguard, I saw and felt a waft" (*whiff*) " of death go forth against him." — — Or in favor of him, George? His life, if thou knew it, has not been a merry thing for this man, now or heretofore! I fancy he has been looking, this long while, to give it up, whenever the Commander-in-chief required. To quit his laborious sentry-post; honorably lay up his arms, and be gone to his rest: — all Eternity to rest in, O George! Was thy own life merry, for example, in the hollow of the tree; clad permanently in leather? And does kingly purple, and governing refractory worlds instead of stitching coarse shoes, make it merrier? The waft of death is not against *him* I think, — perhaps against thee, and me, and others, O George, when the Nell-Gwyn Defender and Two Centuries of all-victorious Cant have come in upon us! My unfortunate George, — — "a waft of death go forth against him; and when I came to him, he looked like a dead man. After I had laid the Sufferings of Friends before him, and had warned him accordingly as I was moved to speak to him, he bade me come to his house. So I returned to Kingston; and, the next day, went up to Hampton Court to speak farther with him. But when I came, Harvey, who was one that waited on him, told me the Doctors were not willing that I should speak with him. So I passed away, and never saw him more."

Friday, the 20th of August, 1658, this was probably the day on which George Fox saw Oliver riding into Hampton Park with his Guards for the last time. That Friday, as we find, his Highness seemed much better: but on the morrow a sad change had taken place; feverish symptoms, for which the Doctors vigorously prescribed quiet. Saturday to Tuesday the symptons continued ever worsening: a kind of tertian ague, "bastard tertian" as the old Doctors name it; for which it was ordered that his Highness should return to Whitehall, as to a more favorable air in that complaint. On Tuesday, accordingly, he quitted Hampton Court;— never to see it more.

"His time was come," says Harvey, "and neither prayers nor tears could prevail with God to lengthen out his life, and continue him longer to us. Prayers abundantly and incessantly poured out on his behalf, both publicly and privately, as was observed, in a more than ordinary way. Besides many a secret sigh, — secret and unheard by men, yet like the cry of Moses, more loud, and strongly laying hold on God, than many spoken supplications. All which, — the hearts of God's People being thus mightily stirred up, — did seem to beget confidence in some, and hopes in all; yea some thoughts in himself, that God would restore him."

"Prayers public and private": they are worth imagining to ourselves. Meetings of Preachers, Chaplains, and Godly Persons; "Owen, Goodwin, Sterry, with a company of others in an adjoining room"; in Whitehall, and elsewhere over religious London and England, fervent outpourings of many a loyal heart. For there were hearts to whom the nobleness of this man was known; and his worth to the Puritan Cause was evident. Prayers, — strange enough to us; in a dialect fallen obsolete, forgotten now. Authentic wrestlings of ancient Human Souls, — who were alive then, with their affections, awe-struck pieties; with their Human Wishes, risen to be *transcendent*, hoping to prevail with the Inexorable. All swallowed now in the depths of dark Time; which is full of such, since the beginning! Truly it is a great scene of World-History, this in old Whitehall: Oliver Cromwell drawing nigh to his end. The exit of Oliver Cromwell, and of English Puritanism; a great Light, one of our few authentic Solar Luminaries, going down now amid the clouds of Death. Like the setting of a great victorious summer Sun — its course now finished. "*So stirbt ein Held*," says Schiller; " So dies a Hero! Sight worthy to be worshipped!" He died, this Hero Oliver, in Resignation to God, as the Brave have all done. " We could not be more desirous he should abide," says the pious Harvey, "than he was content and willing to be gone." The struggle lasted, amid hope and fear, for ten days. . . . .

On Monday, August 30th, there roared and howled all day a mighty storm of wind. Ludlow, coming up to Town from Essex, could not start in the morning for wind; tried it in the afternoon; still could not get along, in his coach, for head-wind; had to stop at Epping. On the morrow, Fleetwood came to him in the Protector's name, to ask, What he wanted here? — Nothing of public concernment, only to see my mother-in-law! answered the solid man. For indeed he did not know that Oliver was dying; that the glorious hour of Disenthralment, and immortal " Liberty " to plunge over precipices with one's self and one's Cause, was so nigh! — It came; and he took the precipices, like a strongboned resolute blind ginhorse, rejoicing in the breakage of its halter, in a very gallant constitutional manner. Adieu, my solid friend; if I go to Vevay, I will read thy Monument there, perhaps not without emotion, after all!

It was on this stormy Monday, while rocking-winds, heard in the sick-room and everywhere, were piping aloud, that Thurloe and an Official person entered to inquire, Who, in case of the worst, was to be his Highness's Successor? The Successor is named in a sealed Paper already drawn up, above a year ago, at Hampton Court; now lying in such and such a place. The Paper was sent for, searched for; it could never be found. Richard's is the name understood to have been written in that Paper: not a good name; but in fact one does not know. In ten years' time, had ten years more been granted, Richard might have become a fitter man; might have been cancelled, if palpably unfit. Or perhaps it was Fleetwood's name, — and the Paper by certain parties was stolen? None knows. On the Thursday night following, "and not till then," his Highness is understood to have formally named " Richard!" — or perhaps it might only be some heavy-laden " Yes, yes!" spoken out of the thick death-slumbers, in answer to Thurloe's *question* " Richard?" The thing is a little uncertain. It was, once more, a matter of much moment; — giving color probably to all the subsequent Centuries of England, this answer! . . . .

Thursday night the writer of our old Pamphlet was himself in attendance on his Highness; and has preserved a trait or two; with which let us hasten to conclude. To-morrow is September Third, always kept as a Thanksgiving-day, since the Victories of Dunbar and Worcester. The wearied one, "that very night before the Lord took him to his everlasting rest," was heard thus, with oppressed voice, speaking: —

"'Truly God is good; indeed, He is; He will not —' then his speech failed him, but, as I apprehended, it was, ' He will not leave me.' This saying, ' God is good,' he freqnently used all along; and would speak it with much cheerfulness, and fervor of spirit, in the midst of his pains. Again he said: 'I would be willing to live to be farther serviceable to God and His People: but my work is done. Yet God will be with His People.'

" He was very restless most part of the night, speaking often to himself. And there being something to drink offered him, he was desired to take the same, and endeavor to sleep. Unto which he answered: 'It is not my desire to drink or sleep; but my design is, to make what haste I can to be gone.'

"Afterwards, towards morning, he used divers holy expressions, implying much inward consolation and peace;

among the rest he spake some exceeding self-debasing words, *annihilating* and judging himself. And truly it was observed, that a public spirit to God's Cause did breathe in him, — as in his lifetime so now to his very last."

When the morrow's sun rose, Oliver was speechless; between three and four in the afternoon, he lay dead. Friday, 3d September, 1658. "The consternation and astonishment of all people," writes Fauconberg, "are inexpressible; their hearts seem as if sunk within them. My poor Wife, — I know not what on earth to do with her. When seemingly quieted, she bursts out again into a passion that tears her very heart to pieces." Husht, poor weeping Mary! Here is a Life-battle right nobly done. Seest thou not,

> The storm is changed into a calm,
>   At His command and will;
> So that the waves which raged before,
>   Now quiet are and still!
>
> Then are *they* glad, — because at rest
>   And quiet now they be:
> So to the haven He them brings
>   Which they desired to see.

"Blessed are the dead that die in the Lord"; blessed are the valiant that have lived in the Lord. "Amen, saith the Spirit," Amen. "They do rest from their labors, and their works follow them."

"Their works follow them." As, I think, this Oliver Cromwell's works have done, and are still doing? We have had our "Revolutions of Eighty-eight," officially called "glorious"; and other Revolutions not yet called glorious, and somewhat has been gained for poor Mankind. Men's ears are not now slit off by rash Officiality; Officiality will, for long henceforth, be more cautious about men's ears. The tyrannous Star-chambers, branding-irons, chimerical Kings and Surplices at All-hallowtide, they are gone, or with immense velocity going, Oliver's works do follow him! — The works of a man, bury them under what guano-mountains and obscene owl-droppings you will, do not perish, cannot perish. What of Heroism, what of Eternal Light was in a Man and his Life, is with very great exactness added to the Eternities, remains forever a new divine portion of the Sum of Things; and no owl's voice, this way or that, in the least, avails in the matter. But we have to end here.

Oliver is gone; and with him England's Puritanism, laboriously built together by this man, and made a thing far-shining miraculous to its own Century, and memorable to all the Centuries, soon goes. Puritanism, without its King, is *kingless*, anarchic; falls into dislocation, self-collision; staggers, plunges into ever deeper anarchy; King, Defender of the Puritan Faith there can none now be found; — and nothing is left but to recall the old disowned Defender with the remnants of his Four Surplices, and Two Centuries of *Hypocrisis* (or Play-acting *not* so called), and put up with all that, the best we may. The Genius of England no longer soars Sunward, world-defiant like an Eagle through the storms, " mewing her mighty youth," as John Milton saw her do: the Genius of England, much more like a greedy Ostrich intent on provender and a whole skin mainly, stands with its *other* extremity Sunward with its Ostrich-head stuck into the readiest bush of old Church-tippets, King-cloaks, or what other " sheltering Fallacy" there may be, and *so* awaits the issue. The issue has been slow; but it is now seen to have been inevitable. No Ostrich, intent on gross terrene provender, and sticking its head into Fallacies, but will be awakened one day, — in a terrible *a posteriori* mahner, if not otherwise! —— Awake before it come to that! God and man bid us awake! The Voices of our Fathers, with thousand-fold stern monition to one and all, bid us awake.

LITTLE BELL.

By T. WESTWOOD.

"He prayeth well, who loveth well
Both man and bird and beast."
              THE ANCIENT MARINER.

PIPED the Blackbird, on the beechwood spray,
"Pretty maid, slow wandering this way,
    What's your name?" quoth he.
"What's your name? Oh! stop and straight unfold,
Pretty maid, with showery curls of gold."
    "Little Bell," said she.

Little Bell sat down beneath the rocks,
Tossed aside her gleaming, golden locks,
    "Bonny bird!" quoth she,
"Sing me your best song, before I go."
"Here's the very finest song, I know,
    Little Bell," said he.

And the Blackbird piped — you never heard
Half so gay a song from any bird;
    Full of quips and wiles,
Now so round and rich, now soft and slow,
All for love of that sweet face below,
    Dimpled o'er with smiles.

And the while that bonny bird did pour
His full heart out, freely, o'er and o'er,
    'Neath the morning skies,

In the little childish heart below,
All the sweetness seemed to grow and grow,
And shine forth in happy overflow
    From the brown, bright eyes.

Down the dell she tripped, and through the glade —
Peeped the squirrel from the hazel shade,
    And, from out the tree,
Swung and leaped and frolicked, void of fear,
While bold Blackbird piped, that all might hear,
    "Little Bell!" piped he.

Little Bell sat down amid the fern:
"Squirrel, Squirrel! to your task return;
    Bring me nuts!" quoth she.
Up, away! the frisky Squirrel hies,
Golden wood-lights glancing in his eyes,
    And adown the tree,
Great ripe nuts, kissed brown by July sun,
In the little lap drop, one by one —
Hark! how Blackbird pipes, to see the fun!
    "*Happy* Bell!" pipes he.

Little Bell looked up and down the glade:
"Squirrel, Squirrel, from the nut-tree shade,
Bonny Blackbird, if you're not afraid,
    Come and share with me!"
Down came Squirrel, eager for his fare,
Down came bonny Blackbird, I declare;
Little Bell gave each his honest share —
    Ah! the merry three!

And the while those frolic playmates twain
Piped and frisked from bough to bough again,
    'Neath the morning skies,

In the little childish heart below,
All the sweetness seemed to grow and grow,
And shine out in happy overflow,
    From her brown, bright eyes.

By her snow-white cot, at close of day,
Knelt sweet Bell, with folded palms, to pray.
    Very calm and clear
Rose the praying voice, to where, unseen,
In blue heaven, an angel shape serene
    Paused awhile to hear.

"What good child is this," the angel said,
"That, with happy heart, beside her bed,
    Prays so lovingly?"
Low and soft, oh! very low and soft,
Crooned the Blackbird in the orchard croft,
    "Bell, *dear* Bell!" crooned he.

"Whom God's creatures love," the angel fair
Murmured, "God doth bless with angels' care;
    Child, thy bed shall be
Folded safe from harm; love, deep and kind,
Shall watch round and leave good gifts behind,
    Little Bell, for thee."

THE MORMON'S WIFE.

By ROSE TERRY.

"'Woe to that man,' his warning voice replied
To all who questioned, or in silence sighed —
'Woe to that man who ventures truth to win,
And seeks his object by the path of sin!'" —
SCHILLER.

"I DON'T think much, my young friend, of those Mormons! I have had some reasons of my own for disliking them!" said Parson Field to me, as we sat together, one August noon, in the porch of his red house at Plainfield.

"Do tell me, sir," said I, settling myself in an easy attitude to hear his story — for a story from Parson Field was not to be despised — his quaint simplicity bringing out, in old-time and expressive phrases, whatever he describes with the clear fidelity of an interior by Mieris. "Do tell me," said I again, with a deeper emphasis; whereat the old gentleman looked at me over his spectacles, and, smiling benignantly into my eager face, began.

"When I first came to Plainfield," said he, "more than thirty years ago, I had been a minister of the Lord only ten years, and I had been settled for that period of time in a large city, where I served acceptably to a worthy congregation; but certain reasons of my own induced me to leave that situation, and come here to live, where also I found acceptance, and not many months after I came there was a considerable reviving of the work in this place, and many believed. Of these was a certain Joseph Frazer, a young

Scotchman, concerning whom I felt much misgiving, lest he should take the wrong path; but he, in due season, joined himself to the church, and edified the brethren in walk and conversation; so that, when he left Plainfield and settled in the West Indies, we were loth to have him go.

"Some years afterwards we heard he was married there to a lady of Spanish extraction, and a Catholic; and, after ten years elapsed, she died, leaving him one child, a daughter, eight years of age, and with her he came to Plainfield, desiring that the child, whom he had named Adeline, after his own mother, should have a New England training.

"But, wonderful are the ways of Providence! On his return to Cuba, he perished in the vessel, which went down in a heavy gale off Cape Hatteras; and when the news came to his mother, old Mrs. Frazer, she sent for me that I should tell the child Adeline, for she had given proofs of a singular nature, ardent and self-confident in the extreme. I took my hat, and went over to Mrs. Frazer's, with a very heavy heart, for the grief of a child is a fearful thing to me, and to be the bringer of evil tidings, that shall stain the pureness and calm of a child's thoughts with the irreparable shadow of death, is no light thing, nor easily to be done. I entered into the house one day in June: it was a very sweet day, and, as I walked quietly into the low kitchen, I saw Adeline, with her head resting on her hands, and her large eyes eagerly gazing out of the window at the gambols of a scarlet-throated humming-bird. I went close to her, and thought to myself that I would speak, but I did not, for I saw that, in her little pale face, which made me more sad than before; and I had it on my lips to say, 'Adeline, are you homesick?' (which was the thing of all others I should not say) when suddenly she turned about, and answered the question before I spoke it.

"'Sir,' said she, 'I wish I was in Cuba. I had just such a humming-bird at home; and I fed it with orange boughs full of white flowers, every day; but you have no orange trees here, and I have no papa!'

"It seemed to me that the child's angel had thus opened the way for me to speak, and I began to say some things about the love of our universal Father, when she laid her little hand on my arm with a fearfully strong pressure. 'Mr. Field,' said she, 'is my papa dead!' I never shall forget the eyes that looked that question into mine. I felt like an unveiled spirit before their eager, piercing stare. I did not answer except by a strong quiver of feeling that would run over my features, for I loved her father even as a kinsman, and I needed to say nothing more, for the child fell at my feet quite rigid, and I called Mrs. Frazer, who tried all her nurse-arts to restore little Adeline; but was forced, at last, to send for a physician, who bled the child, and brought her round.

"In the mean time I had gone home to prepare my sermon, for it was not yet finished, and the day was Friday; but I kept seeing that little lifeless face, all orphaned as it was, and the Scripture, 'As one whom his mother comforteth,' was so borne in upon my mind, that, although I had previously fixed upon one adapted to a setting forth of the doctrine of election, I was wrought upon to make the other the subject of my discourse: and truly the people wept; almost all but Adeline, who sat in the square pew with her great eyes fixed upon me, and her small lips apart, like one who drinks from the stream of a rock.

"The next day I was resting, as my custom is, after the Sabbath; and in a warm, fair day, I find no better rest than to sit by the open window, and breathe the summer air, and fill my eyes and heart with the innumerable love-tokens that God hath set thickly in Nature. I was, therefore, at my usual place, wrapt in thought, and beholding the labors of a small bird which taught her young to fly, when I felt a light, cold touch, and, turning, saw little Adeline beside me.

'Sir,' said she, without any preface, 'when my papa went away, he left with me a letter, which he said I was to give you if he died.' So far she spoke steadily, but there the small voice quivered, and broke down. I took the letter she proffered me, and, breaking the seal, found it a short but touching appeal to me, as the spiritual father of Joseph Frazer, to take his own child under my care, and be as a father to her, inasmuch as his mother was old and feeble, and also to be executor of his will, of which a copy was enclosed. I said this much to the child as shortly as I could, and with her grave voice she replied, ' Sir, I should like to be your little girl, if you will preach me some more sermons.' Now I was affected at this answer; not the less that the leaven of pride, which worketh in every man, was fed by even a baby's praise; and, putting on my hat, I walked over to Mrs. Frazer's house and laid the matter before her. She was not, at first, willing to give Adeline up, but at length, after much converse to and fro, she came to my conclusion, that the child would be better in my hands, inasmuch as she herself could not hope for a long continuance: and as it was ordered, she died the next summer. I sent for my sister Martha, who was somewhat past marriageable years, but kind and good, to come and keep house for me, and from that time Adeline was as my own child. But I must hasten over a time, for I am too long in telling this.

" In course of years the child grew up, tall and slender, of a very stately carriage, and having that Scriptural glory of a woman, long and abundant hair.

" She was still very fervid in her feelings, but reserved and proud, and I fear I had been too tender with her for her good, inasmuch as she thought her own will and pleasure must always be fulfilled; and we all know that is not one of the ordinations of Providence.

" As Adeline came to be a woman, divers youths of my

congregation were given to call of a Sabbath night, with red apples for me, and redder cheeks for Adeline, who was scarcely civil to them, and often left them to my conversation, which they seemed not to relish so much as would have been pleasing to human nature.

"But my sainted mother, who was not wanting in the wisdom of this world, was used to say that every man and woman had their time of crying for the moon, and while some knew it to be a burning fire, and others scornfully called it cheese, and if they got it, either burned their fingers, or despised their desire, still all generations must have their turn, and truly I believed it, when I found that Adeline herself began to have a pining for something which I could not persuade her to specify. The child grew thin and pale, and ceased the singing of psalms at her daily task, and I could not devise what should be done for her; though Martha strongly recommended certain herb teas, which Adeline somewhat unreasonably rebelled against. However, about this time, my attention was a little turned from her, as there was much religious awakening in the place, and among others, whom the deacons singled out as special objects of attention, was one John Henderson, a frequent visitor at our house, and a young man of good parts and kindly feeling, as it seemed, but of a peculiar nature, being easily led into either right or wrong, yet still given to fits of stubbornness, when he could not be drawn, so to speak, with a cart-rope.

"Now Adeline had been a professor of religion for some years, but it did not seem to me that she took a right view of this particular season, for many times she refused to go to the prayer-meetings, even to those which were held with special intentions towards the unconverted; and many times, on my return, I found her with pale cheeks and red eyes, evidently from tears. About this time, also, she began to take long, solitary walks, from which she returned with her hands full of wild flowers, for it was now early spring; but she cared nothing for the flowers, and would scatter them about the house to fade, without a thought. In the mean time, the revival progressed, but, I lament to say, with no visible change in John Henderson. He had gotten into one of his stubborn moods of mind, and neither heaven nor hell seemed to affect him. The only softening I could perceive in the young man was during the singing of hymns, which was well done in our meeting-house, for Adeline led the choir, and I noticed that, whenever that part of the exercises began, John Henderson would lift up his head, and a strange color and tender expression seemed to melt the hard lines of his face.

"Somewhere about the latter end of April, as I was returning from a visit to a sick man, I met John coming from a piece of woods, that lay behind my house about a mile, with his hands full of liverwort blossoms. I do not know why this little circumstance gave me comfort, yet, I have ever observed, that a man who loves the manifestations of God in his works is more likely to be led into religion than a brutal or a mere business man: so I was desirous of speaking to the youth, but when he saw me he turned from the straight path, and, like an evil-doer, fled across the fields another way. I did not call after him, for some experience has constrained me to think that there is no little wisdom in sometimes letting people alone, but I took my own way home, and having put on my cloth shoes to ease my feet, and being in somewhat of a maze of thought, I went up to my study, as it seemed, very quietly, for I entered at the open door and found Adeline sitting in my arm-chair by the window, quite unaware of my nearness. I well remember how like a spirit she looked that day, with her great eyes raised to a cloud that rested in the bright sky, her soft black hair twisted into a crown about her head, and her light dress falling all over the chair, while in her hands, lying between the slight fingers, and by the bluer veins, was clasped a bunch of liverwort blossoms. Then I perceived, for the first time, why my child was crying for the moon, and that John Henderson cared for the singing and not for the hymns, at which I sorrowed. But I sat down by Ada, and taking the flowers out of her cold hands, began to say that I had met John Henderson on the road with some such blossoms, at which she looked at me even as she did when I told her about her father, and, seeing that I smiled, and yet was not dry-eyed, nor quite at rest, the tears began, slowly, to run over her eyelashes, and in a few very resolute words, she told me that Mr. Henderson had asked her that morning to marry him.

"Now I knew not well what to say, but I set myself aside, as far as I could, and tried not to remember how sore a trial it would be to part with Ada, and I reasoned with her calmly about the youth, setting forth, first, that he was not a professing Christian, and that the Scripture seemed plain to me on that matter, though I would not constrain her conscience if she found it clear in this thing; and, second, that he was a man who held fast to this world's goods, and was like to be a follower of Mammon if he learned not to love better things in his youth; and, third, that he was a man who had, as one might say, a streak of granite in his nature, against which a feeling person would continually fall and be hurt, and which no person could work upon, if once it came in the way even of right action. To all this Adeline answered with more reason than I supposed a woman could, only that I noticed, at the end of each answer, she said in a low voice, as if it were the end of all contention, — 'and I love him.' Whereby, seeing that the thing was well past my interference, I gave my consent with many doubts and fears in my heart, and, having blessed the child, I sent her away that I might meditate over this matter.

"When John came in the evening for his answer, I was

enabled to exhort him faithfully, and, in his softened state of feeling, he chose to tell me that he had been seeking religion because he feared I would not give him Adeline unless he were joined to the church, and he could not make a hypocrite of himself, even for that, but he had hoped that in the use of means he might be awakened and converted. At this I was pleased, inasmuch as it showed a spirit of truth in the young man, but I could not avoid setting before him that self-seeking had never led any soul to God, and how cogent a reason he had himself given for his want of success in things pertaining to his salvation; but as I spoke Ada came in by the other door, and John's eyes began to wander so visibly, that I thought it best to conclude, and I must say he appeared grateful. So I went out of the door, leaving Ada stately and blushing as a fair rose-tree, notwithstanding that John Henderson seemed to fancy she needed his support.

"As the year went on, and I could not in conscience let Adeline leave me until her lover had some fixed maintenance, I had many conversations with him, (for he also was an orphan,) and it was at length decided that he should buy, with Ada's portion, a goodly farm in Western New York; and in the ensuing summer, after a year's engagement, they were to marry. So the summer came; I know not exactly what month was fixed for their marriage, though I have the date somewhere, but one thing I recollect, that the hop-vine over this porch was in full bloom, and after I had joined my child and the youth in the bands of wedlock, I went out into the porch to see them safe into the carriage that was to take them to the boat, and there Ada put her arms about my neck, and kissed me for good-by, leaving a hot tear upon my cheek; and a south wind at that moment smote the hop-vine so that its odor of honey and bitterness mingled swept across my face, and always afterward this scent made me think of Adeline. After two years had passed away, during which we heard from her often, we heard that she had a little daughter born, and her letters were full of joy and pride, so that I trembled for the child's spiritual state; but after some three years the little girl with her mother came to Plainfield, and I did not know but Adeline was excusable in her joy, for such a fair and bright child was scarcely ever seen; but the next summer came sad news: little Nelly was dead, and Ada's grief seemed inexhaustible, while her husband fell into one of his sullen states of mind, and the affliction passed over them to no good end, as it seemed.

"Soon after this, the Mormon delusion began to spread rapidly about John Henderson's dwelling-place, and in less than a year after Nelly's death I had a letter from Ada, dated at St. Louis, which I will read to you, for I have it in my pocket-book, having retained it there since yesterday, when I took it out from the desk to consult a date.

"It begins: — 'Dear Uncle,' (I had always instructed the child so to call me, rather than father, seeing we can have but one father, while we may be blessed with numerous uncles) 'I suppose you will wonder how I came to be at St. Louis, and it is just my being here that I write to explain. You know how my husband felt about Nelly's death, but you cannot know how I felt; for, even in my very great sorrow, I hoped all the time, that by her death, John might be led to a love of religion. He was very unhappy, but he would not show it, only that he took even more tender care of me than before. I have always been his darling and pride; he never let me work, because he said it spoiled my hands; but after Nelly died, he was hardly willing I should breathe; and though he never spoke of her, or seemed to feel her loss, yet I have heard him whisper her name in his sleep, and every morning his hair and pillow were damp with crying; but he never knew I saw it. After a few months, there came a Mormon preacher into our neighborhood, a man of a great deal of talent and earnestness, and a firm believer in the revelation to Joseph Smith. At first my husband did not take any notice of him, and then he laughed at him for being a believer in what seemed like nonsense; but one night he was persuaded to go and hear Brother Marvin preach in the school-house, and he came home with a very sober face. I said nothing, but when I found there was to be a meeting the next night, I asked to go with him, and, to my surprise, I heard a most powerful and exciting discourse, not wanting in either sense or feeling, though rather poor as to argument; but I was not surprised that John wanted to hear more, nor that, in the course of a few weeks, he avowed himself a Mormon, and was received publicly into the sect. Dear Uncle, you will be shocked, I know, and you will wonder why I did not use my influence over my husband, to keep him from this delusion; but you do not know how much I have longed and prayed for his conversion to a religious life; until any religion, even one full of errors, seemed to me better than the hardened and listless state of his mind.

"'I could not but feel, that if he were awakened to a sense of the life to come, in any way, his own good sense would lead him right in the end; and there is so much ardor and faith about this strange belief, that I do not regret his having fallen in with it, for I think the true burning of Gospel faith will yet be kindled by means of this strange fire. In the mean time he is very eager and full of zeal for the cause, so much so, that thinking it to be his duty, he resolved to sell our farm at Oakwood, and remove to Utah. If anything could make me grieve over a change, I believe to be for John's spiritual good, it would be this idea: but no regret or sorrow of mine shall ever stand in the way of his soul; so I gave as cheerful a consent as I could to the sale, and I only cried a few tears, over little Nelly's bed, under the great tulip-tree. There my husband has put an iron railing, and I have planted a great many sweet-brier vines over the rock; and Mr. Keeney, who bought the farm, has promised that the spot shall be kept free from weeds, so I leave her in peace. Do write to me, Uncle Field. I feel sure I have done right, because it has not been in my own way, yet sometimes I am almost afraid. I shall be very far away from you, and from home, and my child; but I am so glad now she is in heaven, nothing can trouble her, and I shall not much care about myself, if John goes right.

"'Give my love to Aunt Martha, and please write to your dear child.

"'ADA HENDERSON.'"

"I need not say, my young friend," resumed Parson Field, wiping his spectacles, and clearing his voice with a vigorous ahem!! "that I could not, in conscience, approve of Adeline's course. 'Thou shalt not do evil that good may come,' is a Gospel truth, and cannot be transgressed with good consequences. I did write to Ada; but, inasmuch as the act was done, I said not much concerning it, but bade her take courage, seeing that she had meant to do right, although in the deed she had considered John Henderson before anything else, which was, as you may perceive, her besetting sin, and therefore it seemed good to me to put, at the end of my epistle, (as I was wont always to offer a suitable text of Scripture for her meditation,) these words, 'Little children, keep yourselves from idols!' I did not hear again from Adeline, till she had been two months in the Mormon city, and though she tried her best to seem contented and peaceful, in view of John's new zeal, and his tender care of her, still I could not but think of the hop-blossoms, for I perceived, underneath this present sweetness, a little drop of life and pain working to some unseen end. That year passed away and we heard no more, and the next also, at which I wondered much; but, reflecting on the chances of travel across those deserts, and having a surety of Ada's affection for me, I did not repine, though I felt some regret that there was such uncertainty of carriage; nevertheless, I wrote as usual, that no chance might be lost.

"The third summer was unusually warm in our parts, and its heats following upon a long, wet spring, caused much and grievous sickness, and I was obliged to be out at all hours with the dying, and at funerals, so that my bodily strength was wellnigh exhausted, and at haying-time, just as I was cutting the last swarth on my river meadow, which is low-lying land, and steamed with hot vapor as I laid it bare to the sun, I fell forward across my scythe-snath and fainted. This was the beginning of a long course of fever, of a typhoid character, during which I was either stupid or delirious most of the time, and, while I lay sick, there came a letter to me, from Salt Lake city, written chiefly by John Henderson, who begged me to come on if it was a possible thing and see his wife, who was wasting with a slow consumption, and much bent upon seeing me. I could discern that the letter was not willingly written; it was stiff in speech, though writ with a trembling hand. At the end of it were a few lines from Ada herself; a very impatient and absolute cry for me, as if she could not die till I came. Now Martha had opened this letter, as she was forced to by my great illness, and, having read it, asked the doctor if it was well to propound the contents to me, and he said decidedly that he could not answer for my life if she did: so Martha, like a considerate woman, wrote an answer herself to John Henderson (of which she kept a copy for me to see), setting forth that I was in no state to be moved with such tidings; that, however, I should have the letter as soon as the doctor saw fit, and sending her love and sympathy to Ada, and a recommend that she should try balm tea.

"After a long season of suspense, I was graciously uplifted from fever, and enabled to leave my bed for a few hours daily; and, when I could ride out, which was only by the latter end of October, I was given the child's letter, and my heart sank within me, for I knew how bitterly she had needed my strength to help her. It was a warm autumn day, near to noon, when I read that letter, and, as I leaned back in my chair, the red sunshine came in upon me, and the smell of dead leaves, while upon the hop-vine one late blossom, spared by the white frosts, and dropping across the window, also put forth its scent, bringing Adeline, as it were, right back into my arms, and the faintness passed away from me with some tears, for I was weak, and a man may not always be stronger than his nature. Now, when Martha sounded the horn for dinner, and our hired man came in from the hill-lot, where he was sowing wheat, I saw that he had a letter in his hand of great size and thickness; and, coming into the keeping-room where I sat, he said that Squire White had brought it over from the Post-office as he came along, thinking I would like to have it directly. I was rather loth to open the great packet at first, for I bethought myself it was likely to be some Consociation proceedings, which were never otherwise than irksome to me, and were now weary to think of, seeing the grasshopper had become a burden. I reached my spectacles down from the nail, and found the post-mark to be that of the Mormon city; and with unsteady hand I opened the seal, and found within several sheets of written letter-paper, directed to me in Ada's writing, and a short letter from John Henderson, which ran thus:—

"'DEAR SIR,—

"'My first wife, Adeline Frazer Henderson, departed this life on the sixth of July, at my house in the city of Great Salt Lake. Shortly before dying she called upon me, in the presence of two sisters, and one of the Saints, to deliver into your hands the enclosed packet, and tell you of her death. According to her wish, I send the papers by mail; and, hoping you may yet be called to be a partaker in the faith of the saints below, I remain your afflicted, yet rejoicing friend,

"'JOHN HENDERSON.'

"I was really stunned for a moment, my young friend, not only with grief at my own loss, but with pity and surprise at the entire deadening, as it appeared, of natural affection in the man to whom I had given my daughter; and also my conscience was not free from offence, for I could not but think that a more fervent and wrestling expostulation, on the sin of marrying an unbeliever, might have saved Adeline from sorrow in the flesh. However, I said as much as seemed best at the time, and upon that reflection I rested myself; for he who adheres to a pure intention, need not repent of his deeds afterward; and the next day, when my present anguish and weakness had somewhat abated, I read the manuscript Ada had sent me.

"It was, doubtless, penned with much reluctance, for the child's natural pride was great, and no less weighty subject than her husband's salvation could have forced her to speak of what she wrote for me: and, indeed, I should feel no right to put the confidence into your hands, were not my child beyond the reach of man's judgment, and did I not feel it a sacred duty to protest, so long as life lasts, against this abominable Mormon delusion, and the no less delusive pretext of doing evil that good may come. I cannot read Ada's letter aloud to you, for there is to be a funeral at two o'clock, which I must attend; but I will give you the papers, and you may sit in my chair and read; only, be patient with my bees, if they come too near you, for they like the hop-blossoms, and never sting unless you strike."

So saying, Parson Field gave me his leathern chair and the papers, and I sat down in the hop-crowned porch, to read Adeline Henderson's story, with a sort of reverence for her that prompted me to turn the rustling pages carefully, and feel startled if a door swung to in the quiet house, as if I were eavesdropping; but soon I ceased to hear, absorbed in her letter, which began as the first did.

" DEAR UNCLE, —

" To-day I begged John to write, and ask you to come here. I could not write you since I came here but that once, though your letters have been my great comfort, and I added a few words of entreaty to his, because I am dying, and it seems as if I must see you before I die; yet I fear the letter may not reach you, or you may be sick: and for that reason I write now, to tell you how terrible a necessity urged me to persuade you to such a journey. I can write but little at a time, my side is so painful; they call it slow-consumption here, but I know better; the heart within me is turned to stone, I felt it then —— Ah! you see my mind wandered in that last line; it still will return to the old theme, like a fugue tune, such as we had in the Plainfield singing-school. I remember one that went, 'The Lord is just, is just, is just.' — Is He? Dear Uncle, I must begin at the beginning, or you never will know. I wrote you from St. Louis, did I not? I meant to. From there, we had a dreary journey, not so bad to Fort Leavenworth, but after that inexpressibly dreary, and set with tokens of the dead, who perished before us. A long reach of prairie, day after day, and night after night; grass, and sky, and graves; grass, and sky, and graves; till I hardly knew whether the life I dragged along was life or death, as the thirsty, feverish days wore on into the awful and breathless nights, when every creature was dead asleep, and the very stars in heaven grew dim in the hot, sleepy air — dreadful days! I was too glad to see that bitter inland sea, blue as the fresh lakes, with its gray islands of bare rock, and sparkling sand shores, still more rejoiced to come upon the City itself, the rows of quaint, bare houses, and such cool water-sources, and, over all, near enough to rest both eyes and heart, the sunlit mountains, 'the shadow of a great rock in a weary land.'

"I liked my new house well. It was too large for our need, but pleasanter for its airiness, and the first thing I did was to plant a little hop-vine, that I had brought all the way with such great care, by the east porch. I wanted something like Plainfield in my home. I don't know why I linger so, I must write faster, for I grow weak all the time.

"I liked the City very well for awhile; the neighbors were kind, and John more than that; I could not be unhappy with him —— I thought. We had a pretty garden, for another man had owned the house before us, and we had not to begin everything. Our next door neighbor, Mrs. Colton, was good and kind to me, so was her daughter Lizzy, a pretty girl, with fair hair, — very fair. I wonder John liked it after mine. The first great shock I had was at a Mormon meeting. I cannot very well remember the ceremony, because I grew so faint; but I would not faint away lest some one should see me. I only remember that it was Mrs. Colton's husband with another wife being "sealed" to him, as they say here. You don't know what that means, Uncle Field; it is one part of this religion of Satan, that any man may have, if he will, three or four wives, perhaps more. I only know that shameless man, with grown daughters, and the hair on his head snow-white, has taken two, and his own wife, a firm believer in this — faith! looks on calmly, and lives with them in peace. I know that, and my soul sickened with disgust, but I did not fear; not a thought, not a dream, not a shadow of fear crossed me. I should have despised myself forever if the idea had stained my soul; my husband was *my* husband — mine — before God and man! and our child was in heaven; how glad I was she could never be a Mormon!

"I was sorry for Mrs. Colton, though she did not need it, and when I saw John leaning over their gate, or smoking in the porch with the old man, I thought he felt so, too, and I was glad to see him more sociable than ever he was in the States. After awhile he did not smoke, but talked with Elder Colton, and then would come home and expound out of the book of Mormon to me. I was very glad to have him earnest in his religion, but I could not be. Then he grew very thoughtful, and had a silent fit, but I took no notice of it, though I think now he meant to leave me, but I began to pine a little for home, and when I worked in the garden, and trained the vines about our veranda, I used to wish he would help me as he did Lizzy Colton, but I still remembered how good he was to pity and help them.

"O fool! yet, I had rather be a fool over again than have imagined — that I am glad of, even now — I did not once suspect.

"But one day — I remember every little thing in that day — even the slow ticking of the clock, as I tied up my hop-vine; and after that I went into the garden, and sat down on a little bench under the grape-trellis, and looked at the mountains. How beautiful they were! all purple in the shadow of sunset, and the sky golden green above them, with one scarlet cloud floating slowly upward: I hope I shall never see a red cloud again. Presently, John came and sat by me, and I laid my head on his shoulder; I was so glad to have him there — it cured my homesickness; once or twice he began to say something, and stopped, but I did not mind it. I wanted him to see a low line of mist creeping down a cañon in the mountains, and I stood up to point it out; so he rose, too, and in a strange, hurried way, began to say something about the Mormon faith, and the duties of a believer, which I did not notice either very much — I was so full of admiring the scarlet cloud — when, like a sudden thunder-clap at my ear, I heard this quick, resolute sentence: 'And so, according to the advice and best judgment of the Saints, Elizabeth Colton will be sealed to me, after two days, as my spiritual wife.'

"Then my soul fled out of my lips, in one cry — I was dead — my heart turned to a stone, and nothing can melt it! I did not speak, or sigh, but sat down on the bench, and John talked a great deal; I think he rubbed my hands and kissed me, but I did not feel it. I went away, by and by, when it was dark, into the house and into my room. I locked the door and looked at the wall till morning, then I went down and sat in a chair till night; and I drank, drank, drank, like a fever. All the time cold water, but it never reached my thirst. John came home, but he did not dare touch me; I was a dead corpse, with another spirit in it — not his wife — she was dead, and gone to heaven on a bright cloud. I remember being glad of that.

"In two days more he had a wife, and I was not his any longer. I staid up stairs when he was in the house, and locked my door, till, after a great many days, I began to feel sorry for him. Oh! how sorry! for I knew — I know — he will see himself some day with my eyes, but not till I die. Then I found my lips full of blood one morning, and that pleased me, for I knew it was a promise of the life to come; now I should go to heaven, where there are n't any Mormons.

"I believe, though, people were kind to me all the time; for I remember they came and said things to me, and one shook me a little to see if I felt; and one woman cried. I was glad of that, for I could n't cry. However, after three months, I was better: worse, John said one day, and he brought a doctor, but the man knew as well as I did — so he said nothing at all, and gave me some herb tea; — tell Aunt Martha that.

"Then I could walk out of doors, but I did not care to; only once I smelt the hop-blossoms, and that I could not bear, so I went out and pulled up my hop-vine by the roots, and laid it out, all straight, in the fierce sunshine: it died directly. In the winter, John had another wife sealed to him; I heard somebody say so; he did not tell me, and if he had I could not help it. I found he had taken a little adobe house for those two, and I knew it was out of tenderness for my feelings he did so. Oh! Uncle Field! perhaps he has loved me all this time? I know better, though, than that? Spring came, and I was very weak, and I grew not to care about anything; so I told John he could bring those two women to this house if he wished; I did not care, only nobody must ever come into my room. He looked ashamed, and pleased, too; but he brought them, and nobody ever did come into my room. By and by Elizabeth Colton brought a little baby down stairs, and its name was Clara. Poor child! poor little Mormon child! I hope it will die some time before it grows up; only I should not like it to come my side of heaven, for it had blue eyes like John's.

"Then I grew more and more ill, and now I am really dying, and no letter has come from you! It takes so long — three whole months, and I have been more than a year in the house with John Henderson and the two women. I know I shall never see you, but I must speak, I must, even out of the grave; and I keep hearing that old fugue. 'The Lord is just, is just, is just; the Lord is just and good!' Is he? I know He is; but I forget sometimes. Uncle Field! you must pray for John! you *must!* I cannot die and leave him in his sins, his delusion; he does not think it is sin, but I know it. Pray! pray! dear Uncle: don't be discouraged — do not fear — he *will* be undeceived some time; he will repent, I know! The Lord is just, and I will pray in heaven, and I will tell Nelly to, but *you* must. It says in the Bible, 'the prayer of a righteous man'; and oh! I am not righteous! I should not have married him; it was an unequal yoke, and I have borne the burden; but I loved him so much! Uncle Field, I did not keep myself from idols. Pray! I shall be dead, but he lives. Pray for him, and, if you will, for the little child — because — I am dying. Dear Nelly! — "

"Are you blotting my letter, young man?" said Parson Field, at my elbow, as I deciphered the last broken, trembling line of Ada's story. "Here I have been five minutes, and you did not hear me!" I really had blotted the letter!

BEYOND.

By JOHN GIBSON LOCKHART.

WHEN youthful faith hath fled,
   Of loving take thy leave;
Be constant to the dead, —
   The dead cannot deceive

Sweet modest flowers of spring,
   How fleet your balmy day!
And man's brief year can bring
   No secondary May, —

No earthly burst again
   Of gladness out of gloom;
Fond hope and vision vain,
   Ungrateful to the tomb.

But 't is an old belief
   That on some solemn shore,
Beyond the sphere of grief,
   Dear friends shall meet once more, —

Beyond the sphere of time,
   And sin and fate's control,
Serene in endless prime
   Of body and of soul.

That creed I fain would keep,
   That hope I'll not forego;
Eternal be the sleep,
   Unless to waken so.

AUTOBIOGRAPHICAL PASSAGES

By JOHN MILTON.

FOR although a poet, soaring in the high region of his fancies, with his garland and singing-robes about him, might, without apology, speak more of himself than I mean to do; yet for me sitting here below in the cool element of prose, a mortal thing among many readers, of no empyreal conceit, to venture and divulge unusual things of myself, I shall petition to the gentler sort, it may not be envy to me. I must say, therefore, that after I had, for my first years, by the ceaseless diligence and care of my father, whom God recompense, been exercised to the tongues, and some sciences, as my age would suffer, by sundry masters and teachers, both at home and at the schools, it was found that whether aught was imposed me by them that had the overlooking, or betaken to of mine own choice in English, or other tongue, prosing or versing, but chiefly this latter, the style, by certain vital signs it had, was likely to live. But much latelier, in the private academies of Italy, whither I was favored to resort, perceiving that some trifles which I had in memory, composed at under twenty or thereabout (for the manner is that every one must give some proof of his wit and reading there), met with acceptance above what was looked for; and other things which I had shifted in scarcity of books and conveniences, to patch up amongst them, were received with written encomiums, which the Italian is not forward to bestow on men of this side the Alps, I began thus far to

assent both to them and divers of my friends here at home, and not less to an inward prompting, which now grew daily upon me, that by labor and intent study, (which I take to be my portion in this life,) joined with the strong propensity of nature, I might perhaps leave something so written, to after-times, as they should not willingly let it die. These thoughts at once possessed me, and these other; that if I were certain to write as men buy leases, for three lives and downward, there ought no regard be sooner had than to God's glory, by the honor and instruction of my country. For which cause, and not only for that I knew it would be hard to arrive at the second rank among the Latins, I applied myself to that resolution which Ariosto followed against the persuasions of Bembo, to fix all the industry and art I could unite to the adorning of my native tongue; not to make verbal curiosities the end, (that were a toilsome vanity,) but to be an interpreter and relater of the best and sagest things among mine own citizens throughout this island, in the mother dialect. That what the greatest and choicest wits of Athens, Rome, or modern Italy, and those Hebrews of old did for their country, I, in my proportion, with this over and above, of being a Christian, might do for mine; not caring to be once named abroad, though perhaps I could attain to that, but content with these British islands as my world; whose fortune hath hitherto been, that if the Athenians, as some say, made their small deeds great and renowned by their eloquent writers, England hath had her noble achievements made small by the unskilful handling of monks and mechanics.

Time serves not now, and perhaps I might seem too profuse, to give any certain account of what the mind at home, in the spacious circuits of her musing, hath liberty to propose to herself, though of highest hope and hardest attempting. Whether that epic form, whereof the two poems of Homer, and those other two of Virgil and Tasso are a diffuse, and the book of Job a brief model; or whether the rules of Aristotle herein are strictly to be kept, or nature to be followed, which in them that know art, and use judgment, is no transgression, but an enriching of art. And lastly, what king or knight before the conquest, might be chosen, in whom to lay the pattern of a Christian hero. And as Tasso gave to a prince of Italy his choice, whether he would command him to write of Godfrey's expedition against the infidels, or Belisarius against the Goths, or Charlemagne against the Lombards; if to the instinct of nature and the emboldening of art aught may be trusted, and that there be nothing adverse in our climate, or the fate of this age, it haply would be no rashness, from an equal diligence and inclination, to present the like offer in our own ancient stories. Or whether those dramatic constitutions, wherein Sophocles and Euripides reign, shall be found more doctrinal and exemplary to a nation. The Scripture also affords us a divine pastoral drama in the Song of Solomon, consisting of two persons, and a double chorus, as Origen rightly judges; and the Apocalypse of St. John is the majestic image of a high and stately tragedy, shutting up and intermingling her solemn scenes and acts with a seven-fold chorus of hallelujahs and harping symphonies. And this my opinion, the grave authority of Pareus, commenting that book, is sufficient to confirm. Or if occasion should lead, to imitate those magnific odes and hymns, wherein Pindarus and Callimachus are in most things worthy, some others in their frame judicious, in their matter most an end faulty. But those frequent songs throughout the laws and prophets, beyond all these, not in their divine argument alone, but in the very critical art of composition, may be easily made appear over all the kinds of lyric poesy to be incomparable. These abilities, wheresoever they be found, are the inspired gift of God, rarely bestowed, but yet to some (though most abuse) in every nation: and are of power, beside the office of a pulpit, to inbreed and cherish in a great people the seeds of virtue and public civility; to allay the perturbations of the mind, and set the affections in right tune; to celebrate in glorious and lofty hymns the throne and equipage of God's almightiness, and what he suffers to be wrought with high providence in his church; to sing victorious agonies of martyrs and saints, the deeds and triumphs of just and pious nations, doing valiantly through faith against the enemies of Christ; to deplore the general relapses of kingdoms and states from justice and God's true worship. Lastly, whatsoever in religion is holy and sublime, in virtue amiable or grave, whatsoever hath passion or admiration in all the changes of that which is called fortune from without, or the wily subtleties and refluxes of man's thoughts from within; all these things, with a solid and treatable smoothness, to point out and describe. Teaching over the whole book of sanctity and virtue, through all the instances of example, with such delight to those especially of soft and delicious temper, who will not so much as look upon truth herself, unless they see her elegantly dressed; that whereas the paths of honesty and good life appear now rugged and difficult, though they be indeed easy and pleasant, they will then appear to all men both easy and pleasant, though they were rugged and difficult indeed. And what a benefit this would be to our youth and gentry, may be soon guessed by what we know of the corruption and bane which they suck in daily from the writings and interludes of libidinous and ignorant poetasters, who having scarce ever heard of that which is the main consistence of a true poem, the choice of such persons as they ought to introduce, and what is moral and decent to each one, do for the most part lay up vicious principles in sweet pills, to be swallowed down, and make the taste of virtuous documents harsh and sour. But because the spirit of man cannot demean itself lively in this body, without some recreating intermission of labor and serious things, it were happy for the commonwealth, if our magistrates, as in those famous governments of old, would take into their care, not only the deciding of our contentious law cases and brawls, but the managing of our public sports and festival pastimes, that they might be, not such as were authorized awhile since, the provocations of drunkenness and lust, but such as may inure and harden our bodies, by martial exercises, to all warlike skill and performance; and may civilize, adorn, and make discreet our minds, by the learned and affable meeting of frequent academies, and the procurement of wise and artful recitations, sweetened with eloquent and graceful enticements to the love and practice of justice, temperance, and fortitude, instructing and bettering the nation at all opportunities, that the call of wisdom and virtue may be heard everywhere, as Solomon saith: "She crieth without, she uttereth her voice in the streets, in the top of high places, in the chief concourse, and in the openings of the gates." Whether this may not be only in pulpits, but after another persuasive method, at set and solemn paneguries, in theatres, porches, or what other place or way may win most upon the people, to receive at once both recreation and instruction; let them in authority consult. The thing which I had to say, and those intentions which have lived within me, ever since I could conceive myself anything worth to my country, I return to crave excuse, that urgent reason hath plucked from me, by an abortive and foredated discovery. And the accomplishment of them lies not but in a power above man's to promise; but that none hath by more studious ways endeavored, and with more unwearied spirit that none shall, that I dare almost aver of myself, as far as life and free leisure will extend; and that the land had once enfranchised herself from this impertinent yoke of prelacy, under whose inquisitorious and tyrannical duncery no free and splendid wit can flourish. Neither do I think it shame to covenant with any knowing reader, that for some few years yet I may go on trust with him toward the payment of what I am now indebted, as being a work not to be raised from the heat of youth, or the vapors of wine; like that which flows at waste from the pen of some vulgar amorist, or the trencher-fury of a rhyming parasite; nor to be obtained by the invocation of dame Memory and her syren daughters; but by devout prayer to that eternal Spirit, who can enrich with all utterance and knowledge, and sends out his seraphim with the hallowed fire of his altar, to touch and purify the lips of whom he pleases. To this must be added industrious and select reading, steady observation, insight into all seemly and generous arts and affairs; till which in some measure be compassed, at mine own peril and cost, I refuse not to sustain this expectation from as many as are not loth to hazard so much credulity upon the best pledges that I can give them. Although it nothing content me to have disclosed thus much beforehand, but that I trust hereby to make it manifest with what small willingness I endure to interrupt the pursuit of no less hopes than these, and leave a calm and pleasing solitariness, fed with cheerful and confident thoughts, to embark in a troubled sea of noises and hoarse disputes; from beholding the bright countenance of truth in the quiet and still air of delightful studies, to come into the dim reflection of hollow antiquities sold by the seeming bulk, and there be fain to club quotations with men whose learning and belief lies in marginal stuffings; who when they have, like good sumpters, laid you down their horse-load of citations and fathers at your door, with a rhapsody of who and who were bishops here or there, you may take off their pack-saddles, their day's work is done, and episcopacy, as they think, stoutly vindicated. Let any gentle apprehension that can distinguish learned pains from unlearned drudgery, imagine what pleasure or profoundness can be in this, or what honor to deal against such adversaries. But were it the meanest under-service, if God, by his secretary, conscience, enjoin it, it were sad for me if I should draw back; for me especially, now when all men offer their aid to help, ease, and lighten the difficult labors of the Church to whose service, by the intentions of my parents and friends, I was destined of a child, and in mine own resolutions, till coming to some maturity of years, and perceiving what tyranny had invaded the Church, that he who would take orders, must subscribe slave, and take an oath withal; which unless he took with a conscience that would retch, he must either strait perjure, or split his faith; I thought it better to prefer a blameless silence, before the sacred office of speaking, bought and begun with servitude and forswearing.

WAKENING.

By WILLIAM ALLINGHAM.

A GOLDEN pen I mean to take,
   A book of ivory white,
And in the mornings when I wake
   The kind dream-thoughts to write,
Which come from heaven for love's support,
   Like dews that fall at night.
For soon the delicate gifts decay,
As stirs the mired and smoky day.

"Sleep is like death," and after sleep
   The world seems new begun;
Its earnestness all clear and deep,
   Its true solution won;
White thoughts stand luminous and firm,
   Like statues in the sun;
Refreshed from super-sensuous founts,
The soul to purer vision mounts.

JOHN GRAHAM,

FIRST VISCOUNT OF DUNDEE.

By EDMUND LODGE.

THIS remarkable man, whose name can never be forgotten while military skill and prowess, and the most loyal and active fidelity to an almost hopeless cause, shall challenge recollection, was the eldest son of Sir William Graham, of Claverhouse, in the County of Forfar, by Jane, fourth daughter of John Carnegy, first Earl of Northesk. His family was a scion which branched off from the ancient stock of the great House of Montrose, early in the fifteenth century, by the second marriage of William Lord Graham, of Kincardine, to Mary, second daughter of Robert the Third, King of Scotland, and had gradually acquired considerable estates, chiefly by the bounty of the Crown. He received his education in the University of St. Andrews, which he left to seek on the Continent the more polished qualifications of a private gentleman of large fortune, the sphere to which he seemed to have been destined. In France, however, the latent fire of his character broke forth; he entered as a volunteer into the army of Louis the Fourteenth; and having presently determined to adopt the military profession, accepted in 1672 a commission of Cornet in the Horse Guards of William the Third, Prince of Orange, by whom, in the summer of 1674, he was promoted to be Captain of a troop, for his signal gallantry at the battle of Seneffe, in which indeed he saved the life of that Prince by a personal

effort. He asked soon after for the command of one of the Scottish regiments in the Dutch service, and, strange to tell, was refused, on which he threw up his commission, making the cutting remark, that "the soldier who has not gratitude cannot be brave," and returned to England, bringing with him, however, the warmest recommendations from William to Charles the Second; and Charles, who had been just then misadvised to subdue the obstinacy of the Scottish Covenanters by force of arms, appointed him to lead a body of horse which had been raised in Scotland for that purpose, and gave him full powers to act as he might think fit against them, although under the nominal command of the Duke of Monmouth. His conduct in the performance of this impolitic and cruel commission has left a stain on his memory scarcely to be glossed over by the brilliancy of his subsequent merits. Bred from his infancy in an enthusiastic veneration to monarchy, and to the Established Church, his hatred to the Whigs, as they were then called in Scotland, was almost a part of his nature; and, under the influence of a temper which never allowed him to be lukewarm in any pursuit, his zeal degenerated on this occasion with a frightful facility into a spirit of persecution. He watched and dispersed, with the most severe vigilance, the devotional meetings of those perverse and miserable sectaries, and forced thousands of them to subscribe, at the point of the sword, to an oath utterly subversive of the doctrines which they most cherished. But this was not the worst. On the 1st of July, 1679, having attacked a conventicle on Loudoun Hill, in Ayrshire, the neighboring peasants rose suddenly on a detachment of his troops, and, with that almost supernatural power which a pure thirst of vengeance alone will sometimes confer on mere physical force, defeated them with considerable loss. The fancied disgrace annexed to this check raised Graham's fury to the highest pitch, and he permitted himself to retaliate on the unarmed Whigs by cruelties inconsistent with the character of a brave man. The track of his march was now uniformly marked by carnage; the refusal of his test was punished with instant death; and the practice of these horrible excesses, which was continued for some months, procured for him the appellation of "Bloody Claverhouse"; by which he is still occasionally mentioned in that part of Scotland. He apologized for these horrors by coldly remarking, that "if terror ended or prevented war, it was true mercy."

It may be concluded that this intemperance had the full approbation of the Crown, for we find that he was appointed in 1682 Sheriff of the Shire of Wigton; received soon after a commission of Captain in what was called the Royal Regiment of Horse; was sworn a Privy-Councillor in Scotland; and had a grant from the King of the Castle of Dudhope, and the office of Constable of Dundee. Nor was it less acceptable — such is the rage of party, especially when excited by religious discord — to the Scottish Episcopalians, who from that time seemed to have reposed in him the highest confidence. James, however, in forming on his accession a new Privy Council for that country, was prevailed on to omit his name, on the ground of his having connected himself in marriage with the fanatical family of Cochrane, Earl of Dundonald, but that umbrage was soon removed, and in 1686 he was restored to his seat in the Council, and appointed a Brigadier-General; in 1688 promoted to the rank of Major-General; and, on the 12th of November in that year, created by patent to him, and the heirs male of his body, with remainder, in default of such issue, to his other heirs male, Viscount of Dundee, and Baron Graham of Claverhouse, in Scotland. The gift of these dignities was, in fact, the concluding act of James's expiring government. Graham, who was then attending that unhappy Prince in London, used every effort that good sense and high spirit could suggest, to induce him to remain in his capital, and await there with dignified firmness the arrival of the Prince of Orange; undertaking for himself to collect, with that promptitude which was almost peculiar to him, ten thousand of the King's disbanded troops, and at their head to annihilate the Dutch forces which William had brought with him. Perhaps there existed not on the face of the earth another man so likely to redeem such an engagement; but James, depressed and irresolute, refused the offer. Struck, however, with the zeal and bravery, and indeed with the personal affection, which had dictated it, he intrusted to Dundee the direction of all his military affairs in Scotland, whither that nobleman repaired just at the time that James fled from London.

When he arrived at Edinburgh he found a Convention sitting, as in London, of the Estates of the country, in which he took his place. He complained to that assembly that a design had been formed to assassinate him; required that all strangers should be removed from the town; and, his request having been denied, he left Edinburgh at the head of a troop of horse, which he had hastily formed there of soldiers who had deserted in England from his own regiment. In the short interval afforded by the discussion of this matter, he formed his plans. After a conference with the Duke of Gordon, who then held the Castle for James, he set out for Stirling, where he called a Parliament of the friends of that Prince, and the revolutionists in Scotland saw their influence, even within a few days, dispelled as it were by magic, in obedience to his powerful energies. He was, in a manner, without troops, depending on the affections of those around him, which he had heated to enthusiasm, when a force sent by the Convention to seize his person seemed to remind him that he must have an army. He retired therefore into Lochaber; summoned a meeting of the chiefs of clans in the Highlands, and presently found himself at the head of six thousand of the hardy natives, well armed and accoutred. He now wrote to James, who, in compliance with French counsels, was wasting his time and means in Ireland, conjuring him to embark with a part of his army for Scotland, "where," as he told the king, "there were no regular troops, except four regiments, which William had lately sent down; where his presence would fix the wavering, and intimidate the timid; and where hosts of shepherds would start up warriors at the first wave of his banner upon their mountains." With the candor and plainness of a soldier and a faithful servant, he besought James to be content with the exercise of his own religion, and to leave in Ireland the Earl of Melfort, Secretary of State, between whom and himself some jealousy existed which might be prejudicial to a service in which they were alike devotedly sincere, however they might differ as to the best means of advancing it. James rejected his advice. "Dundee was furnished," says Burnet, "with some small store of arms and ammunition, and had kind promises, encouraging him, and all that joined with him."

Left now to his own discretion and his own resources, he displayed, together with the greatest military qualifications, and the most exalted generosity and disinterestedness, all the subtlety of a refined politician. On his arrival at Inverness he found that a discord had long subsisted between the people of the town and some neighboring chiefs, on an alleged debt from the one to the other, and that the two parties, with their dependants, had assembled in arms to decide the quarrel. He heard the allegations of the principals on each side, with an affectation of the exactness of judicial inquiry, and then, having convened the entire mass of the conflicting parties in public, reproached them with the most cutting severity, that they, "who were all equally friends to King James, should be preparing, at a time when he most needed their friendship, to draw those daggers against each other which ought to be plunged only into the breasts of his enemies." He then paid from his own purse the debt in dispute; and the late litigants, charmed by the grandeur of his conduct, instantly placed themselves in a cordial union under his banner. To certain other chiefs, upon whose estates the Earl of Argyle, who sought to restore his importance by attaching himself to the revolutionary party, had ancient claims in law, and to others, who had obtained grants from the Crown of some of that nobleman's forfeited lands, he represented the peril in which they would be placed by the success of William's enterprise on the British throne, and gained them readily to his beloved cause. He addressed himself with signal effect to all the powerful men of the north of Scotland; fomented the angry feelings of those who thought themselves neglected by the new government; flattered the vanity of those who, indifferent to the affairs of either party, sought simply for power and importance; corrupted several officers of the regiments which were in preparation to be sent against him; and even managed to maintain a constant correspondence with some members of the Privy Council, by whom he was regularly apprised of the plans contrived from time to time to counteract his gigantic efforts. Nay, he contrived to detach, as it were in a moment, from Lord Murray, heir to the Earl of Athol, a body of a thousand men, raised by that nobleman on his father's estates; a defection of Highland vassals which had never till then occurred. " While Murray," says my author, " was reviewing them, they quitted their ranks; ran to an adjoining brook; filled their bonnets with water; drank to King James's health; and, with pipes playing, marched off to Lord Dundee."

So acute and experienced a commander as William could not be long unconscious of the importance of such an enemy. He despatched into Scotland, at the head of between five and six thousand picked troops, General M'Kay, who had long served him in Holland with the highest military reputation. In the mean time, James, who had been apprised of this disposition, sent orders to Dundee not to hazard a battle till the arrival of a force from Ireland, which he now promised. Two months, however, elapsed before it appeared, which Dundee, burning with impatience, was necessitated to pass in the mountains, in marches of unexampled rapidity, in furious partial attacks, and masterly retreats. It has been well said of him, that "the first messenger of his approach was generally his own army in fight, and that the first intelligence of his retreat, brought accounts that he was already out of his enemy's reach." The long-expected aid at length arrived, in the last week of June, 1689, consisting only of five hundred raw and ill-provided recruits, but he instantly made ready for action. He advanced to meet M'Kay, who was preparing to invest the Castle of Blair, in Athol, a fortress the possession whereof enabled James's army to maintain a free communication between the northern and southern Highlands, and determined to attack William's troops on a small plain at the mouth of the pass of Killicranky, after they should have marched through that remarkable defile, on their road to Blair. On the 16th of July, at noon, M'Kay's army arrived on the plain, and discovered Dundee in array on the opposite hills. He had resolved, for reasons abounding with military genius, to defer his onset till the evening, and M'Kay, by various expedients vainly tempted him during the day to descend: at length, half an hour before sunset, his Highlanders rushed down with the celerity and the fury of lions, and William's army was in an instant completely routed. Dundee, who had fought on foot, now mounted his horse, and flew towards the pass, to cut off their retreat, when, looking back, he found that he had outstripped his men, and was nearly alone. He halted, and, wavering his arm in the air, pointed to the pass, as a signal to them to hasten their march, and to occupy it. At that moment a ball from a musket aimed at him lodged in his body, immediately under the arm so raised. He fell from his horse, and, fainting, was carried off the field; but, soon after recovering his senses for a few seconds, he hastily inquired "how things went," and on being answered "all was well," — "Then," said he, "I am well," and expired. William, on hearing of his death, said, "The war in Scotland is now ended."

The memory of this heroic partisan has been cherished in the hearts, and celebrated by the pens, of numbers of his countrymen. A poet thus pathetically addresses his shade, and bewails the loss sustained by Scotland in his death: —

> "Ultime Scotorum, potuit quo sospite solo
> Libertas patriæ salva fuisse tuæ.
> Te moriente novos accepit Scotia cives,
> Accepitque novos te moriente Deos.
> Illa tibi superesse negat, tu non potes illi.
> Ergo Caledonia, nomen inane, vale!
> Tuque vale gentis priscæ fortissime ductor,
> Optime Scotorum, atque ultime, Grame, vale!"

And Sir John Dalrymple has left us some particulars of his military character exquisitely curious and interesting. "In his marches," says that author, "his men frequently wanted bread, salt, and all liquors except water, during several weeks, yet were ashamed to complain, when they observed that their commander lived not more delicately than themselves. If anything good was brought him to eat, he sent it to a faint or sick soldier. If a soldier was weary, he offered to carry his arms. He kept those who were with him from sinking under their fatigues, not so much by exhortation as by preventing them from attending to their sufferings; for this reason he walked on foot with the men; now by the side of one clan, and anon by that of another: he amused them with jokes; he flattered them with his knowledge of their genealogies; he animated them by a recital of the deeds of their ancestors, and of the verses of their bards. It was one of his maxims that no general should fight with an irregular army, unless he was acquainted with every man he commanded. Yet, with these habits of familiarity, the severity of his discipline was dreadful: the only punishment he inflicted was death. All other punishments, he said, disgraced a gentleman, and all who were with him were of that rank; but that death was a relief from the consciousness of crime. It is reported of him that having seen a youth fly in his first action, he pretended he had sent him to the rear on a message. The youth fled a second time — he brought him to the front of the army, and saying that 'a gentleman's son ought not to fall by the hands of a common executioner,' shot him with his own pistol."

In society he is said to have been as much distinguished by a delicacy and softness of manners and temper, and by the most refined politeness, as he was by his sternness in war. Sir Walter Scott, in his Romance of *Old Mortality*, in which facts and fiction are blended with an uncommon felicity, gives us the following picture of his person and demeanor, evidently not the work of fancy, and probably in substance the result of respectable and inveterate tradition: —

" Graham of Claverhouse was rather low of stature, and slightly, though elegantly, formed; his gesture, language, and manners, were those of one whose life had been spent among the noble and the gay. His features exhibited even feminine regularity. An oval face, a straight and well-formed nose, dark hazel eyes, a complexion just sufficiently tinged with brown to save it from the charge of effeminacy, a short upper lip, curved upwards like that of a Grecian statue, and slightly shaded by small mustachios of light brown, joined to a profusion of long curled locks of the same color, which fell down on each side of his face, contributed to form such a countenance as limners like to paint, and ladies to look upon. The severity of his character, as well as the higher attributes of undaunted and enterprising valor which even his enemies were compelled to admit, lay concealed under an exterior which seemed adapted to the court or the saloon rather than to the field. The same gentleness and gayety of expression which reigned in his features seemed to inspire his actions and gestures ; and, on the whole, he was generally esteemed, at first sight, rather qualified to be the votary of pleasure than of ambition. But under this soft exterior was hidden a spirit unbounded in daring and in aspiring, yet cautious and prudent as that of Machiavel himself. Profound in politics, and imbued, of course, with that disregard for individual rights which its intrigues usually generate, this leader was cool in pursuing success, careless of death himself, and ruthless in inflicting it upon others. Such are the characters formed in times of civil discord, when the highest qualities, perverted by party spirit, and inflamed by habitual opposition, are too often combined with vices and excesses, which deprive them at once of their merit and of their lustre."

THE BURIAL-MARCH OF DUNDEE.*

By W. EDMONDSTOUNE AYTOUN.

SOUND the fife, and cry the slogan,—
Let the pribroch shake the air
With its wild triumphal music,
    Worthy of the freight we bear.
Let the ancient hills of Scotland
    Hear once more the battle-song
Swell within their glens and valleys
    As the clansmen march along!
Never from the field of combat,
    Never from the deadly fray,
Was a nobler trophy carried
    Than we bring with us to-day,—
Never, since the valiant Douglas
    On his dauntless bosom bore
Good King Robert's heart — the priceless —
    To our dear Redeemer's shore!
Lo! we bring with us the hero,—
    Lo! we bring the conquering Græme,
Crowned as best beseems a victor
    From the altar of his fame;
Fresh and bleeding from the battle
    Whence his spirit took its flight,

---

* John Graham of Claverhouse, Viscount Dundee, was killed at the battle of Killiecrankie in Scotland.

Midst the crashing charge of squadrons,
   And the thunder of the fight!
Strike, I say, the notes of triumph,
   As we march o'er moor and lea!
Is there any here will venture
   To bewail our dead Dundee?
Let the widows of the traitors
   Weep until their eyes are dim!
Wail ye may full well for Scotland,—
   Let none dare to mourn for him!
See! above his glorious body
   Lies the royal banner's fold;
See! his valiant blood is mingled
   With its crimson and its gold.
See how calm he looks, and stately,
   Like a warrior on his shield,
Waiting till the flush of morning
   Breaks along the battle-field!
See — O never more, my comrades,
   Shall we see that falcon eye
Redden with its inward lightning,
   As the hour of fight drew nigh!
Never shall we hear the voice that
   Clearer than the trumpet's call,
Bade us strike for King and Country,
   Bade us win the field, or fall!
On the heights of Killiecrankie
   Yester-morn our army lay:
Slowly rose the mist in columns
   From the river's broken way;
Hoarsely roared the swollen torrent,
   And the Pass was wrapt in gloom,
When the clansmen rose together
   From their lair amidst the broom.

Then we belted on our tartans,
  And our bonnets down we drew,
And we felt our broadswords' edges,
  And we proved them to be true;
And we prayed the prayer of soldiers,
  And we cried the gathering-cry,
And we clasped the hands of kinsmen,
  And we swore to do or die!
Then our leader rode before us
  On his war-horse black as night,—
Well the Cameronian rebels
  Know that charger in the fight!—
And a cry of exultation
  From the bearded warriors rose;
For we loved the house of Claver'se,
  And we thought of good Montrose.
But he raised his hand for silence—
  "Soldiers! I have sworn a vow:
Ere the evening star shall glisten
  On Schehallion's lofty brow,
Either we shall rest in triumph,
  Or another of the Græmes
Shall have died in battle-harness
  For his Country and King James!
Think upon the Royal Martyr,—
  Think of what his race endure,—
Think of him whom butchers murdered
  On the field of Magus Muir:—
By his sacred blood I charge ye,
  By the ruined hearth and shrine,—
By the blighted hopes of Scotland,
  By your injuries and mine,—
Strike this day as if the anvil
  Lay beneath your blows the while,

Be they covenanting traitors,
    Or the brood of false Argyle!
Strike! and drive the trembling rebels
    Backwards o'er the stormy Forth;
Let them tell their pale Convention
    How they fared within the North.
Let them tell that Highland honor
    Is not to be bought nor sold,
That we scorn their prince's anger
    As we loathe his foreign gold.
Strike! and when the fight is over,
    If ye look in vain for me,
Where the dead are lying thickest,
    Search for him that was Dundee!"

Loudly then the hills re-echoed
    With our answer to his call,
But a deeper echo sounded
    In the bosoms of us all.
For the lands of wide Breadalbane,
    Not a man who heard him speak
Would that day have left the battle.
    Burning eye and flushing cheek
Told the clansmen's fierce emotion,
    And they harder drew their breath;
For their souls were strong within them,
    Stronger than the grasp of death.
Soon we heard a challenge-trumpet
    Sounding in the Pass below,
And the distant tramp of horses,
    And the voices of the foe:
Down we crouched amid the bracken,
    Till the Lowland ranks drew near,
Panting like the hounds in summer,
    When they scent the stately deer.

From the dark defile emerging,
    Next we saw the squadrons come,
Leslie's foot and Leven's troopers
    Marching to the tuck of drum;
Through the scattered wood of birches,
    O'er the broken ground and heath,
Wound the long battalion slowly,
    Till they gained the plain beneath;
Then we bounded from our covert,—
    Judge how looked the Saxons then,
When they saw the rugged mountains
    Start to life with armèd men!
Like a tempest down the ridges
    Swept the hurricane of steel,
Rose the slogan of Macdonald,—
    Flashed the broadsword of Lochiel!
Vainly sped the withering volley
    'Mongst the foremost of our band,—
On we poured until we met them,
    Foot to foot, and hand to hand.
Horse and man went down like drift-wood
    When the floods are black at Yule,
And their carcasses are whirling
    In the Garry's deepest pool.
Horse and man went down before us,—
    Living foe there tarried none
On the field of Killiecrankie,
    When that stubborn fight was done!

And the evening star was shining
    On Schehallion's distant head,
When we wiped our bloody broadswords,
    And returned to count the dead.
There we found him gashed and gory,
    Stretched upon the cumbered plain,

As he told us where to seek him,
  In the thickest of the slain.
And a smile was on his visage,
  For within his dying ear
Pealed the joyful note of triumph,
  And the clansmen's clamorous cheer:
So, amidst the battle's thunder,
  Shot, and steel, and scorching flame,
In the glory of his manhood
  Passed the spirit of the Græme!

Open wide the vaults of Atholl,
  Where the bones of heroes rest,—
Open wide the hallowed portals
  To receive another guest!
Last of Scots, and last of freemen,—
  Last of all that dauntless race,
Who would rather die unsullied
  Than outlive the land's disgrace!
O thou lion-hearted warrior!
  Reck not of the after-time;
Honor may be deemed dishonor,
  Loyalty be called a crime.
Sleep in peace with kindred ashes
  Of the noble and the true,
Hands that never failed their country,
  Hearts that never baseness knew.
Sleep!— and till the latest trumpet
  Wakes the dead from earth and sea,
Scotland shall not boast a braver
  Chieftain than our own Dundee!

MIGNON AS AN ANGEL.

By GOETHE.

IT chanced that the birthday of two twin-sisters, whose behavior had been always very good, was near; I promised that, on this occasion, the little present they had so well deserved should be delivered to them by an angel. They were on the stretch of curiosity regarding this phenomenon. I had chosen Mignon for the part; and accordingly, at the appointed day, I had her suitably equipped in a long light snow-white dress. She was, of course, provided with a golden girdle round her waist, and a golden fillet on her hair. I at first proposed to omit the wings; but the young ladies who were decking her, insisted on a pair of large golden pinions, in preparing which they meant to show their highest art. Thus did the strange apparition, with a lily in the one hand, and a little basket in the other, glide in among the girls: she surprised even me. "There comes the angel!" said I. The children all shrank back; at last they cried: "It is Mignon!" yet they durst not venture to approach the wondrous figure.

"Here are your gifts," said she, putting down the basket. They gathered around her, they viewed, they felt, they questioned her.

"Art though an angel?" asked one of them.

"I wish I were," said Mignon.

"Why dost thou bear a lily?"

"So pure and so open should my heart be; then were I happy."
" What wings are these? Let us see them!"
"They represent far finer ones, which are not yet unfolded."
And thus significantly did she answer all their other childlike, innocent inquiries. The little party having satisfied their curiosity, and the impression of the show beginning to abate, we were for proceeding to undress the little angel. This, however, she resisted: she took her cithern; she seated herself here, on this high writing-table, and sang a little song with touching grace: —

> Such let me seem, till such I be;
> Take not my snow-white dress away;
> Soon from this dusk of earth I flee
> Up to the glittering lands of day.
>
> There first a little space I rest,
> Then wake so glad, to scene so kind;
> In earthly robes no longer drest,
> This band, this girdle left behind.
>
> And those calm shining sons of morn,
> They ask not who is maid or boy;
> No robes, no garments there are worn,
> Our body pure from sin's alloy.
>
> Through little life not much I toiled,
> Yet anguish long this heart has wrung,
> Untimely woe my blossom spoiled;
> Make me again forever young!

THE CAGE AT CRANFORD.

By MRS. GASKELL.

HAVE I told you anything about my friends at Cranford since the year 1856? I think not.
You remember the Gordons, don't you? She that was Jessie Brown, who married her old love, Major Gordon: and from being poor became quite a rich lady: but for all that never forgot any of her old friends in Cranford.

Well! the Gordons were travelling abroad, for they were very fond of travelling; people who have had to spend part of their lives in a regiment always are, I think. They were now at Paris, in May, 1856, and were going to stop there, and in the neighborhood all summer, but Mr. Ludovic was coming to England soon; so Mrs. Gordon wrote me word. I was glad she told me, for just then I was waiting to make a little present to Miss Pole, with whom I was staying; so I wrote to Mrs. Gordon, and asked her to choose me out something pretty and new and fashionable, that would be acceptable to Miss Pole. Miss Pole had just been talking a great deal about Mrs. Fitz Adam's caps being so unfashionable, which I suppose made me put in that word fashionable; but afterwards I wished I had sent to say my present was not to be too fashionable; for there *is* such a thing, I can assure you! The price of my present was not to be more than twenty shillings, but that is a very handsome sum if you put it in that way, though it may not sound so much if you only call it a sovereign.

Mrs. Gordon wrote back to me, pleased, as she always was, with doing anything for her old friends. She told me she had been out for a day's shopping before going into the country, and had got a cage for herself of the newest and most elegant description, and had thought that she could not do better than get another like it as my present for Miss Pole, as cages were so much better made in Paris than anywhere else. I was rather dismayed when I read this letter, for however pretty a cage might be, it was something for Miss Pole's own self, and not for her parrot, that I had intended to get. Here had I been finding ever so many reasons against her buying a new cap at Johnson's fashion-show, because I thought that the present which Mrs. Gordon was to choose for me in Paris might turn out to be an elegant and fashionable head-dress; a kind of cross between a turban and a cap, as I see those from Paris mostly are; and now I had to veer round, and advise her to go as fast as she could, and secure Mr. Johnson's cap before any other purchaser snatched it up. But Miss Pole was too sharp for me.

"Why, Mary," said she, "it was only yesterday you were running down that cap like anything. You said, you know, that lilac was too old a color for me; and green too young; and that the mixture was very unbecoming."

"Yes, I know," said I; "but I have thought better of it. I thought about it a great deal last night, and I think — I thought — they would neutralize each other; and the shadows of any color are, you know — something I know — complementary colors." I was not sure of my own meaning, but I had an idea in my head, though I could not express it. She took me up shortly.

"Child, you don't know what you are saying. And besides, I don't want compliments at my time of life. I lay awake, too, thinking of the cap. I only buy one ready-made once a year, and of course it's a matter for consideration; and I came to the conclusion that you were quite right."

"O dear Miss Pole! I was quite wrong; if you only knew — I did think it a very pretty cap — only —"

"Well! do just finish what you've got to say. You're almost as bad as Miss Matty in your way of talking, without being half as good as she is in other ways; though I'm very fond of you, Mary, I don't mean I am not; but you must see you're very off and on, and very muddle-headed. It's the truth, so you will not mind my saying so."

It was just because it did seem like the truth at that time that I did mind her saying so; and, in despair, I thought I would tell her all.

"I did not mean what I said; I don't think lilac too old or green too young: and I think the mixture very becoming to you; and I think you will never get such a pretty cap again, at least in Cranford." It was fully out, so far, at least.

"Then, Mary Smith, will you tell me what you did mean, by speaking as you did, and convincing me against my will, and giving me a bad night?"

"I meant — O Miss Pole, I meant to surprise you with a present from Paris; and I thought it would be a cap. Mrs. Gordon was to choose it, and Mr. Ludovic to bring it. I dare say it is in England now; only it's not a cap. And I did not want you to buy Johnson's cap, when I thought I was getting another for you."

Miss Pole found this speech "muddle-headed," I have no doubt, though she did not say so, only making an odd noise of perplexity. I went on: "I wrote to Mrs. Gordon, and asked her to get you a present — something new and pretty. I meant it to be a dress, but I suppose I did not say so; I thought it would be a cap, for Paris is so famous for caps, and it is —"

"You're a good girl, Mary," (I was past thirty, but did not object to being called a girl; and, indeed, I generally felt like a girl at Cranford, where everybody was so much older than I was,) "but when you want a thing, say what you want; it is the best way in general. And now I suppose Mrs. Gordon has bought something quite different? — a pair of shoes, I dare say, for people talk a deal of Paris shoes. Anyhow, I'm just as much obliged to you, Mary, my dear. Only you should not go and spend your money on me."

"It was not much money; and it was not a pair of shoes. You'll let me go and get the cap, won't you? It was so pretty — somebody will be sure to snatch it up."

"I don't like getting a cap that's sure to be unbecoming."

"But it is not; it was not. I never saw you look so well in anything," said I.

"Mary, Mary, remember who is the father of lies!"

"But he's not my father," exclaimed I, in a hurry, for I saw Mrs. FitzAdam go down the street in the direction of Johnson's shop. "I'll eat my words; they were all false: only just let me run down and buy you that cap — that pretty cap."

"Well! run off, child. I liked it myself till you put me out of taste with it."

I brought it back in triumph from under Mrs. FitzAdam's very nose, as she was hanging in meditation over it; and the more we saw of it, the more we felt pleased with our purchase. We turned it on this side, and we turned it on that; and though we hurried it away into Miss Pole's bedroom at the sound of a double knock at the door, when we found it was only Miss Matty and Mr. Peter, Miss Pole could not resist the opportunity of displaying it, and said in a solemn way to Miss Matty: "Can I speak to you for a few minutes in private?" And I knew feminine delicacy too well to explain what this grave prelude was to lead to; aware how immediately Miss Matty's anxious tremor would be allayed by the sight of the cap. I had to go on talking to Mr. Peter, however, when I would far rather have been in the bedroom, and heard the observations and comments.

We talked of the new cap all day; what gowns it would suit; whether a certain bow was not rather too coquettish for a woman of Miss Pole's age. "No longer young," as she called herself, after a little struggle with the words, though at sixty-five she need not have blushed as if she were telling a falsehood. But at last the cap was put away, and with a wrench we turned our thoughts from the subject. We had been silent for a little while, each at our work with a candle between us, when Miss Pole began: —

"It was very kind of you, Mary, to think of giving me a present from Paris."

"Oh, I was only too glad to be able to get you something! I hope you will like it, though it is not what I expected."

"I am sure I shall like it. And a surprise is always so pleasant."

"Yes; but I think Mrs. Gordon has made a very odd choice."

"I wonder what it is. I don't like to ask, but there's a great deal in anticipation; I remember hearing dear Miss Jenkyns say that 'anticipation was the soul of enjoyment,' or something like that. Now there is no anticipation in a surprise; that's the worst of it."

"Shall I tell you what it is?"

"Just as you like, my dear. If it is any pleasure to you, I am quite willing to hear."

"Perhaps I had better not. It is something quite different to what I expected, and meant to have got; and I'm not sure if I like it as well."

"Relieve your mind, if you like, Mary. In all disappointments sympathy is a great balm."

"Well, then, it's something not for you; it's for Polly. It's a cage. Mrs. Gordon says they make such pretty ones in Paris."

I could see that Miss Pole's first emotion was disappointment. But she was very fond of her cockatoo, and the thought of his smartness in his new habitation made her be reconciled in a moment; besides that she was really grateful to me for having planned a present for her.

"Polly! Well, yes; his old cage is very shabby; he is so continually pecking at it with his sharp bill. I dare say Mrs. Gordon noticed it when she called here last October. I shall always think of you, Mary, when I see him in it. Now we can have him in the drawing-room, for I dare say a French cage will be quite an ornament to the room."

And so she talked on, till we worked ourselves up into high delight at the idea of Polly in his new abode, presentable in it even to the Honorable Mrs. Jamieson. The next morning Miss Pole said she had been dreaming of Polly with her new cap on his head, while she herself sat on a perch in the new cage and admired him. Then, as if ashamed of having revealed the fact of imagining "such arrant nonsense" in her sleep, she passed on rapidly to the philosophy of dreams, quoting some book she had lately been reading, which was either too deep in itself, or too confused in her repetition for me to understand it. After breakfast, we had the cap out again; and that in its different aspects occupied us for an hour or so; and then, as it was a fine day, we turned into the garden, where Polly was hung on a nail outside the kitchen window. He clamored and screamed at the sight of his mistress, who went to look for an almond for him. I examined his cage meanwhile, old discolored wicker-work, clumsily made by a Cranford basket-maker. I took out Mrs. Gordon's letter; it was dated the 15th, and this was the 20th, for I had kept it secret for two days in my pocket. Mr. Ludovic was on the point of setting out for England when she wrote.

"Poor Polly!" said I, as Miss Pole, returning, fed him with the almond.

"Ah! Polly does not know what a pretty cage he is going to have," said she, talking to him as she would have done to a child; and then turning to me, she asked when I thought it would come? We reckoned up dates, and made out that it might arrive that very day. So she called to her little stupid servant-maiden Fanny, and bade her go out and buy a great brass-headed nail, very strong, strong enough to bear Polly and the new cage, and we all three weighed the cage in our hands, and on her return she was to come up into the drawing-room with the nail and a hammer.

Fanny was a long time, as she always was, over her errands; but as soon as she came back, we knocked the nail, with solemn earnestness, into the house-wall, just outside the drawing-room window; for, as Miss Pole observed, when I was not there she had no one to talk to, and as in summertime she generally sat with the window open, she could combine two purposes, the giving air and sun to Polly-Cockatoo, and the having his agreeable companionship in her solitary hours.

"When it rains, my dear, or even in a very hot sun, I shall take the cage in. I would not have your pretty present spoilt for the world. It was very kind of you to think of it; I am quite come round to liking it better than any present of mere dress; and dear Mrs. Gordon has shown all her usual pretty observation in remembering my Polly-Cockatoo."

"Polly-Cockatoo" was his grand name; I had only once or twice heard him spoken of by Miss Pole in this formal manner, except when she was speaking to the servants; then she always gave him his full designation, just as most people call their daughters Miss, in speaking of them to strangers or servants. But since Polly was to have a new cage, and all the way from Paris too, Miss Pole evidently thought it necessary to treat him with unusual respect.

We were obliged to go out to pay some calls; but we left

strict orders with Fanny what to do if the cage arrived in our absence, as (we had calculated) it might. Miss Pole stood ready bonneted and shawled at the kitchen door, I behind her, and cook behind Fanny, each of us listening to the conversation of the other two.

"And Fanny, mind if it comes you coax Polly-Cockatoo nicely into it. He is very particular, and may be attached to his old cage, though it is so shabby. Remember, birds have their feelings as much as we have! Don't hurry him in making up his mind."

"Please, ma'am, I think an almond would help him to get over his feelings," said Fanny, dropping a curtsey at every speech, as she had been taught to do at her charity school.

"A very good idea, very. If I have my keys in my pocket I will give you an almond for him. I think he is sure to like the view up the street from the window; he likes seeing people, I think."

"It's but a dull look-out into the garden; nowt but dumb flowers," said cook, touched by this allusion to the cheerfulness of the street, as contrasted with the view from her own kitchen window.

"It's a very good look-out for busy people," said Miss Pole, severely. And then, feeling she was likely to get the worst of it in an encounter with her old servant, she withdrew with meek dignity, being deaf to some sharp reply; and of course I, being bound to keep order, was deaf too. If the truth must be told, we rather hastened our steps, until we had banged the street door behind us.

We called on Miss Matty, of course; and then on Mrs. Hoggins. It seemed as if ill-luck would have it that we went to the only two households of Cranford where there was the encumbrance of a man, and in both places the man was where he ought not to have been — namely, in his own house, and in the way. Miss Pole — out of civility to me, and because she really was full of the new cage for Polly, and because we all in Cranford relied on the sympathy of our neighbors in the veriest trifle that interested us — told Miss Matty, and Mr. Peter, and Mr. and Mrs. Hoggins; he was standing in the drawing-room, booted and spurred, and eating his hunk of bread and cheese in the very presence of his aristocratic wife, my lady that was. As Miss Pole said afterwards, if refinement was not to be found in Cranford, blessed as it was with so many scions of county families, she did not know where to meet with it. Bread and cheese in a drawing-room! Onions next.

But for all Mr. Hoggins's vulgarity, Miss Pole told him of the present she was about to receive.

"Only think! a new cage for Polly — Polly — Polly-Cockatoo, you know, Mr. Hoggins. You remember him, and the bite he gave me once because he wanted to be put back in his cage, pretty bird?"

"I only hope the new cage will be strong as well as pretty, for I must say a ——" He caught a look from his wife, I think, for he stopped short. "Well, we're old friends, Polly and I, and he put some practice in my way once. I shall be up the street this afternoon, and perhaps I shall step in and see this smart Parisian cage."

"Do!" said Miss Pole, eagerly. "Or, if you are in a hurry, look up at my drawing-room window; if the cage is come, it will be hanging out there, and Polly in it."

We had passed the omnibus that met the train from London some time ago, so we were not surprised as we returned home to see Fanny half out of the window, and cook evidently either helping or hindering her. Then they both took their heads in; but there was no cage hanging up. We hastened up the steps.

Both Fanny and the cook met us in the passage.

"Please, ma'am," said Fanny, "there's no bottom to the cage, and Polly would fly away."

"And there's no top," exclaimed cook. "He might get out at the top quite easy."

"Let me see," said Miss Pole, brushing past, thinking no doubt that her superior intelligence was all that was needed to set things to rights. On the ground lay a bundle, or a circle of hoops, neatly covered over with calico, no more like a cage for Polly-Cockatoo than I am like a cage. Cook took something up between her finger and thumb, and lifted the unsightly present from Paris. How I wish it had stayed there!—but foolish ambition has brought people to ruin before now; and my twenty shillings are gone, sure enough, and there must be some use or some ornament intended by the maker of the thing before us.

"Don't you think it's a mousetrap, ma'am?" asked Fanny, dropping her little curtsey.

For reply, the cook lifted up the machine, and showed how easily mice might run out; and Fanny shrank back abashed. Cook was evidently set against the new invention, and muttered about its being all of a piece with French things — French cooks, French plums, (nasty dried-up things,) French rolls (as had no substance in 'em.)

Miss Pole's good manners, and desire of making the best of things in my presence, induced her to try and drown cook's mutterings.

"Indeed, I think it will make a very nice cage for Polly-Cockatoo. How pleased he will be to go from one hoop to another, just like a ladder, and with a board or two at the bottom, and nicely tied up at the top ——"

Fanny was struck with a new idea.

"Please, ma'am, my sister-in-law has got an aunt as lives lady's-maid with Sir John's daughter — Miss Arley. And they did say as she wore iron petticoats all made of hoops ——"

"Nonsense, Fanny!" we all cried; for such a thing had not been heard of in all Drumble, let alone Cranford, and I was rather looked upon in the light of a fast young woman by all the laundresses of Cranford, because I had two corded petticoats.

"Go mind thy business, wench," said cook, with the utmost contempt; "I'll warrant we'll manage th' cage without thy help."

"It is near dinner-time, Fanny, and the cloth not laid," said Miss Pole, hoping the remark might cut two ways; but cook had no notion of going. She stood on the bottom step of the stairs, holding the Paris perplexity aloft in the air.

"It might do for a meat-safe," said she. "Cover it o'er wi' canvas, to keep th' flies out. It is a good framework, I reckon, anyhow!" She held her head on one side, like a connoisseur in meat-safes, as she was.

Miss Pole said, "Are you sure Mrs. Gordon called it a cage, Mary? Because she is a woman of her word, and would not have called it so if it was not."

"Look here; I have the letter in my pocket."

"'I have wondered how I could best fulfil your commission for me to purchase something to the value of' — um, um, never mind — 'fashionable and pretty for dear Miss Pole, and at length I have decided upon one of the new kind of "cages"' (look here, Miss Pole; here is the word, C A G E), 'which are made so much lighter and more elegant in Paris than in England. Indeed, I am not sure if they have ever reached you, for it is not a month since I saw the first of the kind in Paris.'"

"Does she say anything about Polly-Cockatoo?" asked Miss Pole. "That would settle the matter at once, as showing that she had him in her mind."

"No — nothing."

Just then Fanny came along the passage with the tray full of dinner things in her hands. When she had put them down, she stood at the door of the dining-room taking a distant view of the article. "Please, ma'am, it looks like a petticoat without any stuff in it; indeed it does, if I'm to be whipped for saying it."

But she only drew down upon herself a fresh objurgation from the cook; and sorry and annoyed, I seized the opportunity of taking the thing out of cook's hand, and carrying it up stairs, for it was full time to get ready for dinner. But we had very little appetite for our meal, and kept constantly making suggestions, one to the other, as to the nature and purpose of this Paris "cage," but as constantly snubbing poor little Fanny's reiteration of "Please, ma'am, I do believe it's a kind of petticoat — indeed I do." At length Miss Pole turned upon her with almost as much vehemence as cook had done, only in choicer language.

"Don't be so silly, Fanny. Do you think ladies are like children, and must be put in go-carts; or need wire-guards like fires to surround them; or can get warmth out of bits of whalebone and steel; a likely thing indeed! Don't keep talking about what you don't understand."

So our maiden was mute for the rest of the meal. After dinner we had Polly brought up stairs in her old cage, and I held out the new one, and we turned it about in every way. At length Miss Pole said: —

"Put Polly-Cockatoo back, and shut him up in his cage. You hold this French thing up," (alas! that my present should be called a "thing,") "and I'll sew a bottom on to it. I'll lay a good deal, they've forgotten to sew in the bottom before sending it off." So I held and she sewed; and then she held, and I sewed, till it was all done. Just as we had put Polly-Cockatoo in, and were closing up the top with a pretty piece of old yellow ribbon — and, indeed, it was not a bad-looking cage after all our trouble — Mr. Hoggins came up stairs, having been seen by Fanny before he had time to knock at the door.

"Hallo!" said he, almost tumbling over us, as we were sitting on the floor at our work. "What's this?"

"It's this pretty present for Polly-Cockatoo," said Miss Pole, raising herself up with as much dignity as she could, "that Mary has had sent from Paris for me." Miss Pole was in great spirits now we had got Polly in; I can't say that I was.

Mr. Hoggins began to laugh in his boisterous vulgar way. "For Polly — ha! ha! It's meant for you, Miss Pole — ha! ha! It's a new invention to hold your gowns out — ha! ha!"

"Mr. Hoggins! you may be a surgeon, and a very clever one, but nothing — not even your profession — gives you a right to be indecent."

Miss Pole was thoroughly roused, and I trembled in my shoes. But Mr. Hoggins only laughed the more. Polly screamed in concert, but Miss Pole stood in stiff rigid propriety, very red in the face.

"I beg your pardon, Miss Pole, I am sure. But I am pretty certain I am right. It's no indecency that I can see; my wife and Mrs. FitzAdam take in a Paris fashion-book between 'em, and I can't help seeing the plates of fashions sometimes — ha! ha! ha! Look, Polly has got out of his queer prison — ha! ha! ha!"

Just then Mr. Peter came in; Miss Matty was so curious to know if the expected present had arrived. Mr. Hoggins took him by the arm, and pointed to the poor thing lying on the ground, but could not explain for laughing. Miss Pole said: —

"Although I am not accustomed to give an explanation of my conduct to gentlemen, yet, being insulted in my own house by — by Mr. Hoggins, I must appeal to the brother of my old friend — my very oldest friend. Is this article a lady's petticoat, or a bird's cage?"

She held it up as she made this solemn inquiry. Mr. Hoggins seized the moment to leave the room, in shame, as I supposed, but, in reality, to fetch his wife's fashion-book;

and, before I had completed the narration of the story of my unlucky commission, he returned, and, holding the fashion-plate open by the side of the extended article, demonstrated the identity of the two.

But Mr. Peter had always a smooth way of turning off anger, by either his fun or a compliment. "It is a cage," said he, bowing to Miss Pole; "but it is a cage for an angel, instead of a bird! Come along, Hoggins, I want to speak to you!"

And, with an apology, he took the offending and victorious surgeon out of Miss Pole's presence. For a good while we said nothing; and we were now rather shy of little Fanny's superior wisdom when she brought up tea. But towards night our spirits revived, and we were quite ourselves again, when Miss Pole proposed that we should cut up the pieces of steel or whalebone — which, to do them justice, were very elastic — and make ourselves two good comfortable English calashes out of them with the aid of a piece of dyed silk which Miss Pole had by her.

VERSES ON SIR PHILIP SIDNEY.

By EDMUND SPENSER.

YOU knew — who knew not? — Astrophel.
   (That I should live to say I knew,
And have not in possession still!)
   Things known permit me to renew:
     Of him you know his merit such,
     I cannot say — you hear — too much.

Within these woods of Arcady,
   He chief delight and pleasure took;
And on the mountain Partheny,
   Upon the crystal liquid brook,
     The Muses met him every day,
     That taught him song to write and say.

When he descended from the mount,
   His personage seemed most divine;
A thousand graces one might count
   Upon his lovely cheerful eyne.
     To hear him speak and sweetly smile,
     You were in Paradise the while.

A sweet attractive kind of grace,
   A full assurance given by looks;
Continual comfort in a face,
   The lineaments of Gospel books:

I trow that countenance cannot lie,
Whose thoughts are legible in th' eye.

Above all others, this is he,
  Which erst approvèd in his song
That love and honor might agree,
  And that pure love will do no wrong.
    Sweet saints, it is no sin or blame
    To love a man of virtuous name.

Did never love so sweetly breathe
  In any mortal breast before:
Did never Muse inspire beneath
  A poet's brain with finer store.
    He wrote of love with high conceit,
    And beauty rear'd above her height.

PRESCOTT'S INFIRMITY OF SIGHT.

By GEORGE TICKNOR.

WHEN the "Ferdinand and Isabella" was published, in the winter of 1837-8, its author was nearly forty-two years old. His character, some of whose traits had been prominent from childhood, while others had been slowly developed, was fully formed. His habits were settled for life. He had a perfectly well-defined individuality, as everybody knew who knew anything about his occupations and ways.

Much of what went to constitute this individuality was the result of his infirmity of sight, and of the unceasing struggle he had made to overcome the difficulties it entailed upon him. For, as we shall see hereafter, the thought of this infirmity, and of the embarrassments it brought with it, was ever before him. It colored, and in many respects it controlled, his whole life.

The violent inflammation that resulted from the fierce attack of rheumatism in the early months of 1815 first startled him, I think, with the apprehension that he might possibly be deprived of sight altogether, and that thus his future years would be left in "total eclipse, without all hope of day." But from this dreary apprehension, his recovery, slow, and partial as it was, and the buoyant spirits that entered so largely into his constitution, at last relieved him. He even, from time to time, as the disease fluctuated to and fro, had hopes of an entire restoration of his sight.

But before long, he began to judge things more exactly as they were, and saw plainly that anything like a full recovery of his sight was improbable, if not impossible. He turned his thoughts, therefore, to the resources that would still remain to him. The prospect was by no means a pleasant one, but he looked at it steadily and calmly. All thought of the profession which had long been so tempting to him he gave up. He saw that he could never fulfil its duties. But intellectual occupation he could not give up It was a gratification and resource which his nature demanded, and would not be refused. The difficulty was to find out how it could be obtained. During the three months of his confinement in total darkness at St. Michael's, he first began to discipline his thoughts to such orderly composition in his memory as he might have written down on paper, if his sight had permitted it. "I have cheated," he says, in a letter to his family written at the end of that discouraging period, — "I have cheated many a moment of tedium by compositions which were soon banished from my mind for want of an amanuensis."

Among these compositions was a Latin ode to his friend Gardiner, which was prepared wholly without books, but which, though now lost, like the rest of his Latin verses, he repeated years afterwards to his Club, who did not fail to think it good. It is evident, however, that, for a considerable time, he resorted to such mental occupations and exercises rather as an amusement than as anything more serious. Nor did he at first go far with them even as a light and transient relief from idleness; for, though he never gave them up altogether, and though they at last became a very important element in his success as an author, he soon found an agreeable substitute for them, at least so far as his immediate, every-day wants were concerned.

The substitute to which I refer, but which itself implied much previous reflection and thought upon what he should

7*

commit to paper, was an apparatus to enable the blind to write. He heard of it in London during his first residence there in the summer of 1816. A lady, at whose house he visited frequently, and who became interested in his misfortune, "told him," as he says in a letter to his mother, "of a newly invented machine by which blind people are enabled to write. I have," he adds, "before been indebted to Mrs. Delafield for an ingenious candle-screen. If this machine can be procured, you will be sure to feel the effects of it."

He obtained it at once; but he did not use it until nearly a month afterwards, when, on the 24th of August, at Paris, he wrote home his first letter with it, saying, " It is a very happy invention for me." And such it certainly proved to be, for he never ceased to use it from that day; nor does it now seem possible that, without the facilities it afforded him, he ever would have ventured to undertake any of the works which have made his name what it is.

The machine — if machine it can properly be called — is an apparatus invented by one of the well-known Wedgewood family, and is very simple both in its structure and use. It looks, as it lies folded up on the table, like a clumsy portfolio, bound in morocco, and measures about ten inches by nine when unopened. Sixteen stout parallel brass wires fastened on the right-hand side into a frame of the same size with the cover, much like the frame of a school-boy's slate, and crossing it from side to side, mark the number of lines that can be written on a page, and guide the hand in its blind motions. This framework of wires is folded down upon a sheet of paper thoroughly impregnated with a black substance, especially on its under surface, beneath which lies the sheet of common paper that is to receive the writing. There are thus, when it is in use, three layers on the right-hand side of the opened apparatus; viz. the wires, the blackened sheet of paper, and the white sheet, — all lying successively in contact with each other, the two that are underneath being held firmly in their places by the framework of wires which is uppermost. The whole apparatus is called a *noctograph*.

When it has been adjusted, as above described, the person using it writes with an ivory style, or with a style made of some harder substance, like agate, on the upper surface of the blackened paper, which, wherever the style presses on it, transfers the coloring matter of its under surface to the white paper beneath it, — the writing thus produced looking much like that done with a common black-lead pencil.

The chief difficulty in the use of such an apparatus is obvious. The person employing it never looks upon his work; never sees one of the marks he is making. He trusts wholly to the wires for the direction of his hand. He makes his letters and words only from mechanical habit. He must, therefore, write straight forward, without any opportunity for correction, however gross may be the mistakes he has made, or however sure he may be that he has made them; for, if he were to go back in order to correct an error, he would only make his page still more confused, and probably render it quite illegible. When, therefore, he has made a mistake, great or small, all he can do is to go forward, and rewrite further on the word or phrase he first intended to write, rarely attempting to strike out what was wrong, or to insert, in its proper place, anything that may have been omitted. It is plain, therefore, that the person who resorts to this apparatus as a substitute for sight ought previously to prepare and settle in his memory what he wishes to write, so as to make as few mistakes as possible.

With the best care his manuscript will not be very legible. Without it, he may be sure it can hardly be deciphered at all.

That Mr. Prescott, under his disheartening infirmities, — I refer not only to his imperfect sight, but to the rheumatism from which he was seldom wholly free, — should, at the age of five-and-twenty or thirty, with no help but this simple apparatus, have aspired to the character of a historian dealing with events that happened in times and countries far distant from his own, and that are recorded chiefly in foreign languages and by authors whose conflicting testimony was often to be reconciled by laborious comparison, is a remarkable fact in literary history. It is a problem the solution of which was, I believe, never before undertaken; certainly never before accomplished. Nor do I conceive that he himself could have accomplished it, unless to his uncommon intellectual gifts had been added great animal spirits, a strong, persistent will, and a moral courage which was to be daunted by no obstacle that he might deem it possible to remove by almost any amount of effort.*

That he was not insensible to the difficulties of his undertaking, we have partly seen, as we have witnessed how his hopes fluctuated while he was struggling through the arrangements for beginning to write his "Ferdinand and Isabella," and, in fact, during the whole period of its composition. But he showed the same character, the same fertility of resource, every day of his life, and provided, both by forecast and self-sacrifice, against the embarrassments of his condition as they successively presented themselves.

The first thing to be done, and the thing always to be repeated day by day, was to strengthen, as much as possible, what remained of his sight, and at any rate, to do nothing

* The case of Thierry — the nearest known to me — was different. His great work, "Histoire de la Conquête de l' Angleterre par les Normands," was written before he became blind. What he published afterward was dictated, — wonderful, indeed, all of it, but especially all that relates to what he did for the commission of the government concerning the Tiers État, to be found in that grand collection of "Documents inédits sur l'Histoire de France," begun under the auspices and influence of M. Guizot, when he was minister of Louis-Philippe.

that should tend to exhaust its impaired powers. In 1821, when he was still not without some hope of its recovery, he made this memorandum. "I will make it my principal purpose to restore my eye to its primitive vigor, and will do nothing habitually that can seriously injure it." To this end he regulated his life with an exactness that I have never known equalled. Especially in whatever related to the daily distribution of his time, whether in regard to his intellectual labors, to his social enjoyments, or to the care of his physical powers, including his diet, he was severely exact,— managing himself, indeed, in this last respect, under the general directions of his wise medical adviser, Dr. Jackson, but carrying out these directions with an ingenuity and fidelity all his own.

He was an early riser, although it was a great effort for him to be such. From boyhood it seemed to be contrary to his nature to get up betimes in the morning. He was, therefore, always awaked, and after silently, and sometimes slowly and with reluctance, counting twenty, so as fairly to arouse himself, he resolutely sprang out of bed; or, if he failed, he paid a forfeit, as a memento of his weakness, to the servant who had knocked at his chamber-door.* His failures, however, were rare. When he was called, he was told the state of the weather and of the thermometer. This was important, as he was compelled by his rheumatism — almost always present, and, when not so, always apprehended — to regulate his dress with care; and, finding it difficult to do so in any other way, he caused each of its heavier external portions to be marked by his tailor with

---

* When he was a bachelor, the servant, after waiting a certain number of minutes at the door without receiving an answer, went in and took away the bed-clothes. This was, at that period, the office of faithful Nathan Webster, who was remembered kindly in Mr. Prescott's will, and who was for nearly thirty years in the family, a true and valued friend of all its members.

the number of ounces it weighed, and then put them on according to the temperature, sure that their weight would indicate the measure of warmth and protection they would afford.*

As soon as he was dressed, he took his early exercise in the open air. This, for many years, was done on horseback, and, as he loved a spirited horse and was often thinking more of his intellectual pursuits than of anything else while he was riding, he sometimes caught a fall. But he was a good rider, and was sorry to give up this form of exercise and resort to walking or driving, as he did, by order of his physician, in the last dozen years of his life. No weather, except a severe storm, prevented him at any period from thus, as he called it, "winding himself up." Even in the coldest of our very cold winter mornings, it was his habit, so long as he could ride, to see the sun rise on a particular spot three or four miles from town. In a letter to Mrs. Ticknor, who was then in Germany, dated March, 1836, — at the end of a winter memorable for its extreme severity, — he says, "You will give me credit for some spunk when I tell you that I have not been frightened by the cold a single morning from a ride on horseback to Jamaica Plain and back again before breakfast. My mark has been to see the sun rise by Mr. Greene's school, if you remember where that is." When the rides here referred to were taken, the thermometer was often below zero of Fahrenheit.

On his return home, after adjusting his dress anew, with reference to the temperature within doors, he sat down, almost always in a very gay humor, to a moderate and even spare breakfast, — a meal he much liked, because, as he said,

---

* As in the case of the use of wine, hereafter to be noticed, he made, from year to year, the most minute memoranda about the use of clothes, finding it necessary to be exact on account of the rheumatism which, besides almost constantly infesting his limbs, always affected his sight when it became severe.

he could then have his family with him in a quiet way, and so begin the day happily. From the breakfast-table he went at once to his study. There, while busied with what remained of his toilet, or with the needful arrangements for his regular occupations, Mrs. Prescott read to him, generally from the morning papers, but sometimes from the current literature of the day. At a fixed hour — seldom later than ten — his reader, or secretary, came. In this, as in everything, he required punctuality; but he noted tardiness only by looking significantly at his watch; for it is the testimony of all his surviving secretaries, that he never spoke a severe word to either of them in the many years of their familiar intercourse.

When they had met in the study, there was no thought but of active work for about three hours.* His infirmities, however, were always present to warn him how cautiously it must be done, and he was extremely ingenious in the means he devised for doing it without increasing them. The shades and shutters for regulating the exact amount of light which should be admitted; his own position relatively to its direct rays, and to those that were reflected from surrounding objects; the adaptation of his dress and of the temperature of the room to his rheumatic affections; and the different contrivances for taking notes from the books that were read to him, and for impressing on his memory, with the least possible use of his sight, such portions of

---

* I speak here of the time during which he was busy with his Histories. In the intervals between them, as, for instance, between the "Ferdinand and Isabella" and the "Mexico," between the "Mexico" and "Peru," &c., his habits were very different. At these periods he indulged, sometimes for many months, in a great deal of light, miscellaneous reading, which he used to call "literary loafing." This he thought not only agreeable, but refreshing and useful; though sometimes he complained bitterly of himself for carrying his indulgences of this sort too far.

each as were needful for his immediate purpose, — were all of them the result of painstaking experiments, skilfully and patiently made. But their ingenuity and adaptation were less remarkable than the conscientious consistency with which they were employed from day to day for forty years.

In relation to all such arrangements, two circumstances should be noted.

The first is, that the resources of his eye were always very small and uncertain, except for a few years, beginning in 1840, when, from his long-continued prudence or from some inscrutable cause, there seemed to be either an increase of strength in the organ, or else such a diminution of its sensibility as enabled him to use it more, though its strength might really be diminished.

Thus, for instance, he was able to use his eye very little in the preparation of the "Ferdinand and Isabella," not looking into a book sometimes for weeks and even months together, and yet occasionally he could read several hours in a day if he carefully divided the whole into short portions, so as to avoid fatigue. While engaged in the composition of the "Conquest of Mexico," on the contrary, he was able to read with considerable regularity, and so he was while working on the "Conquest of Peru," though, on the whole, with less.*

* How uncertain was the state of his eye, even when it was strongest, may be seen from memoranda made at different times, within less than two years of each other. The first is in January, 1829, when he was full of grateful feelings for an unexpected increase of his powers of sight. "By the blessing of Heaven," he says, "I have been enabled to have the free use of my eye in the daytime during the last weeks, without the exception of a single day, although deprived, for nearly a fortnight, of my accustomed exercise. I hope I have not abused this great privilege." But this condition of things did not last long. Great fluctuations followed. In August and September he was much discouraged by severe inflammations; and in October, 1830, when he had been slowly writing the "Ferdinand

But he had, during nearly all this time, another difficulty to encounter. There had come on prematurely that gradual alteration of the eye which is the consequence of advancing years, and for which the common remedy is spectacles. Even when he was using what remained to him of sight on the "Conquest of Mexico" with a freedom which not a little animated him in his pursuits, he perceived this discouraging change. In July, 1841, he says: "My eye, for some days, feels dim. 'I guess and fear,' as Burns says." And in June, 1842, when our families were spending together at Lebanon Springs a few days which he has recorded as otherwise very happy, he spoke to me more than once in a tone of absolute grief, that he should never again enjoy the magnificent spectacle of the starry heavens. To this sad deprivation he, in fact, alludes himself in his Memoranda of that period, where, in relation to his eyes, he says: "I find a misty veil increasing over them, quite annoying when reading. The other evening B—— said, 'How beautiful the heavens are with so many stars!' I could hardly see two. It made me sad."

Spectacles, however, although they brought their appropriate relief, brought also an inevitable inconvenience. They fatigued his eye. He could use it, therefore, less and less, or if he used it at all, beyond a nicely adjusted amount, the excess was followed by a sort of irritability, weakness, and pain in the organ which he had not felt for many years. This went on increasing with sad regularity. But he knew that it was inevitable, and submitted to it patiently. In the latter part of his life he was able to use his eye very little indeed for the purpose of reading, — in the last year, hardly at all. Even in several of the years pre-

and Isabella" for about a year, his sight for a time became so much impaired that he was brought — I use his own words — "seriously to consider what steps he should take in relation to that work, if his sight should fail him altogether."

ceding, he used it only thirty-five minutes in each day, divided exactly by the watch into portions of five minutes each, with at least half an hour between, and always stopping the moment pain was felt, even if it were felt at the first instant of opening the book. I doubt whether a more persistent, conscientious care was ever taken of an impaired physical power. Indeed, I do not see how it could have been made more thorough. But all care was unavailing, and he at last knew that it was so. The decay could not be arrested. He spoke of it rarely, but when he perceived that in the evening twilight he could no longer walk about the streets that were familiar to him with his accustomed assurance, he felt it deeply. Still he persevered, and was as watchful of what remained of his sight as if his hopes of its restoration had continued unchecked. Indeed, I think he always trusted that he was saving something by his anxious care; he always believed that great prudence on one day would enable him to do a little more work on the next than he should be able to do without so much caution.

The other circumstance that should be noticed in relation to the arrangements for his pursuits is, the continually increased amount of light he was obliged to use, and which he could use without apparent injury.

In Bedford Street, where he first began his experiments, he could, from the extreme sensitiveness of his eye, bear very little light. But, even before he left that quiet old mansion, he cut out a new window in his working-room, arranging it so that the light should fall more strongly and more exclusively upon the book he might be using. This did very well for a time. But when he removed to Beacon Street, the room he built expressly for his own use contained six contiguous windows; two of which, though large, were glazed each with a single sheet of the finest plate-glass, nicely protected by several curtains of delicate fabric and of a light-blue color, one or more of which could be drawn up over each window to temper the light while the whole light that was admitted through any one opening could be excluded by solid wooden shutters. At first, though much light was commonly used, these appliances for diminishing it were all more or less required. But, gradually, one after another of them was given up, and, at last, I observed that none was found important. He needed and used all the light he could get.

The change was a sad one, and he did not like to allude to it. But during the last year of his life, after the first slight access of paralysis, which much disturbed the organ for a time, and rendered its action very irregular, he spoke plainly to me. He said he must soon cease to use his eye for any purpose of study, but fondly trusted that he should always be able to recognize the features of his friends, and should never become a burden to those he loved by needing to be led about. His hopes were, indeed, fulfilled, but not without the sorrow of all. The day before his sudden death he walked the streets as freely as he had done for years.

Still, whatever may have been the condition of his eye at any period, — from the fierce attack of 1815 to the very end of his life, — it was always a paramount subject of anxiety with him. He never ceased to think of it, and to regulate the hours, and almost the minutes, of his daily life by it. Even in its best estate he felt that it must be spared; in its worst, he was anxious to save something by care and abstinence. He said, " he reckoned time by eyesight, as distances on railroads are reckoned by hours."

One thing in this connection may be noted as remarkable. He knew that, if he would give up literary labor altogether, his eye would be better at once, and would last longer. His physicians all told him so, and their opinion was rendered certain by his own experience; for whenever he ceased to work for some time, as during a visit to New York in

1842 and a visit to Europe in 1850, — in short, whenever he took a journey or indulged himself in holidays of such a sort as prevented him from looking into books at all or thinking much about them, — his general health immediately became more vigorous than might have been expected from a relief so transient, and his sight was always improved; sometimes materially improved. But he would not pay the price. He perferred to submit, if it should be inevitable, to the penalty of ultimate blindness, rather than give up his literary pursuits.

He never liked to work more than three hours consecutively. At one o'clock, therefore, he took a walk of about two miles, and attended to any little business abroad that was incumbent on him, coming home generally refreshed and exhilarated, and ready to lounge a little and gossip. Dinner followed, for the greater part of his life about three o'clock, although, during a few years, he dined in winter at five or six, which he preferred, and which he gave up only because his health demanded the change. In the summer he always dined early, so as to have the late afternoon for driving and exercise during our hot season.

He enjoyed the pleasures of the table, and even its luxuries, more than most men. But he restricted himself carefully in the use of them, adjusting everything with reference to its effect on the power of using his eye immediately afterwards, and especially on his power of using it the next day. Occasional indulgence when dining out or with friends at home he found useful, or at least not injurious, and was encouraged in it by his medical counsel. But he dined abroad, as he did everything of the sort, at regulated intervals, and not only determined beforehand in what he should deviate from his settled habits, but often made a record of the result for his future government.

The most embarrassing question, however, as to diet, regarded the use of wine, which, if at first it sometimes seemed to be followed by bad consequences, was yet, on the whole, found useful, and was prescribed to him. To make everything certain, and settle the precise point to which he should go, he instituted a series of experiments, and between March, 1818, and November, 1820, — a period of two years and nine months, — he recorded the exact quantity of wine that he took every day, except the few days when he entirely abstained. It was Sherry or Madeira. In the great majority of cases — four fifths, I should think — it ranged from one to two glasses, but went up sometimes to four or five, and even to six. He settled at last, upon two or two and a half as the quantity best suited to his case, and persevered in this as his daily habit, until the last year of his life, during which a peculiar regimen was imposed upon him from the peculiar circumstances of his health. In all this I wish to be understood that he was rigorous with himself, — much more so than persons thought who saw him only when he was dining with friends, and when, but equally upon system and principle, he was much more free.

He generally smoked a single weak cigar after dinner, and listened at the same time to light reading from Mrs. Prescott. A walk of two miles — more or less — followed; but always enough, after the habit of riding was given up, to make the full amount of six miles' walking for the day's exercise, and then, between five and eight, he took a cup of tea, and had his reader with him for work two hours more.

The labors of the day were now definitively ended. He came down from his study to his library, and either sat there or walked about while Mrs. Prescott read to him from some amusing book, generally a novel, and, above all other novels, those of Scott and Miss Edgeworth. In all this he took great solace. He enjoyed the room as well as the reading, and, as he moved about, would often stop before the books, — especially his favorite books, — and be sure that they were all in their proper places, drawn up exactly to the front of their respective shelves, like soldiers on a dress-parade, — sometimes speaking of them, and almost to them, as if they were personal friends.

At half past ten, having first taken nearly another glass of wine, he went to bed, fell asleep quickly, and slept soundly and well. Suppers he early gave up, although they were a form of social intercourse much liked in his father's house, and common thirty or forty years ago in the circle to which he belonged. Besides all other reasons against them, he found that the lights commonly on the table shot their horizontal rays so as to injure his suffering organ. Larger evening parties, which were not so liable to this objection, he liked rather for their social influences than for the pleasure they gave him; but he was seen in them to the last, though rarely and only for a short time in each. Earlier in life, when he enjoyed them more and stayed later, he would, in the coldest winter nights, after going home, run up and down on a plank walk, so arranged in the garden of the Bedford-Street house that he could do it with his eyes shut, for twenty minutes or more, in order that his system might be refreshed, and his sight invigorated, for the next morning's work.* Later, unhappily, this was not needful. His eye had lost the sensibility that gave its value to such a habit.

In his exercise, at all its assigned hours, he was faithful and exact. If a violent storm prevented him from going out, or if the bright snow on sunny days in winter rendered it dangerous for him to expose his eye to its brilliant reflec-

---

* Some persons may think this to have been a fancy of my friend, or an over-nice estimate of the value of the open air. But others have found the same benefit who needed it less. Sir Charles Bell says, in his journal, that he used to sit in the open air a great deal, and read or draw, because *on the following day* he found himself so much better able to work. Some of the best passages in his great treatises were, he says, written under these circumstances.

tion, he would dress himself as for the street and walk vigorously about the colder parts of the house, or he would saw and chop fire-wood, under cover, being, in the latter case, read to all the while.

The result he sought, and generally obtained, by these efforts was not, however, always to be had without suffering. The first mile or two of his walk often cost him pain — sometimes sharp pain — in consequence of the rheumatism, which seldom deserted his limbs; but he never on this account gave it up; for regular exercise in the open air was, as he well knew, indispensable to the preservation of whatever remained of his decaying sight. He persevered, therefore, through the last two suffering years of his life, when it was peculiarly irksome and difficult for him to move; and even in the days immediately preceding his first attack of paralysis, when he was very feeble, he was out at his usual hours. His will, in truth, was always stronger than the bodily ills that beset him, and prevailed over them to the last.*

* On one occasion, when he was employed upon a work that interested him because it related to a friend, he was attacked with pains that made a sitting posture impossible. But he would not yield. He took his noctograph to a sofa, and knelt before it so as to be able to continue his work. This resource, however, failed, and then he laid himself down flat upon the floor. This extraordinary operation went on during portions of nine successive days.

BEATRICE.

By DANTE.

THIS most gentle lady reached such favor among the people, that when she passed along the way persons ran to see her, which gave me wonderful delight. And when she was near any one, such modesty took possession of his heart, that he did not dare to raise his eyes or to return her salutation; and to this, should any one doubt it, many, as having experienced it, could bear witness for me. She, crowned and clothed with humility, took her way, displaying no pride in that which she saw and heard. Many, when she had passed, said, "This is not a woman; rather is she one of the most beautiful angels of heaven." Others said, "She is a miracle. Blessed be the Lord who can perform such a marvel!" I say that she showed herself so gentle and so full of all beauties, that those who looked on her felt within themselves a pure and sweet delight such as they could not tell in words; nor was there any who could look at her and not feel need at first to sigh. These and more wonderful things proceeded from her, marvellously and with power. Wherefore I, thinking on all this, proposed to say some words, in which I would exhibit her marvellous and excellent influences, to the end that not only those who might actually behold her, but also others, might know of her whatever words could tell. Then I wrote this sonnet:—

So gentle and so modest doth appear
  My lady when she giveth her salute,
  That every tongue becometh trembling mute,
  Nor do the eyes to look upon her dare.
And though she hears her praises, she doth go
  Benignly clothed with humility,
  And like a thing come down she seems to be
  From heaven to earth, a miracle to show.
So pleaseth she whoever cometh nigh,
  She gives the heart a sweetness through the eyes,
  Which none can understand who doth not prove.
And from her lip there seems indeed to move
  A spirit sweet and in Love's very guise,
  Which goeth saying to the soul, "Ah, sigh!"

A LOVE STORY.*

By ROBERT SOUTHEY.

CHAPTER I.

RASH MARRIAGES. AN EARLY WIDOWHOOD. AFFLICTION RENDERED A BLESSING TO THE SUFFERERS; AND TWO ORPHANS LEFT, THOUGH NOT DESTITUTE, YET FRIENDLESS.

> Love built a stately house; where Fortune came,
> And spinning fancies, she was heard to say
> That her fine cobwebs did support the frame;
> Whereas they were supported by the same.
> But Wisdom quickly swept them all away.
> HERBERT.

MRS. DOVE was the only child of a clergyman who held a small vicarage in the West Riding. Leonard Bacon, her father, had been left an orphan in early youth. He had some wealthy relations by whose contributions he was placed at an endowed grammar-school in the country, and having through their influence gained a scholarship, to which his own deserts might have entitled him, they continued to assist him — sparingly enough indeed — at the University, till he succeeded to a fellowship. Leonard was made of Nature's finest clay, and Nature had tempered it with the choicest dews of heaven.

He had a female cousin about three years younger than himself, and in like manner an orphan, equally destitute, but

---

* Southey always intended to complete this story, but he did not live to fulfil his purpose. It is here brought together for the first time in America, from the pages of that admirable work which has now taken its place as an English classic, — "The Doctor."

far more forlorn. Man hath a fleece about him which enables him to bear the buffetings of the storm;—but woman when young, and lovely, and poor, is as a shorn lamb for which the wind has not been tempered.

Leonard's father and Margaret's had been bosom friends. They were subalterns in the same regiment, and, being for a long time stationed at Salisbury, had become intimate at the house of Mr. Trewbody, a gentleman of one of the oldest families in Wiltshire. Mr. Trewbody had three daughters. Melicent, the eldest, was a celebrated beauty, and the knowledge of this had not tended to improve a detestable temper. The two youngest, Deborah and Margaret, were lively, good-natured, thoughtless, and attractive. They danced with the two lieutenants, played to them on the spinnet, sung with them and laughed with them, — till this mirthful intercourse became serious, and, knowing that it would be impossible to obtain their father's consent, they married the men of their hearts without it. Palmer and Bacon were both without fortune, and without any other means of subsistence than their commissions. For four years they were as happy as love could make them; at the end of that time Palmer was seized with an infectious fever. Deborah was then far advanced in pregnancy, and no solicitations could induce Bacon to keep from his friend's bedside. The disease proved fatal; it communicated to Bacon and his wife; the former only survived his friend ten days, and he and Deborah were then laid in the same grave. They left an only boy of three years old, and in less than a month the widow Palmer was delivered of a daughter.

In the first impulse of anger at the flight of his daughters, and the degradation of his family, (for Bacon was the son of a tradesman, and Palmer was nobody knew who,) Mr. Trewbody had made his will, and left the whole sum, which he had designed for his three daughters, to the eldest. Whether the situation of Margaret and the two orphans might have touched him, is perhaps doubtful, — for the family were either light-hearted or hard-hearted, and his heart was of the hard sort; but he died suddenly a few months before his sons-in-law. The only son, Trewman Trewbody, Esq., a Wiltshire fox-hunter, like his father, succeeded to the estate; and as he and his eldest sister hated each other cordially, Miss Melicent left the manor-house, and established herself in the Close at Salisbury, where she lived in that style which a portion of £6,000 enabled her in those days to support.

The circumstance which might appear so greatly to have aggravated Mrs. Palmer's distress, if such distress be capable of aggravation, prevented her perhaps from eventually sinking under it. If the birth of her child was no alleviation of her sorrow, it brought with it new feelings, new duties, new cause for exertion, and new strength for it. She wrote to Melicent and to her brother, simply stating her own destitute situation, and that of the orphan Leonard; she believed that their pride would not suffer them either to let her starve or go to the parish for support, and in this she was not disappointed. An answer was returned by Miss Trewbody, informing her that she had nobody to thank but herself for her misfortunes; but that, notwithstanding the disgrace which she had brought upon the family, she might expect an annual allowance of ten pounds from the writer, and a like sum from her brother; upon this she must retire into some obscure part of the country, and pray God to forgive her for the offence she had committed, in marrying beneath her birth, and against her father's consent.

Mrs. Palmer had also written to the friends of Lieutenant Bacon, — her own husband had none who could assist her. She expressed her willingness and her anxiety to have the care of her sister's orphan, but represented her forlorn state. They behaved more liberally than her own kin had done, and promised five pounds a year as long as the boy should require it. With this and her pension she took a cottage in a retired village. Grief had acted upon her heart like the rod of Moses upon the rock in the desert; it had opened it, and the well-spring of piety had gushed forth. Affliction made her religious, and religion brought with it consolation, and comfort, and joy. Leonard became as dear to her as Margaret. The sense of duty educed a pleasure from every privation to which she subjected herself for the sake of economy; and, in endeavoring to fulfil her duties in that state of life to which it had pleased God to call her, she was happier than she had ever been in her father's house, and not less so than in her marriage state. Her happiness indeed was different in kind, but it was higher in degree. For the sake of these dear children she was contented to live, and even prayed for life; while, if it had respected herself only, death had become to her rather an object of desire than of dread. In this manner she lived seven years after the loss of her husband, and was then carried off by an acute disease, to the irreparable loss of the orphans, who were thus orphaned indeed.

CHAPTER II.

A LADY DESCRIBED WHOSE SINGLE LIFE WAS NO BLESSEDNESS EITHER TO HERSELF OR OTHERS. A VERACIOUS EPITAPH AND AN APPROPRIATE MONUMENT.

> Beauty! my Lord,—'t is the worst part of woman!
> A weak, poor thing, assaulted every hour
> By creeping minutes of defacing time;
> A superficies which each breath of care
> Blasts off; and every humorous stream of grief,
> Which flows from forth these fountains of our eyes,
> Washeth away, as rain doth winter's snow.
> GOFF.

MISS TREWBODY behaved with perfect propriety upon the news of her sister's death. She closed her front windows for two days; received no visitors for a week; was much indisposed, but resigned to the will of Providence, in reply to messages of condolence; put her servants in mourning, and sent for Margaret, that she might do her duty to her sister's child by breeding her up under her own eye. Poor Margaret was transferred from the stone floor of her mother's cottage to the Turkey carpet of her aunt's parlor. She was too young to comprehend at once the whole evil of the exchange; but she learned to feel and understand it during years of bitter dependence, unalleviated by any hope, except that of one day seeing Leonard, the only creature on earth whom she remembered with affection.

Seven years elapsed, and during all those years Leonard was left to pass his holidays, summer and winter, at the grammar-school where he had been placed at Mrs. Palmer's death: for although the master regularly transmitted with his half-yearly bill the most favorable accounts of his disposition and general conduct, as well as of his progress in learning, no wish to see the boy had ever arisen in the hearts of his nearest relations; and no feeling of kindness, or sense of decent humanity, had ever induced either the fox-hunter Trewman, or Melicent his sister, to invite him for Midsummer or Christmas. At length in the seventh year a letter announced that his school-education had been completed, and that he was elected to a scholarship at —— College, Oxford, which scholarship would entitle him to a fellowship in due course of time: in the intervening years some little assistance from his *liberal benefactors* would be required; and the liberality of those *kind friends* would be well bestowed upon a youth who bade so fair to do honor to himself, and to reflect *no disgrace upon his honorable connections*. The head of the family promised his part, with an ungracious expression of satisfaction at thinking that, "thank God, there would soon be an end of these demands upon him." Miss Trewbody signified her assent in the same amiable and religious spirit. However much her sister had disgraced her family, she replied, " Please God, it should never be said that she refused to do her duty."

The whole sum which these wealthy relations contributed was not very heavy,— an annual ten pounds each; but they contrived to make their nephew feel the weight of every separate portion. The Squire's half came always with a brief note, desiring that the receipt of the enclosed sum might be acknowledged without delay, — not a word of kindness or courtesy accompanied it: and Miss Trewbody never failed to administer with her remittance a few edifying remarks upon the folly of his mother in marrying beneath herself; and the improper conduct of his father in connecting himself with a woman of family, against the consent of her relations; the consequence of which was, that he had left a child dependent upon those relations for support. Leonard received these pleasant preparations of charity only at distant intervals, when he regularly expected them, with his half-yearly allowance. But Margaret meantime was dieted upon the food of bitterness, without one circumstance to relieve the misery of her situation.

At the time of which I am now speaking, Miss Trewbody was a maiden lady of forty-seven, in the highest state of preservation. The whole business of her life had been to take care of a fine person, and in this she had succeeded admirably. Her library consisted of two books: "Nelson's Festivals and Fasts" was one, the other was "The Queen's Cabinet Unlocked"; and there was not a cosmetic in the latter which she had not faithfully prepared. Thus by means, as she believed, of distilled waters of various kinds, May-dew and buttermilk, her skin retained its beautiful texture still, and much of its smoothness; and she knew at times how to give it the appearance of that brilliancy which it had lost. But that was a profound secret. Miss Trewbody, remembering the example of Jezebel, always felt conscious that she was committing a sin when she took the rouge-box in her hand, and generally ejaculated in a low voice, the Lord forgive me! when she laid it down: but, looking in the glass at the same time, she indulged a hope that the nature of the temptation might be considered as an excuse for the transgression. Her other great business was to observe with the utmost precision all the punctilios of her situation in life; and the time which was not devoted to one or other of these worthy occupations, was employed in scolding her servants, and tormenting her niece. This employment, for it was so habitual that it deserved that name, agreed excellently with her constitution. She was troubled with no acrid humors, no fits of bile, no diseases of the spleen, no vapors or hysterics. The morbid matter was all collected in her temper, and found a regular vent at her tongue. This kept the lungs in vigorous health; nay, it even seemed to supply the place of wholesome exercise, and to stimulate the system like a perpetual blister, with this peculiar advantage, that instead of an inconvenience it was a pleasure to herself, and all the annoyance was to her dependants.

Miss Trewbody lies buried in the Cathedral at Salisbury, where a monument was erected to her memory worthy of remembrance itself for its appropriate inscription and accompaniments. The epitaph recorded her as a woman eminently pious, virtuous, and charitable, who lived universally respected, and died sincerely lamented, by all who had the happiness of knowing her. This inscription was upon a marble shield supported by two Cupids, who bent their heads over the edge, with marble tears larger than gray pease, and something of the same color, upon their cheeks. These were the only tears which her death occasioned, and the only Cupids with whom she had ever any concern.

CHAPTER III.

A SCENE WHICH WILL PUT SOME OF THOSE READERS WHO HAVE BEEN MOST IMPATIENT WITH THE AUTHOR, IN THE BEST HUMOR WITH HIM.

There is no argument of more antiquity and elegancy than is the matter of Love; for it seems to be as old as the world, and to bear date from the first time that man and woman was: therefore in this, as in the finest metal, the freshest wits have in all ages shown their best workmanship.

ROBERT WILMOT.

WHEN Leonard had resided three years at Oxford, one of his college-friends invited him to pass the long vacation at his father's house, which happened to be within an easy ride of Salisbury. One morning, therefore, he rode to that city, rung at Miss Trewbody's door, and having sent in his name, was admitted into the parlor, where there was no one to receive him, while Miss Trewbody adjusted her head-dress at the toilette, before she made her appearance. Her feelings while she was thus employed were not of the pleasantest kind toward this unexpected guest; and she was prepared to accost him with a reproof for his extravagance in undertaking so long a journey, and with some mortifying questions concerning the business which brought him there. But this amiable intention was put to flight, when Leonard, as soon as she entered the room, informed her, that having accepted an invitation into that neighborhood, from his friend and fellow-collegian, the son of Sir Lambert Bowles, he had taken the earliest opportunity of coming to pay his respects to her, and acknowledging his obligations, as bound alike by duty and inclination. The name of Sir Lambert Bowles acted upon Miss Trewbody like a charm; and its mollifying effect was not a little aided by the tone of her nephew's address, and the sight of a fine youth in the first bloom of manhood, whose appearance and manners were such, that she could not be surprised at the introduction he had obtained into one of the first families in the county. The scowl, therefore, which she brought into the room upon her brow, passed instantly away, and was succeeded by so gracious an aspect, that Leonard, if he had not divined the cause, might have mistaken this gleam of sunshine for fair weather.

A cause which Miss Trewbody could not possibly suspect had rendered her nephew's address thus conciliatory. Had he expected to see no other person in that house, the visit would have been performed as an irksome obligation, and his manner would have appeared as cold and formal as the reception which he anticipated. But Leonard had not forgotten the playmate and companion with whom the happy years of his childhood had been passed. Young as he was at their separation, his character had taken its stamp during those peaceful years, and the impression which it then received was indelible. Hitherto hope had never been to him so delightful as memory. His thoughts wandered back into the past more frequently than they took flight into the future; and the favorite form which his imagination called up was that of the sweet child, who in winter partook his bench in the chimney-corner, and in summer sat with him in the porch, and strung the fallen blossoms of jessamine upon stalks of grass. The snowdrop and the crocus reminded him of their little garden, the primrose of their sunny orchard-bank, and the bluebells and the cowslip of the fields, wherein they were allowed to run wild, and gather them in the merry month of May. Such as she then was he saw her frequently in sleep, with her blue eyes, and rosy cheeks, and flaxen curls: and in his daydreams he sometimes pictured her to himself such as he supposed she now might be, and dressed up the image with all the magic of ideal beauty. His heart, therefore, was at his lips when he inquired for his cousin. It was not without something like fear, and an apprehension of disappointment, that he awaited her appearance; and he was secretly condemning himself for the romantic folly which he had encouraged, when the door opened, and a creature came in, — less radiant, indeed, but more winning than his fancy had created, for the loveliness of earth and reality was about her.

"Margaret," said Miss Trewbody, "do you remember your cousin Leonard?"

Before she could answer, Leonard had taken her hand. "'T is a long while, Margaret, since we parted! — ten years! — But I have not forgotten the parting — nor the blessed days of our childhood."

She stood trembling like an aspen leaf, and looked wistfully in his face for a moment, then hung down her head, without power to utter a word in reply. But he felt her tears fall fast upon his hand, and felt also that she returned its pressure.

Leonard had some difficulty to command himself, so as to bear a part in conversation with his aunt, and keep his eyes and his thoughts from wandering. He accepted, however, her invitation to stay and dine with her with undissembled satisfaction, and the pleasure was not a little heightened when she left the room to give some necessary orders in consequence. Margaret still sate trembling and in silence. He took her hand, pressed it to his lips, and said in a low earnest voice, "Dear, dear Margaret!" She raised her eyes, and fixing them upon him with one of those looks, the perfect remembrance of which can never be effaced from the heart to which they have been addressed, replied in a lower but not less earnest tone, "Dear Leonard!" and from that moment their lot was sealed for time and for eternity.

CHAPTER IV.

MORE CONCERNING LOVE AND THE DREAM OF LIFE.

> Happy the bonds that hold ye;
> Sure they be sweeter far than liberty,
> There is no blessedness but in such bondage;
> Happy that happy chain; such links are heavenly.
> BEAUMONT AND FLETCHER.

I WILL not describe the subsequent interviews between Leonard and his cousin, short and broken, but precious as they were; nor that parting one, in which hands were plighted with the sure and certain knowledge that hearts had been interchanged. Remembrance will enable some of my readers to portray the scene, and then perhaps a sigh may be heaved for the days that are gone : Hope will picture it to others — and with them the sigh will be for the days that are to come.

There was not that indefinite deferment of hope in this case at which the heart sickens. Leonard had been bred up in poverty from his childhood; a parsimonious allowance, grudgingly bestowed, had contributed to keep him frugal at college, by calling forth a pardonable if not a commendable sense of pride in aid of a worthier principle. He knew that he could rely upon himself for frugality, industry, and a cheerful as well as a contented mind. He had seen the miserable state of bondage in which Margaret existed with her aunt, and his resolution was made to deliver her from that bondage as soon as he could obtain the smallest benefice on which it was possible for them to subsist. They agreed to live rigorously within their means, however poor, and put their trust in Providence. They could not be deceived in each other, for they had grown up together; and they knew that they were not deceived in themselves. Their love had the freshness of youth, but prudence and forethought were not wanting; the resolution which they had taken brought with it peace of mind, and no misgiving was felt in either heart when they prayed for a blessing upon their purpose. In reality it had already brought a blessing with it; and this they felt; for love, when it deserves that name, produces in us what may be called a regeneration of its own — a second birth — dimly, but yet in some degree, resembling that which is effected by Divine Love when its redeeming work is accomplished in the soul.

Leonard returned to Oxford happier than all this world's wealth or this world's honors could have made him. He had now a definite and attainable hope — an object in life which gave to life itself a value. For Margaret, the world no longer seemed to her like the same earth which she had till then inhabited. Hitherto she had felt herself a forlorn and solitary creature, without a friend; and the sweet sounds and pleasant objects of nature, had imparted as little cheerfulness to her as to the debtor who sees green fields in sunshine from his prison, and hears the lark singing at liberty. Her heart was open now to all the exhilarating and all the softening influences of birds, fields, flowers, vernal suns, and melodious streams. She was subject to the same daily and hourly exercise of meekness, patience, and humility; but the trial was no longer painful; with love in her heart, and hope and sunshine in her prospect, she found even a pleasure in contrasting her present condition with that which was in store for her.

In these our days every young lady holds the pen of a ready writer, and words flow from it as fast as it can indent its zigzag lines, according to the reformed system of writing, — which said system improves handwritings by making them all alike and all illegible. At that time women wrote better and spelt worse; but letter-writing was not one of their accomplishments. It had not yet become one of the general pleasures and luxuries of life, — perhaps the greatest gratification which the progress of civilization has given us. There was then no mail-coach to waft a sigh across the country at the rate of eight miles an hour. Letters came slowly and with long intervals between; but when they came, the happiness which they imparted to Leonard and Margaret lasted during the interval, however long. To Leonard it was as an exhilarant and a cordial which rejoiced and strengthened him. He trod the earth with a lighter and more elated movement on the day when he received a letter from Margaret, as if he felt himself invested with an importance which he had never possessed till the happiness of another human being was inseparably associated with his own.

> So proud a thing it was for him to wear
> Love's golden chain,
> With which it is best freedom to be bound.*

Happy, indeed, if there be happiness on earth, as that same sweet poet says, is he

> Who love enjoys, and placed hath his mind
> Where fairest virtues fairest beauties grace,
> Then in himself such store of worth doth find
> That he deserves to find so good a place.*

This was Leonard's case; and when he kissed the paper which her hand had pressed, it was with a consciousness of the strength and sincerity of his affection, which at once rejoiced and fortified his heart. To Margaret his letters were like summer dew upon the herb that thirsts for such refreshment. Whenever they arrived, a headache became the cause or pretext for retiring earlier than usual to her chamber, that she might weep and dream over the precious lines.

> True gentle love is like the summer dew,
> Which falls around when all is still and hush;
> And falls unseen until its bright drops strew
> With odors, herb and flower, and bank and bush.

* Drummond.

O love!—when womanhood is in the flush,
And man's a young and an unspotted thing,
His first-breathed word, and her half-conscious blush,
Are fair as light in heaven, or flowers in spring.*

CHAPTER V.

AN EARLY BEREAVEMENT. TRUE LOVE ITS OWN COMFORTER. A LONELY FATHER AND AN ONLY CHILD.

> Read ye that run the awful truth,
> With which I charge my page;
> A worm is in the bud of youth,
> And at the root of age.
> COWPER.

LEONARD was not more than eight-and-twenty when he obtained a living, a few miles from Doncaster. He took his bride with him to the vicarage. The house was as humble as the benefice, which was worth less than £50 a year; but it was soon made the neatest cottage in the country round, and upon a happier dwelling the sun never shone. A few acres of good glebe were attached to it; and the garden was large enough to afford healthful and pleasurable employment to its owners. The course of true love never ran more smoothly; but its course was short.

> O how this spring of love resembleth
> The uncertain glory of an April day,
> Which now shows all the beauty of the sun,
> And by and by a cloud takes all away!†

Little more than five years from the time of their marriage had elapsed, before a head-stone in the adjacent churchyard told where the remains of Margaret Bacon had been deposited, in the thirtieth year of her age.

* Allan Cunningham. † Shakespeare.

When the stupor and the agony of that bereavement had passed away, the very intensity of Leonard's affection became a source of consolation. Margaret had been to him a purely ideal object during the years of his youth; death had again rendered her such. Imagination had beautified and idolized her then; faith sanctified and glorified her now. She had been to him on earth all that he had fancied, all that he had hoped, all that he had desired. She would again be so in heaven. And this second union nothing could impede, nothing could interrupt, nothing could dissolve. He had only to keep himself worthy of it by cherishing her memory, hallowing his heart to it while he performed a parent's duty to their child; and so doing to await his own summons, which must one day come, which every day was brought nearer, and which any day might bring.

'T is the only discipline we are born for;
All studies else are but as circular lines,
And death the centre where they must all meet.*

The same feeling which from his chidhood had refined Leonard's heart, keeping it pure and undefiled, had also corroborated the natural strength of his character, and made him firm of purpose. It was a saying of Bishop Andrewes; that "good husbandry is good divinity"; "the truth whereof," says Fuller, "no wise man will deny." Frugality he had always practised as a needful virtue, and found that, in an especial manner, it brings with it its own reward. He now resolved upon scrupulously setting apart a fourth of his small income to make a provision for his child, in case of her surviving him, as in the natural course of things might be expected. If she should be removed before him — for this was an event the possibility of which he always bore in mind — he had resolved, that whatever should have been accumulated with this intent, should be disposed of to some

* Massinger.

other pious purpose, — for such, within the limits to which his poor means extended, he properly considered this. And having entered on this prudential course with a calm reliance upon Providence, in case his hour should come before that purpose could be accomplished, he was without any earthly hope or fear, — those alone excepted from which no parent can be free.

The child had been christened Deborah, after her maternal grandmother, for whom Leonard ever gratefully retained a most affectionate and reverential remembrance. She was a healthy, happy creature in body and in mind; at first

> one of those little prating girls
> Of whom fond parents tell such tedious stories; *

afterwards, as she grew up, a favorite with the village schoolmistress, and with the whole parish; docile, good-natured, lively and yet considerate, always gay as a lark and busy as a bee. One of the pensive pleasures in which Leonard indulged was to gaze on her unperceived, and trace the likeness to her mother.

> O Christ!
> How that which was the life's life of our being,
> Can pass away, and we recall it thus! †

That resemblance which was strong in childhood lessened as the child grew up; for Margaret's countenance had acquired a cast of meek melancholy during those years in which the bread of bitterness had been her portion; and, when hope came to her, it was that "hope deferred," which takes from the cheek its bloom, even when the heart, instead of being made sick, is sustained by it. But no unhappy circumstances depressed the constitutional buoyancy of her daughter's spirits. Deborah brought into the world the

* Dryden. † Isaac Comnenus.

happiest of all nature's endowments, an easy temper and a light heart. Resemblant therefore as the features were, the dissimiltude of expression was more apparent; and when Leonard contrasted in thought the sunshine of hilarity that lit up his daughter's face, with the sort of moonlight loveliness which had given a serene and saint-like character to her mother's, he wished to persuade himself, that as the early translation of the one seemed to have been thus prefigured, the other might be destined to live for the happiness of others till a good old age, while length of years in their course should ripen her for heaven.

CHAPTER VI.

OBSERVATIONS WHICH SHOW, THAT WHATEVER PRIDE MEN MAY TAKE IN THE APPELLATIONS THEY ACQUIRE IN THEIR PROGRESS THROUGH THE WORLD, THEIR DEAREST NAME DIES BEFORE THEM.

> Thus they who reach
> Gray hairs, die piecemeal. — SOUTHEY.

THE name of Leonard must now be dropped as we proceed. Some of the South American tribes, among whom the Jesuits labored with such exemplary zeal, and who take their personal appellations (as most names were originally derived) from beasts, birds, plants, and other visible objects, abolish upon the death of every individual the name by which he was called, and invent another for the thing from which it was taken, so that their language, owing to this curiously inconvenient custom, is in a state of continual change. An abolition almost as complete with regard to the person had taken place in the present instance. The name, Leonard, was consecrated to him by all his dearest and fondest recollections. He had been known by it on his mother's knees, and in the humble cottage of that aunt who had been to him a second mother; and by the wife of his bosom, his first, last, and only love. Margaret had never spoken to him, never thought of him, by any other name. From the hour of her death, no human voice ever addressed him by it again. He never heard himself so called, except in dreams. It existed only in the dead letter; he signed it mechanically in the course of business, but it had ceased to be a living name.

Men willingly prefix a handle to their names, and tack on to them any two or more honorary letters of the alphabet as a tail; they drop their surnames for a dignity, and change them for an estate or a title. They are pleased to be Doctor'd and Professor'd; to be Captain'd, Major'd, Colonel'd, General'd, or Admiral'd; to be Sir John'd, my-Lorded, or your-Grace'd. "You and I," says Cranmer in his Answer to Gardiner's book upon Transubstantiation — "you and I were delivered from our surnames when we were consecrated Bishops; sithence which time we have so commonly been used of all men to be called Bishops, you of Winchester, and I of Canterbury, that the most part of the people know not that your name is Gardiner, and mine Cranmer. And I pray God, that we being called to the name of Lords, have not forgotten our own baser estates, that once we were simple squires!"—But the emotion with which the most successful suitor of Fortune hears himself first addressed by a new and honorable title, conferred upon him for his public deserts, touches his heart less (if that heart be sound at the core), than when after long absence, some one who is privileged so to use it, accosts him by his christian name,—that household name which he has never heard but from his nearest relations, and his old familiar friends. By this it is that we are known to all around us in childhood; it is used only by our parents and our nearest kin when that stage is passed; and, as they drop off, it dies as to its oral uses with them.

It is because we are remembered more naturally in our family and paternal circles by our baptismal than our hereditary names, and remember ourselves more naturally by them, that the Roman Catholic, renouncing, upon a principle of perverted piety, all natural ties when he enters a convent, and voluntarily dies to the world, assumes a new one. This is one manifestation of that intense selfishness which the law of monastic life inculcates, and affects to sanctify. Alas, there need no motives of erroneous religion to wean us from the ties of blood and of affection! They are weakened and dissolved by fatal circumstances, and the ways of the world, too frequently and too soon.

"Our men of rank," said my friend one day when he was speaking upon this subject, "are not the only persons who go by different appellations in different parts of their lives. We all moult our names in the natural course of life. I was Dan in my father's house, and should still be so with my uncle William and Mr. Guy, if they were still living. Upon my removal to Doncaster, my master and mistress called me Daniel, and my acquaintance Dove. In Holland I was Mynheer Duif. Now I am the Doctor, and not among my patients only; friends, acquaintance, and strangers, address me by this appellation; even my wife calls me by no other name; and I shall never be anything but the Doctor again, — till I am registered at my burial by the same name as at my christening."

CHAPTER VII.

THE DOCTOR IS INTRODUCED, BY THE SMALL-POX, TO HIS FUTURE WIFE.

> Long-waiting love doth entrance find
> Into the slow-believing mind.
> SYDNEY GODOLPHIN.

WHEN Deborah was about nineteen, the small-pox broke out in Doncaster, and soon spread over the surrounding country, occasioning everywhere a great mortality. At that time inoculation had very rarely been practised in the provinces; and the prejudice against it was so strong, that Mr. Bacon, though convinced in his own mind that the practice was not only lawful, but advisable, refrained from having his daughter inoculated till the disease appeared in his own parish. He had been induced to defer it during her childhood, partly because he was unwilling to offend the prejudices of his parishioners, which he hoped to overcome by persuasion and reasoning when time and opportunity might favor; still more, because he thought it unjustifiable to introduce such a disease into his own house, with imminent risk of communicating it to others, which were otherwise in no danger, in which the same preparations would not be made, and where, consequently, the danger would be greater. But when the malady had shown itself in the parish, then he felt that his duty as a parent required him to take the best apparent means for the preservation of his child; and that as a pastor also it became him now in his own family to set an example to his parishioners.

Deborah, who had the most perfect reliance upon her father's judgment, and lived in entire accordance with his will in all things, readily consented; and seemed to regard the beneficial consequences of the experiment to others with hope, rather than to look with apprehension to it for herself. Mr. Bacon therefore went to Doncaster and called upon Mr. Dove. "I do not," said he, "ask whether you would advise me to have my daughter inoculated; where so great a risk is to be incurred, in the case of an only child, you might hesitate to advise it. But if you see nothing in her present state of health, or in her constitutional tendencies, which would render it more than ordinarily dangerous, it is her own wish and mine, after due consideration on my part, that she should be committed to your care, — putting our trust in Providence."

Hitherto there had been no acquaintance between Mr. Bacon and the Doctor, farther than that they knew each other by sight and by good report. This circumstance led to a growing intimacy. During the course of his attendance, the Doctor fell in friendship with the father, and the father with him.

"Did he fall in love with his patient?"

"No, ladies."

You have already heard that he once fell in love, and how it happened. And you have also been informed that he caught love once, though I have not told you how, because it would have led me into too melancholy a tale. In this case he neither fell in love, nor caught it, nor ran into it, nor walked into it; nor was he overtaken in it, as a boon companion in liquor, or a runaway in his flight. Yet there was love between the parties at last, and it was love for love, to the heart's content of both. How this came to pass will be related at the proper time and in the proper place.

For here let me set before the judicious reader certain pertinent remarks by the pious and well-known author of a popular treatise upon the Right Use of Reason,— a treatise which has been much read to little purpose. That author observes, that "those writers and speakers whose chief business is to amuse or delight, to allure, terrify, or persuade mankind, do not confine themselves to any natural order, but in a cryptical or hidden method, adapt everything to their designed ends. Sometimes they omit those things which might injure their design, or grow tedious to their hearers, though they seem to have a necessary relation to the point in hand; sometimes they add those things which have no great reference to the subject, but are suited to allure or refresh the mind and the ear. They dilate sometimes, and flourish long upon little incidents, and they skip over, and but lightly touch the dryer part of the theme. They omit things essential which are not beautiful; they insert little needless circumstances, and beautiful digressions: they invert times and actions, in order to place everything in the most affecting light; — they place the first things last, and the last things first with wondrous art; and yet so manage it as to conceal their artifice, and lead the senses and passions of their hearers into a pleasing and powerful captivity."

CHAPTER VIII.

MR. BACON'S PARSONAGE. CHRISTIAN RESIGNATION. TIME AND CHANGE. WILKIE AND THE MONK IN THE ESCURIAL.

> The idea of her life shall sweetly creep
> Into his study of imagination;
> And every lovely organ of her life
> Shall come apparelled in more precious habit,
> More moving delicate, and full of life,
> Into the eye and prospect of his soul,
> Than when she lived indeed.
>
> SHAKESPEARE.

In a Scotch village the Manse is sometimes the only good house, and generally it is the best; almost, indeed, what in old times the Mansion used to be in an English one. In Mr. Bacon's parish, the vicarage, though humble as the benefice itself, was the neatest. The cottage in which he and Margaret passed their childhood, had been remarkable for that comfort which is the result and the reward of order and neatness: and when the reunion which blessed them both rendered the remembrance of those years delightful, they returned in this respect to the way in which they had been trained up, practised the economy which they had learned there, and loved to think how entirely their course of life, in all its circumstances, would be after the heart of that person, if she could behold it, whose memory they both with equal affection cherished. After his bereavement, it was one of the widower's pensive pleasures to keep everything in the same state as when Margaret was living. Nothing was neglected that she used to do, or that she would have done. The flowers were tended as carefully as if she were still to enjoy their fragrance and their beauty; and the birds who came in winter for their crumbs, were fed as duly for her sake, as they had formerly been by her hands.

There was no superstition in this, nor weakness. Immoderate grief, if it does not exhaust itself by indulgence, easily assumes the one character or the other, or takes a type of insanity. But he had looked for consolation, where, when sincerely sought, it is always to be found; and he had experienced that religion effects in a true believer all that philosophy professes, and more than all that mere philosophy can perform. The wounds which stoicism would cauterize, religion heals.

There is a resignation with which, it may be feared, most of us deceive ourselves. To bear what must be borne, and submit to what cannot be resisted, is no more than what the unregenerate heart is taught by the instinct of animal nature. But to acquiesce in the afflictive dispensations of Providence, — to make one's own will conform in all things to that of our Heavenly Father, — to say to him in the sincerity of faith, when we drink of the bitter cup, " Thy will be done ! " — to bless the name of the Lord as much from the heart when he takes away as when he gives, and with a depth of feeling, of which, perhaps, none but the afflicted heart is capable, — this is the resignation which religion teaches, this the sacrifice which it requires.* This sacrifice Leonard had made, and he felt that it was accepted.

---

* This passage was written when Southey was bowing his head under the sorest and saddest of his many troubles. He thus alludes to it in a letter to J. W. Warter, dated October 5, 1834.

"On the next leaf is the passage of which I spoke in my letter from York. It belongs to an early chapter in the third volume; and very remarkable it is that it should have been written just at that time."

Severe, therefore, as his loss had been, and lasting as its effects were, it produced in him nothing like a settled sorrow, nor even that melancholy which sorrow leaves behind. Gibbon has said to himself, that as a mere philosopher he could not agree with the Greeks, in thinking that those who die in their youth are favored by the Gods:

*Ὃν οἱ θεοὶ φιλοῦσιν ἀποθνήσκει νέος.

It was because he was "a mere philosopher," that he failed to perceive a truth which the religious heathen acknowledged, and which is so trivial, and of such practical value, that it may now be seen inscribed upon village tombstones. The Christian knows that "Blessed are the dead which die in the Lord; even so saith the Spirit." And the heart of the Christian mourner, in its deepest distress, hath the witness of the Spirit to that consolatory assurance.

In this faith Leonard regarded his bereavement. His loss, he knew, had been Margaret's gain. What, if she had been summoned in the flower of her years, and from a state of connubial happiness which there had been nothing to disturb or to alloy? How soon might that flower have been blighted, — how surely must it have faded, — how easily might that happiness have been interrupted, by some of those evils which flesh is heir to! And as the separation was to take place, how mercifully had it been appointed that he, who was the stronger vessel, should be the survivor! Even for their child this was the best, greatly as she needed, and would need, a mother's care. His paternal solicitude would supply that care, as far as it was possible to supply it; but had he been removed, mother and child must have been left to the mercy of Providence, without any earthly protector, or any means of support.

For her to die was gain; in him, therefore, it were sinful as well as selfish to repine, and of such selfishness and sin his heart acquitted him. If a wish could have recalled her to life, no such wish would ever have by him been uttered, nor ever have by him been felt; certain he was, that he loved her too well to bring her again into this world of instability and trial. Upon earth there can be no safe happiness.

> *Ah! male* FORTUNÆ *devota est ara* MANENTI.
> *Fallit, et hæc nullas accipit ara preces.**

All things here are subject to Time and Mutability:

> *Quod tibi largâ dedit Hora dextrâ,*
> *Hora furaci rapiet sinistrâ.†*

We must be in eternity before we can be secure against change. " The world," says Cowper, " upon which we close our eyes at night, is never the same with that on which we open them in the morning."

It was to the perfect Order he should find in that state upon which he was about to enter, that the judicious Hooker looked forward at his death with placid and profound contentment. Because he had been employed in contending against a spirit of insubordination and schism which soon proved fatal to his country; and because his life had been passed under the perpetual discomfort of domestic discord, the happiness of Heaven seemed, in his estimation, to consist primarily in Order, as, indeed, in all human societies this is the first thing needful. The discipline which Mr. Bacon had undergone was very different in kind: what he delighted to think was, that the souls of those whom death and redemption have made perfect, are in a world where there is no change, nor parting, — where nothing fades, nothing passes away and is no more seen, but the good and the beautiful are permanent.

> *Miser, chi speme in cosa mortal pone;*
> *Ma, chi non ve la pone ? ‡*

---

* Wallius. † Casimir. ‡ Petrarch.

A LOVE STORY. 195

When Wilkie was in the Escurial looking at Titian's famous picture of the Last Supper, in the refectory there, an old Jeronimite said to him, "I have sat daily in sight of that picture for now nearly threescore years; during that time my companions have dropped off, one after another,— all who were my seniors, all who were my contemporaries, and many, or most of those who were younger than myself; more than one generation has passed away, and there the figures in the picture have remained unchanged! I look at them till I sometimes think that they are the realities, and we but shadows!"*

I wish I could record the name of the monk by whom that natural feeling was so feelingly and strikingly expressed.

"The shows of things are better than themselves,"

says the author of the Tragedy of Nero, whose name also I could wish had been forthcoming; and the classical reader will remember the lines of Sophocles:—

'Ορῶ γὰρ ἡμᾶς οὐδὲν ὄντας ἄλλο, πλὴν
Εἴδωλ', ὅσοιπερ ζῶμεν, ἢ κούφην σκιάν. †

These are reflections which should make us think

 Of that same time when no more change shall be,
 But steadfast rest of all things, firmly stayd
 Upon the pillars of Eternity,
 That is contraire to mutability;
 For all that moveth doth in change delight:
 But thenceforth all shall rest eternally
 With Him that is the God of Sabaoth hight,
 O that great Sabaoth God grant me that sabbath's sight.‡

---

 * See the very beautiful lines of Wordsworth in the "Yarrow Revisited." The affecting incident is introduced in "Lines on a Portrait."
 † Sophocles.   ‡ Spenser.

CHAPTER IX.

A COUNTRY PARISH. SOME WHOLESOME EXTRACTS, SOME TRUE ANECDOTES, AND SOME USEFUL HINTS, WHICH WILL NOT BE TAKEN BY THOSE WHO NEED THEM MOST.

Non è inconveniente, che delle cose delettabili alcune ne sieno utili, cosi come dell' utili molte ne sono delettabili, et in tutte due alcune si truovano honeste.

LEONE MEDICO (HEBREO.)

MR. BACON'S parsonage was as humble a dwelling in all respects as the cottage in which his friend Daniel was born. A best kitchen was its best room, and in its furniture an Observantine Friar would have seen nothing that he could have condemned as superfluous. His college and later school books, with a few volumes which had been presented to him by the more grateful of his pupils, composed his scanty library: they were either books of needful reference, or such as upon every fresh perusal might afford new delight. But he had obtained the use of the Church Library at Doncaster by a payment of twenty shillings, according to the terms of the foundation. Folios from that collection might be kept three months, smaller volumes, one or two, according to their size; and as there were many works in it of solid contents as well as sterling value, he was in no such want of intellectual food, as too many of his brethren are, even at this time. How much good might have been done, and how much evil might probably have been prevented, if Dr. Bray's design for the foundation of parochial libraries had been everywhere carried into effect!

The parish contained between five and six hundred souls. There was no one of higher rank among them than entitled him, according to the custom of those days, to be styled gentleman upon his tombstone. They were plain people, who had neither manufactories to corrupt, alehouses to brutalize, nor newspapers to mislead them. At first coming among them he had won their good-will by his affability and benign conduct, and he had afterwards gained their respect and affection in an equal degree.

There were two services at his church, but only one sermon, which never fell short of fifteen minutes in length, and seldom extended to half an hour. It was generally abridged from some good old divine. His own compositions were few, and only upon points on which he wished carefully to examine and digest his own thoughts, or which were peculiarly suited to some or other of his hearers. His whole stock might be deemed scanty in these days; but there was not one in it which would not well bear repetition, and the more observant of his congregation liked that they should be repeated.

Young ministers are earnestly advised long to refrain from preaching their own productions, in an excellent little book addressed by a Father to his Son, preparatory to his receiving holy orders. Its title is a "Monitor for Young Ministers," and every parent who has a son so circumstanced would do well to put it into his hands. "It is not possible," says this judicious writer, "that a young minister can at first be competent to preach his sermons with effect, even if his abilities should qualify him to write well. His very youth and youthful manner, both in his style of writing and in his delivery, will preclude him from being effective. Unquestionably it is very rare indeed for a man of his age to have his mental abilities sufficiently chastened, or his method sufficiently settled, to be equal to the composition of a sermon fit for public use, even if it should receive the advantage of chaste and good delivery. On every account, therefore, it is wise and prudent to be slow and backward in venturing to produce his own efforts, or in thinking that they are fit for the public ear. There is an abundant field of the works of others open to him from the wisest and the best of men, the weight of whose little fingers, in argument or instruction, will be greater than his own loins even at his highest maturity. There is clearly no *want* of new compositions, excepting on some new or occasional emergencies: for there is not an open subject in the Christian religion, which has not been discussed by men of the greatest learning and piety, who have left behind them numerous works for our assistance and edification. Many of these are so neglected that they are become almost new ground for our generation. To these he may freely resort, — till experience and a rational and chastened confidence shall warrant him in believing himself qualified to work upon his own resources."

"He that learns of young men," says Rabbi Jose Bar Jehudah, "is like a man that eats unripe grapes, or that drinks wine out of the wine-press; but he that learneth of the ancient, is like a man that eateth ripe grapes, and drinketh wine that is old." *

It was not in pursuance of any judicious advice like this that Mr. Bacon followed the course here pointed out, but from his own good sense and natural humility. His only ambition was to be useful; if a desire may be called ambitious which orginated in the sincere sense of duty. To think of distinguishing himself in any other way, would for him, he well knew, have been worse than an idle dream. The time expended in composing a sermon as a perfunctory official business, would have been worse than wasted for himself, and the time employed in delivering it, no better than wasted upon his congregation. He was especially careful never to weary them, and, therefore, never to preach anything which was not likely to engage their attention, and make at least some present impression. His own ser-

* Lightfoot.

mons effected this, because they were always composed with some immediate view, or under the influence of some deep and strong feeling: and in his adopted ones, the different manner of the different authors produced an awakening effect. Good sense is as often to be found among the illiterate, as among those who have enjoyed the opportunities of education. Many of his hearers who knew but one meaning of the word style, and had never heard it used in any other, perceived a difference in the manner of Bishops Hall and Sanderson and Jeremy Taylor, of Barrow and South and Scott, without troubling themselves about the cause, or being in the slightest degree aware of it.

Mr. Bacon neither undervalued his parishioners, nor overvalued the good which could be wrought among them by direct instruction of this kind. While he used perspicuous language, he knew that they who listened to it would be able to follow the argument; and as he drew always from the wells of English undefiled, he was safe on that point. But that all even of the adults would listen, and that all even of those who did, would do anything more than hear, he was too well acquainted with human nature to expect.

A woman in humble life was asked one day on the way back from church, whether she had understood the sermon; a stranger had preached, and his discourse resembled one of Mr. Bacon's neither in length nor depth. "Wud I hae the persumption?" was her simple and contented answer. The quality of the discourse signified nothing to her; she had done her duty, as well as she could, in hearing it; and she went to her house justified rather than some of those who had attended to it critically; or who had turned to the text in their Bibles when it was given out.

"Well, Master Jackson," said his minister, walking homeward after service with an industrious laborer, who was a constant attendant; "well, Master Jackson, Sunday must be a blessed day of rest for you, who work so hard all the week! And you make a good use of the day, for you are always to be seen at church!"—"Ay, sir," replied Jackson, "it is indeed a blessed day; I works hard enough all the week, and then I comes to church o' Sundays, and sets me down, and lays my legs up, and thinks o' nothing."

"Let my candle go out in a stink, when I refuse to confess from whom I have lighted it."* The author to whose little book † I am beholden for this true anecdote, after saying, "Such was the religion of this worthy man," justly adds, "and such must be the religion of most men of his station. Doubtless, it is a wise dispensation that it is so. For so it has been from the beginning of the world, and there is no visible reason to suppose that it can ever be otherwise."

"In spite," says this judicious writer, "of all the zealous wishes and efforts of the most pious and laborious teachers, the religion of the bulk of the people must and will ever be little more than mere habit, and confidence in others. This must of necessity be the case with all men, who, from defect of nature or education, or from other worldy causes, have not the power or the disposition to think; and it cannot be disputed that the far greater number of mankind are of this class. These facts give peculiar force to those lessons which teach the importance and efficacy of good example from those who are blessed with higher qualifications; and they strongly demonstrate the necessity, that the zeal of those who wish to impress the people with the deep and awful mysteries of religion should be tempered by wisdom and discretion, no less than by patience, forbearance, and a great latitude of indulgence for uncontrollable circumstances. They also call upon us most powerfully to do all we can to provide such teachers, and imbue them with such principles as shall not endanger the good cause by over

---

* Fuller.   † Few Words on many Subjects.

earnest efforts to effect more than, in the nature of things, can be done; or disturb the existing good by attempting more than will be borne, or by producing hypocritical pretences of more than can be really felt."

CHAPTER X.

SHOWING HOW THE VICAR DEALT WITH THE JUVENILE PART OF HIS FLOCK; AND HOW HE WAS OF OPINION THAT THE MORE PLEASANT THE WAY IN WHICH CHILDREN ARE TRAINED UP TO GO CAN BE MADE FOR THEM, THE LESS LIKELY THEY WILL BE TO DEPART FROM IT.

> Sweet were the sauce would please each kind of taste,
> The life, likewise, were pure that never swerved;
> For spiteful tongues, in cankered stomachs placed,
> Deem worst of things which best, percase, deserved.
> But what for that? This medicine may suffice,
> To scorn the rest, and seek to please the wise.
> SIR WALTER RALEIGH.

THE first thing which Mr. Bacon had done after taking possession of his vicarage, and obtaining such information about his parishioners as the more considerate of them could impart, was to inquire into the state of the children in every household. He knew that to win the mother's good-will was the surest way to win that of the family, and to win the children was a good step toward gaining that of the mother. In those days reading and writing were thought as little necessary for the lower class, as the art of spelling for the class above them, or indeed for any except the learned. Their ignorance in this respect was sometimes found to be inconvenient, but by none, perhaps, except here and there by a conscientious and thoughtful clergyman, was it felt to be an evil, — an impediment in the way of that moral and religious instruction, without which men are in danger of becoming as the beasts that perish. Yet the common wish of advancing their children in the world, made most parents in this station desire to obtain the advantage of what they called book-learning for any son, who was supposed to manifest a disposition likely to profit by it. To make him a scholar was to raise him a step above themselves.

> *Qui ha les lettres, ha l'adresse*
> *Au double d'un qui n'en ha point.**

Partly for this reason, and still more that industrious mothers might be relieved from the care of looking after their children, there were few villages in which, as in Mr. Bacon's parish, some poor woman in the decline of life and of fortune did not obtain day-scholars enough to eke out her scanty means of subsistence.

The village schoolmistress, such as Shenstone describes in his admirable poem, and such as Kirke White drew from the life, is no longer a living character. The new system of education has taken from this class of women the staff of their declining age, as the spinning-jennies have silenced the domestic music of the spinning-wheel. Both changes have come on unavoidably in the progress of human affairs. It is well when any change brings with it nothing worse than some temporary and incidental evil; but if the moral machinery can counteract the great and growing evils of the manufacturing system, it will be the greatest moral miracle that has ever been wrought.

Sunday schools, which make Sunday a day of toil to the teachers, and the most irksome day of the week to the children, had not at that time been devised as a palliative for the profligacy of large towns, and the worsened and worsening condition of the poor. Mr. Bacon endeavored to make the parents perform their religious duty toward their children, either by teaching them what they could themselves teach, or by sending them where their own want of knowl-

---

* Baif.

edge might be supplied. Whether the children went to school or not, it was his wish that they should be taught their prayers, the Creed, and the Commandments, at home. These he thought were better learned at the mother's knees than from any other teacher; and he knew also how wholesome for the mother it was, that the child should receive from her its first spiritual food, the milk of sound doctrine. In a purely agricultural parish, there were at that time no parents in a state of such brutal ignorance as to be unable to teach these, though they might never have been taught to read. When the father or mother could read, he expected that they should also teach their children the Catechism; in other cases this was left to his humble coadjutrix, the schoolmistress.

During the summer and part of the autumn, he followed the good old usage of catechising the children, after the second lesson in the evening service. His method was to ask a few questions in succession, and only from those who he knew were able to answer them; and after each answer he entered into a brief exposition suited to their capacity. His manner was so benevolent, and he had made himself so familiar in his visits, which were at once pastoral and friendly, that no child felt alarmed at being singled out; they regarded it as a mark of distinction, and the parents were proud of seeing them thus distinguished. This practice was discontinued in winter; because he knew that to keep a congregation in the cold is not the way either to quicken or cherish devotional feeling. Once a week during Lent he examined all the children, on a week-day; the last examination was in Easter week, after which each was sent home happy with a homely cake, the gift of a wealthy parishioner, who by this means contributed not a little to the good effect of the pastor's diligence.

The foundation was thus laid by teaching the rising generation their duty towards God and towards their neighbor, and so far training them in the way that they should go. In the course of a few years every household, from the highest to the lowest, (the degrees were neither great nor many,) had learned to look upon him as their friend. There was only one in the parish whose members were upon a parity with him in manners, none in literary culture; but in good-will, and in human sympathy, he was upon a level with them all. Never interfering in the concerns of any family, unless his interference was solicited, he was consulted upon all occasions of trouble or importance. Incipient disputes, which would otherwise have afforded grist for the lawyer's mill, were adjusted by his mediation; and anxious parents, when they had cause to apprehend that their children were going wrong, knew no better course than to communicate their fears to him, and request that he would administer some timely admonition. Whenever he was thus called on, or had of himself perceived that reproof or warning was required, it was given in private, or only in presence of the parents, and always with a gentleness which none but an obdurate disposition could resist. His influence over the younger part of his flock was the greater because he was no enemy to any innocent sports, but, on the contrary, was pleased to see them dance round the May-pole, encouraged them to dress their doors with oaken boughs on the day of King Charles's happy restoration, and to wear an oaken garland in the hat, or an oak-apple on its sprig in the button-hole; went to see their bonfire on the 5th of November, and entertained the morris-dancers when they called upon him in their Christmas rounds.

Mr. Bacon was in his parish what a moralizing old poet wished himself to be, in these pleasing stanzas:—

> I would I were an excellent divine,
> That had the Bible at my fingers' ends,

That men might hear out of this mouth of mine
How God doth make his enemies his friends;
Rather than with a thundering and long prayer
Be led into presumption, or despair.

This would I be, and would none other be
But a religious servant of my God:
And know there is none other God but He
And willingly to suffer Mercy's rod,
Joy in his grace and live but in his love,
And seek my bliss but in the world above.

And I would frame a kind of faithful prayer
For all estates within the state of grace;
That careful love might never know despair,
Nor servile fear might faithful love deface;
And this would I both day and night devise
To make my humble spirits exercise.

And I would read the rules of sacred life,
Persuade the troubled soul to patience,
The husband care, and comfort to the wife,
To child and servant due obedience,
Faith to the friend and to the neighbor peace,
That love might live, and quarrels all might cease;

Pray for the health of all that are diseased,
Confession unto all that are convicted,
And patience unto all that are displeased,
And comfort unto all that are afflicted,
And mercy unto all that have offended,
And grace to all, that all may be amended.*

* N. B., supposed to be Nicholas Breton.

CHAPTER XI.

SOME ACCOUNT OF A RETIRED TOBACCONIST AND HIS FAMILY.

Non fumum ex fulgore, sed ex fumo dare lucem.
HORACE.

IN all Mr. Bacon's views he was fortunate enough to have the hearty concurrence of the wealthiest person in the parish. This was a good man, Allison by name, who, having realized a respectable fortune in the metropolis as a tobacconist, and put out his sons in life according to their respective inclinations, had retired from business at the age of threescore, and established himself with an unmarried daughter, and a maiden sister some ten years younger than himself, in his native village, that he might there, when his hour should come, be gathered to his fathers.

"The providence of God," says South, "has so ordered the course of things, that there is no action, the usefulness of which has made it the matter of duty and of a profession, but a man may bear the continual pursuit of it, without loathing or satiety. The same shop and trade that employs a man in his youth, employs him also in his age. Every morning he rises fresh to his hammer and his anvil: custom has naturalized his labor to him; his shop is his element, and he cannot, with any enjoyment of himself, live out of it." The great preacher contrasts this with the wearisomeness of an idle life, and the misery of a continual round of what the world calls pleasure. "But now," says he, "if God has interwoven such a contentment with the works of our ordinary calling, how much superior and more refined must that be that arises from the survey of a pious and well-governed life?"

This passage bears upon Mr. Allison's case, partly in the consolatory fact which it states, and wholly in the application which South has made of it. At the age of fourteen he had been apprenticed to an uncle in Bishopsgate Street Within; and twenty years after, on that uncle's death, had succeeded to his old and well-established business. But though he had lived there prosperously and happily six and twenty years longer, he had contracted no such love for it as to overcome the recollections of his childhood. Grateful as the smell of snuff and tobacco had become to him, he still remembered that cowslips and violets were sweeter; and that the breath of a May morning was more exhilarating than the air of his own shop, impregnated as it was with the odor of the best Virginia. So having buried his wife, who was a Londoner, and made over the business to his eldest son, he returned to his native place, with the intention of dying there; but he was in sound health of body and mind, and his green old age seemed to promise, — as far as anything can promise, — length of days.

Of his two other sons, one had chosen to be a clergyman, and approved his choice both by his parts and diligence; for he had gone off from Merchant-Tailors' School to St. John's, Oxford, and was then a fellow of that college. The other was a mate in the Merchants' service, and would soon have the command of a ship in it. The desire of seeing the world led him to this way of life; and that desire had been unintentionally implanted by his father, who, in making himself acquainted with everything relating to the herb out of which his own fortune was raised, had become fond of reading voyages and travels. His conversation induced the lad to read these books, and the books confirmed the inclination which had already been excited; and, as the boy was of an adventurous temper, he thought it best to let him follow the pursuit on which his mind was bent.

The change to a Yorkshire village was not too great for Mr. Allison, even after residing nearly half a century in Bishopsgate Street Within. The change in his own household, indeed, rendered it expedient for him to begin, in this sense, a new life. He had lost his mate; the young birds were full-fledged and had taken flight; and it was time that he should look out a retreat for himself and the single nestling that remained under his wing, now that his son and successor had brought home a wife. The marriage had been altogether with his approbation; but it altered his position in the house; and in a still greater degree his sister's; moreover, the nest would soon be wanted for another brood. Circumstances thus compelled him to put in effect what had been the dream of his youth, and the still remote intention of his middle age.

Miss Allison, like her brother, regarded this removal as a great and serious change, preparatory to the only greater one in this world that now remained for both; but, like him, she regarded it rather seriously than sadly, or sadly only in the old sober meaning of the word; and there was a soft, sweet, evening sunshine in their prospect, which both partook, because both had retained a deep affection for the scenes of their childhood. To Betsey, her niece, nothing could be more delightful than the expectation of such a removal. She, who was then only entering her teens, had nothing to regret in leaving London; and the place to which she was going was the very spot which, of all others in this wide world, from the time in which she was conscious of forming a wish, she had wished most to see. Her brother, the sailor, was not more taken with the story of Pocahontas and Captain Smith, or Dampier's Voyages, than she was with her aunt's details of the farm and the dairy at Thaxted Grange, the May-games and the Christmas gambols, the days that were gone, and the elders who were departed. To one born and bred in the heart of London, who had scarcely ever seen a flock of sheep, except when they were driven through the streets to or from Smithfield, no fairy tale could present more for the imagination than a description of green fields and rural life. The charm of truth heightened it, and the stronger charm of natural piety; for the personages of the tale were her near kin, whose names she had learned to love, and whose living memory she revered, but whose countenances she never could behold till she should be welcomed by them in the everlasting mansions of the righteous.

None of the party were disappointed when they had established themselves at the Grange. Mr. Allison found full occupation at first in improving the house, and afterwards in his fields and garden. Mr. Bacon was just such a clergyman as he would have chosen for his parish priest, if it had been in his power to choose, only he would have had him provided with a better benefice. The single thing on which there was a want of agreement between them was, that the Vicar neither smoked nor took snuff; he was not the worst company on this account, for he had no dislike to the fragrance of a pipe; but his neighbor lost the pleasure which he would have had in supplying him with the best Pig-tail, and with Strasburg or Rappee. Miss Allison fell into the habits of her new station the more easily, because they were those which she had witnessed in her early youth; she distilled waters, dried herbs, and prepared conserves, — which were at the service of all who needed them in sickness. Betsey attached herself at first sight to Deborah, who was about five years elder, and soon became to her as a sister. The aunt rejoiced in finding so suitable a friend and companion for her niece; and as this connection was a pleasure and an advantage to the Allisons, so was it of the greatest benefit to Deborah.

> What of her ensues
> I list not prophesy, but let Time's news
> Be known, when 't is brought forth. Of this allow
> If ever you have spent time worse ere now:
> If never yet, the Author then doth say,
> He wishes earnestly you never may.*

* Shakespeare.

CHAPTER XII.

MORE CONCERNING THE AFORESAID TOBACCONIST.

I doubt nothing at all but that you shall like the man every day better than other; for verily I think he lacketh not of those qualities which should become any honest man to have, over and besides the gift of nature wherewith God hath above the common rate endued him.

ARCHBISHOP CRANMER.

MR. ALLISON was as quiet a subject as Peter Hopkins, but he was not like him a political quietist from indifference, for he had a warm sense of loyalty, and a well-rooted attachment to the constitution of his country in church and state. His ancestors had suffered in the Great Rebellion, and much the greater part of their never large estates had been alienated to raise the fines imposed upon them as delinquents. The uncle, whom he succeeded in Bishopsgate Street, had, in his early apprenticeship, assisted at burning the Rump, and in maturer years had joined as heartily in the rejoicings when the Seven Bishops were released from the Tower: he subscribed to Walker's "Account of the Sufferings of the Clergy," and had heard sermons preached by the famous Dr. Scott (which were afterwards incorporated in his great work upon the Christian Life) in the church of St. Peter-le-Poor (oddly so called, seeing that there are few districts within the City of London so rich, insomuch that the last historian of the metropolis believed the parish to have scarcely a poor family in it), — and in All-hallows, Lombard Street, where, during the reign of the Godly, the puritanical vestry passed a resolution, that if any persons should come to the church "on the day called Christ's birthday," they should be compelled to leave it.

In these principles Mr. Allison had grown up; and without any profession of extra religion, or ever wearing a sanctified face, he had in the evening of his life attained "the end of the commandment, which is charity, proceeding from a pure heart, and a good conscience, and a faith unfeigned." London in his days was a better school for young men in trade than it ever was before, or has been since. The civic power had quietly and imperceptibly put an end to that club-law which once made the apprentices a turbulent and formidable body, at any moment armed as well as ready for a riot; and masters exercised a sort of parental control over the youth intrusted to them, which in later times it may be feared has not been so conscientiously exerted, because it is not likely to be so patiently endured. Trade itself had not then been corrupted by that ruinous spirit of competition, which, more than any other of the evils now pressing upon us, deserves to be called the curse of England in the present age. At all times men have been to be found, who engaged in hazardous speculations, gamester like, according to their opportunities, or who, mistaking the means for the end, devoted themselves with miserable fidelity to the service of Mammon. But "Live and let live," had not yet become a maxim of obsolete morality. We had our monarchy, or hierarchy, and our aristocracy,— God be praised for the benefits which have been derived from all three, and God in his mercy continue them to us! but we had no plutarchy, no millionnaires, no great capitalists to break down the honest and industrious trader with the weight of their overbearing and overwhelming wealth. They who had enriched themselves in the course of regular and honorable commerce withdrew from business, and left the field to others. Feudal tyranny had passed away, and moneyed tyranny had not yet arisen in its stead, — a tyranny baser in its origin, not more merciful in its operations, and with less in its appendages to redeem it.

Trade, in Mr. Allison's days, was a school of thrift and probity, as much as of profit and loss; such his shop had been when he succeeded to it upon his uncle's decease, and such it continued to be when he transmitted it to his son. Old Mr. Strahan the printer (the founder of his typarchical dynasty) said to Dr. Johnson, that "there are few ways in which a man can be more innocently employed than in getting money"; and he added, that "the more one thinks of this the juster it will appear." Johnson agreed with him; and though it was a money-maker's observation, and though the more it is considered now, the more fallacious it will be found, the general system of trade might have justified it at that time. The entrance of an exciseman never occasioned any alarm or apprehension at No. 113 Bishopsgate Street Within, nor any uncomfortable feeling, unless the officer happened to be one who, by giving unnecessary trouble, and by gratuitous incivility in the exercise of authority, made an equitable law odious in its execution. They never there mixed weeds with their tobacco, nor adulterated it in any worse way; and their snuff was never rendered more pungent by stirring into it a certain proportion of pounded glass. The duties were honestly paid, with a clear perception that the impost fell lightly upon all whom it affected, and affected those only who chose to indulge themselves in a pleasure which was still cheap, and which, without any injurious privation, they might forego. Nay, when our good man expatiated upon the uses of tobacco, which Mr. Bacon demurred at, and the Doctor sometimes playfully disputed, he ventured an opinion, that among the final causes for which so excellent an herb had been created, the facilities afforded by it towards raising the revenue in a well-governed country like our own, might be one.

There was a strong family likeness between him and his sister, both in countenance and disposition. Elizabeth Allison was a person for whom the best and wisest man might have thanked Providence if she had been allotted to him for helpmate. But though she had, in Shakespeare's language, "withered on the virgin thorn," hers had not been a life of single blessedness : she had been a blessing first to her parents; then to her brother and her brother's family, where she relieved an amiable but sickly sister-in-law from those domestic offices which require activity and forethought; lastly, after the dispersion of his sons, the transfer of the business to the eldest, and the breaking-up of his old establishment, to the widower and his daughter, the only child who cleaved to him, — not like Ruth to Naomi, by a meritorious act of duty, for in her case it was in the ordinary course of things, without either sacrifice or choice; but the effect in endearing her to him was the same.

In advanced stages of society, and nowhere more than in England at this time, the tendency of all things is to weaken the relations between parent and child, and frequently to destroy them, reducing human nature in this respect nearer to the level of animal life. Perhaps the greater number of male children who are "born into the world," in our part of it, are *put out* at as early an age, proportionately, as the young bird is driven from its nest, or the young beast turned off by its dam as being capable of feeding and protecting itself; and in many instances they are as totally lost to the parent, though not in like manner forgotten. Mr. Allison never saw all his children together after his removal from London. The only time when his three sons met at the Grange was when they came there to attend their father's funeral; nor would they then have been assembled, if the Captain's ship had not happened to have recently arrived in port.

This is a state of things more favorable to the wealth than to the happiness of nations. It was a natural and pious custom in patriarchal times that the dead should be gathered unto their people. "Bury me," said Jacob, when he gave his dying charge to his sons, — "bury me with my fathers in the cave that is in the field of Machpelah, which is before Mamre in the land of Canaan, which Abraham bought with the field of Ephron the Hittite, for a possession of a burying-place. There they buried Abraham and Sarah his wife; there they buried Isaac and Rebecca his wife; and there I buried Leah." Had such a passage occurred in Homer, or in Dante, all critics would have concurred in admiring the truth and beauty of the sentiment. He had buried his beloved Rachel by the way where she died; but, although he remembered this at his death, the orders which he gave were, that his own remains should be laid in the sepulchre of his fathers. The same feeling prevails among many, or most of those savage tribes who are not utterly degraded. With them the tree is not left to lie where it falls. The body of one who dies on an expedition is interred on the spot, if distance or other circumstances render it inconvenient to transport the corpse; but, however long the journey, it is considered as a sacred duty that the bones should at some time or other be brought home. In Scotland, where the common rites of sepulture are performed with less decency than in any other Christian country, the care with which family burial-grounds in the remoter parts are preserved, may be referred as much to natural feeling as to hereditary pride.

But as indigenous flowers are eradicated by the spade and plough, so this feeling is destroyed in the stirring and bustling intercourse of commercial life. No room is left for it; as little of it at this time remains in wide America as in thickly-peopled England. That to which soldiers and sailors are reconciled by the spirit of their profession, and the chances of war and of the seas, the love of adventure and the desire of advancement cause others to regard with the same indifference; and these motives are so prevalent, that the dispersion of families and the consequent disruption of natural ties, if not occasioned by necessity, would now in most instances be the effect of choice. Even those to whom it is an inevitable evil, and who feel it deeply as such, look upon it as something in the appointed course of things, as much as infirmity and age and death.

It is well for us that in early life we never think of the vicissitudes which lie before us; or look to them only with pleasurable anticipations as they approach.

> Youth
> Knows naught of changes: Age hath traced them oft,
> Expects and can interpret them.*

The thought of them, when it comes across us in middle life, brings with it only a transient sadness, like the shadow of a passing cloud. We turn our eyes from them while they are in prospect; but when they are in retrospect many a longing, lingering look is cast behind. So long as Mr. Allison was in business, he looked to Thaxted Grange as the place where he hoped one day to enjoy the blessings of retirement, — that *otium cum dignitate*, which in a certain sense the prudent citizen is more likely to attain than the successful statesman. It was the pleasure of recollection that gave this hope its zest and its strength. But after the object which during so many years he had held in view had been obtained, his day-dreams, if he had allowed them to take their course, would have recurred more frequently to Bishopsgate Street than they had ever wandered from thence to the scenes of his boyhood. They recurred thither oftener than he wished, although few men have been more masters of themselves; and then the remembrance of his wife, whom he had lost by a lingering disease in middle age; and of the children, those who had died during their childhood, and those who in reality were almost as much lost to him in the ways of the world, made him alway turn for comfort to the prospect of that better state of existence in which they should once more all be gathered

* Isaac Comnenus.

together, and where there would be neither change nor parting. His thoughts often fell into this train, when on summer evenings he was taking a solitary pipe in his arbor, with the church in sight, and the churchyard wherein, at no distant time, he was to be laid in his last abode. Such musings induced a sense of sober piety, — of thankfulness for former blessings, contentment with the present, and humble yet sure and certain hope for futurity, which might vainly have been sought at prayer-meetings or evening lectures, where indeed little good can ever be obtained without some deleterious admixture, or alloy of baser feelings.

The happiness which he had found in retirement was of a different kind from what he had contemplated; for the shades of evening were gathering when he reached the place of his long wished for rest, and the picture of it which had imprinted itself on his imagination was a morning view. But he had been prepared for this by that slow change, of which we are not aware during its progress till we see it reflected in others, and are thus made conscious of it in ourselves; and he found a satisfaction in the station which he occupied there, too worthy in its nature to be called pride, and which had not entered into his anticipations. It is said to have been a saying of George the Third, that the happiest condition in which an Englishman could be placed, was just below that wherein it would have been necessary for him to act as a Justice of the Peace, and above that which would have rendered him liable to parochial duties. This was just Mr. Allison's position; there was nothing which brought him into rivalry or competition with the surrounding Squirarchy, and the yeomen and peasantry respected him for his own character, as well as for his name's sake. He gave employment to more persons than when he was engaged in trade, and his indirect influence over them was greater; that of his sister was still more. The elders of the village remembered her in her youth, and loved her for what she then had been, as well as for what she now was; the young looked up to her as the Lady Bountiful, to whom no one that needed advice or assistance ever applied in vain. She it was who provided those much approved plum-cakes, not the less savory for being both homely and wholesome, the thought of which induced the children to look on to their Lent examination with hope, and prepare for it with alacrity. Those offices in a parish which are the province of the Clergyman's wife, when he has made choice of one who knows her duty, and has both will and ability to discharge it, Miss Allison performed; and she rendered Mr. Bacon the farther, and to him individually the greater, service of imparting to his daughter those instructions which she had no mother to impart. Deborah could not have had a better teacher; but as the present chapter has extended to a sufficient length,

*Diremo il resto in quel che vien dipoi,
Per non venire a noja a me e voi.**

CHAPTER XIII.

A FEW PARTICULARS CONCERNING NO. 113 BISHOPSGATE STREET WITHIN; AND OF THE FAMILY AT THAXTED GRANGE.

Opinion is the rate of things,
From hence our peace doth flow;
I have a better fate than kings,
Because I think it so.
KATHARINE PHILIPS.

THE house wherein Mr. Allison realized by fair dealing and frugality the modest fortune which enabled him to repurchase the homestead of his fathers, is still a Tobacconist's, and has continued to be so from "the palmy days"

* Orlando Innamorato.

of that trade, when King James vainly endeavored, by the expression of his royal dislike, to discountenance the newly-imported practice of smoking; and Joshua Sylvester thundered from Mount Helicon a Volley of Holy Shot, thinking that thereby "Tobacco" should be "battered, and the Pipes shattered, about their ears that idly idolize so base and barbarous a weed, or at least-wise overlove so loathsome vanity." * For he said, —

> If there be any Herb in any place
> Most opposite to God's good Herb of Grace,
> 'T is doubtless this; and this doth plainly prove it,
> That for the most, most graceless men do love it.

Yet it was not long before the dead and unsavory odor of that weed, to which a Parisian was made to say that "sea-coal smoke seemed a very Portugal perfume," prevailed as much in the raiment of the more coarsely clad part of the community, as the scent of lavender among those who were clothed in fine linen, and fared sumptuously every day: and it had grown so much in fashion, that it was said children "began to play with broken pipes, instead of corals, to make way for their teeth."

Louis XIV. endeavored just as ineffectually to discourage the use of snuff-taking. His *valets de chambre* were obliged to renounce it when they were appointed to their office; and the Duke of Harcourt was supposed to have died of apoplexy in consequence of having, to please his Majesty, left off at once a habit which he had carried to excess.

I know not through what intermediate hands the business at No. 113 has passed, since the name of Allison was withdrawn from the firm; nor whether Mr. Evans, by whom it is now carried on there, is in any way related by descent with that family. Matters of no greater importance to most

---

* Old Burton's was a modified opinion. See Anatomie of Melancholy, Part ii. § 2, mem. 2, subs. 2.

men have been made the subject of much antiquarian investigation; and they who busy themselves in such investigations must not be said to be ill-employed, for they find harmless amusement in the pursuit, and sometimes put up a chance truth of which others, soon or late, discover the application. The house has at this time a more antiquated appearance than any other in that part of the street, though it was modernized some forty or fifty years after Mr. Bacon's friend left it. The first floor then projected several feet farther over the street than at present, and the second several feet farther over the first; and the windows, which still extend the whole breadth of the front, were then composed of small casement panes. But in the progress of those improvements which are now carrying on in the city with as much spirit as at the western end of the metropolis, and which have almost reached Mr. Evans's door, it cannot be long before the house will be either wholly removed, or so altered as no longer to be recognized.

The present race of Londoners little know what the appearance of the city was a century ago; — their own city, I was about to have said; but it was the city of their great-grandfathers, not theirs, from which the elder Allisons retired in the year 1746. At that time the kennels (as in Paris) were in the middle of the street, and there were no footpaths; spouts projected the rain-water in streams, against which umbrellas, if umbrellas had been then in use, could have afforded no defence; and large signs, such as are now only to be seen at country inns, were suspended before every shop,* from posts which impeded the way, or from iron supports strongly fixed into the front of the house. The swinging of one of these broad signs in a high wind, and the weight of the iron on which it acted, sometimes

* The counting of these signs "from Temple Bar, the furthest Conduit in Cheapside," &c., is quoted as a remarkable instance of Fuller's Memory. Life, &c., p. 76, ed. 1662.

brought the wall down; and it is recorded that one frontfall of this kind in Fleet Street maimed several persons, and killed "two young ladies, a cobbler, and the King's jeweller."

The sign at No. 113 was an Indian Chief smoking the calumet. Mr. Allison had found it there; and when it became necessary that a new one should be substituted, he retained the same figure, — though, if he had been to choose, he would have greatly preferred the head of Sir Walter Raleigh, by whom, according to the common belief, he supposed tobacco had been introduced into this country. The Water-Poet imputed it to the Devil himself, and published

A Proclamation,
Or Approbation,
From the King of Execration
To every Nation,
For Tobacco's propagation.

Mr. Allison used to shake his head at such libellous aspersions. Raleigh was a great favorite with him, and held, indeed, in especial respect, though not as the Patron of his old trade, as St. Crispin is of the Gentle Craft, yet as the founder of his fortune. He thought it proper, therefore, that he should possess Sir Walter's History of the World, though he had never found inclination, or summoned up resolution, to undertake its perusal.

Common sense has been defined by Sir Egerton Brydges, "to mean nothing more than an uneducated judgment, arising from a plain and coarse understanding exercised upon common concerns, and rendered effective rather by experience, than by any regular process of the intellectual powers. If this," he adds, "be the proper meaning of that quality, we cannot wonder that books are little fitted for its cultivation." Except that there was no coarseness in his nature, this would apply to Mr Allison. He had been bred up with the notion, that it behoved him to attend to his business, and that reading formed to part of it. Nevertheless he had acquired some liking for books, by looking casually now and then over the leaves of those unfortunate volumes with which the shop was continually supplied for its daily consumption.

> Many a load of criticism,
> Elaborate products of the midnight toil
> Of Belgian brains,*

went there; and many a tome of old law, old physic, and old divinity; old history as well; books of which many were at all times rubbish; some which, though little better, would now sell for more shillings by the page than they then cost pence by the pound; and others, the real value of which is perhaps as little known now, as it was then. Such of these as in latter years caught his attention, he now and then rescued from the remorseless use to which they had been condemned. They made a curious assortment with his wife's books of devotion or amusement wherewith she had sometimes beguiled, and sometimes soothed, the weary hours of long and frequent illness. Among the former were Scott's "Christian Life," Bishop Bayly's "Practice of Piety," Bishop Taylor's "Holy Living and Dying," Drelincourt on Death, with De Foe's lying story of Mrs. Veal's ghost as a puff preliminary, and the Night Thoughts. Among the latter were Cassandra, the Guardian and Spectator, Mrs. Rowe's Letters, Richardson's Novels, and Pomfret's Poems.

Mrs. Allison had been able to do little for her daughter of that little, which, if her state of health and spirits had permitted, she might have done; this, therefore, as well as the more active duties of the household, devolved upon Elizabeth, who was of a better constitution in mind as well

* Akenside.

as body. Elizabeth, before she went to reside with her brother, had acquired all the accomplishments which a domestic education in the country could in those days impart. Her book of receipts, culinary and medical, might have vied with the "Queen's Cabinet Unlocked." The spelling indeed was such as ladies used in the reign of Queen Anne, and in the old time before her, when every one spelt as she thought fit; but it was written in a well-proportioned Italian hand, with fine down-strokes and broad up-ones, equally distinct and beautiful. Her speech was good Yorkshire, that is to say, good provincial English, not the worse for being provincial, and a little softened by five-and-twenty years' residence in London. Some sisters, who in those days kept a boarding-school of the first repute, in one of the midland counties, used to say, when they spoke of an old pupil, "*her went to school to we.*" Miss Allison's language was not of this kind, — it savored of rusticity, not of ignorance; and where it was peculiar, as in the metropolis, it gave raciness to the conversation of an agreeable woman.

She had been well instructed in ornamental work as well as ornamental penmanship. Unlike most fashions, this had continued to be in fashion because it continued to be of use; though no doubt some of the varieties which Taylor, the Water-Poet, enumerates in his praise of the Needle, might have been then as little understood as now : —

> Tent-work, Raised-work, Laid-work, Prest-work, Net-work,
> Most curious Pearl, or rare Italian Cut-work,
> Fine Fern-stitch, Finny-stitch, New-stitch and Chain-stitch,
> Brave Bred-stitch, Fisher-stitch, Irish-stitch and Queen-stitch,
> The Spanish-stitch, Rosemary-stitch and Maw-stitch,
> The smarting Whip-stitch, Back-stitch and the Cross-stitch.
>   All these are good, and these we must allow;
>   And these are everywhere in practice now.

There was a book published in the Water-Poet's days,

with the title of "School House for the Needle"; it consisted of two volumes in oblong quarto, that form being suited to its plates "of sundry sorts of patterns and examples"; and it contained a "Dialogue in Verse between Diligence and Sloth." If Betsey Allison had studied in this "School House," she could not have been a greater proficient with the needle than she became under her Aunt's teaching: nor would she have been more

versed in the arts
Of pies, puddings, and tarts,*

if she had gone through a course of practical lessons in one of the Pastry Schools which are common in Scotland, but were tried without success in London, about the middle of the last century. Deborah partook of these instructions at her father's desire. In all that related to the delicacies of a country table, she was glad to be instructed, because it enabled her to assist her friend; but it appeared strange to her that Mr. Bacon should wish her to learn ornamental work, for which she neither had, nor could forsee any use. But if the employment had been less agreeable than she found it in such company, she would never have disputed, nor questioned his will.

For so small a household, a more active or cheerful one could nowhere have been found than at the Grange. Ben Jonson reckoned among the happinesses of Sir Robert Wroth that of being "with unbought provision blest." This blessing Mr. Allison enjoyed in as great a degree as his position in life permitted; he neither killed his own meat nor grew his own corn; but he had his poultry-yard, his garden and his orchard; he baked his own bread, brewed his own beer, and was supplied with milk, cream, and butter from his own dairy. It is a fact not unworthy of notice, that the most intelligent farmers in the neighborhood of London are persons who have taken to farming as a busi-

* T. Warton.

ness, because of their strong inclination for rural employments; one of the very best in Middlesex, when the Survey of that County was published by the Board of Agriculture, had been a tailor. Mr. Allison did not attempt to manage the land which he kept in his own hands; but he had a trusty bailiff, and soon acquired knowledge enough for superintending what was done. When he retired from trade he gave over all desire for gain, which indeed he had never desired for his own sake; he sought now only wholesome occupation, and those comforts which may be said to have a moral zest. They might be called luxuries, if that word could be used in a virtuous sense without something so to qualify it. It is a curious instance of the modification which words undergo in different countries, that luxury has always a sinful acceptation in the southern languages of Europe, and lust an innocent one in the northern; the harmless meaning of the latter word, we have retained in the verb *to list*.

Every one who looks back upon the scenes of his youth, has one spot upon which the last light of the evening sunshine rests. The Grange was that spot in Deborah's retrospect.

CHAPTER XIV.

A REMARKABLE EXAMPLE, SHOWING THAT A WISE MAN, WHEN HE RISES IN THE MORNING, LITTLE KNOWS WHAT HE MAY DO BEFORE NIGHT.

> Now I love,
> And so as in so short a time I may,
> Yet so as time shall never break that so,
> And therefore so accept of Elinor.
> ROBERT GREENE.

ONE summer evening the Doctor, on his way back from a visit in that direction, stopped, as on such opportunities he usually did, at Mr. Bacon's wicket, and looked in at the open casement to see if his friends were within. Mr. Bacon was sitting there alone, with a book open on the table before him; and looking round when he heard the horse stop, "Come in, Doctor," said he, "if you have a few minutes to spare. You were never more welcome."

The Doctor replied, "I hope nothing ails either Deborah or yourself?"

"No," said Mr. Bacon, "God be thanked! but something has occurred which concerns both."

When the Doctor entered the room, he perceived that the wonted serenity of his friend's countenance was overcast by a shade of melancholy thought. "Nothing," said he, "I hope, has happened to distress you?"

"Only to disturb us," was the reply. "Most people would probably think that we ought to consider it a piece of good fortune. One who would be thought a good match for her, has proposed to marry Deborah."

"Indeed!" said the Doctor; "and who is he?" feeling, as he asked the question, an unusual warmth in his face.

"Joseph Hebblethwaite, of the Willows. He broke his mind to me this morning, saying that he thought it best to speak with me before he made any advances himself to the young woman: indeed he had had no opportunity of so doing, for he had seen little of her; but he had heard enough of her character to believe that she would make him a good wife; and this, he said, was all he looked for, for he was well to do in the world."

"And what answer did you make to this matter-of-fact way of proceeding?"

"I told him that I commended the very proper course he had taken, and that I was obliged to him for the good opinion of my daughter which he was pleased to entertain: that marriage was an affair in which I should never attempt to direct her inclinations, being confident that she would never give me cause to oppose them; and that I would talk with her upon the proposal, and let him know the result. As soon as I mentioned it to Deborah, she colored up to her eyes; and with an angry look, of which I did not think those eyes had been capable, she desired me to tell him that he had better lose no time in looking elsewhere, for his thinking of her was of no use. 'Do you know any ill of him?' said I. 'No,' she replied, 'but I never heard any good, and that's ill enough. And I do not like his looks.'"

. "Well said, Deborah!" cried the Doctor: clapping his hands so as to produce a sonorous token of satisfaction.

"'Surely, my child,' said I, 'he is not an ill-looking person?' 'Father,' she replied, 'you know he looks as if he had not one idea in his head to keep company with another.'"

"Well said, Deborah!" repeated the Doctor.

"Why, Doctor, do you know any ill of him?

"None. But, as Deborah says, I know no good; and if there had been any good to be known, it must have come within my knowledge. I cannot help knowing who the persons are to whom the peasantry in my rounds look with respect and good-will, and whom they consider their friends as well as their betters. And, in like manner, I know who they are from whom they never expect either courtesy or kindness."

"You are right, my friend; and Deborah is right. Her answer came from a wise heart; and I was not sorry that her determination was so promptly made, and so resolutely pronounced. But I wish, if it had pleased God, the offer had been one which she could have accepted with her own willing consent, and with my full approbation."

"Yet," said the Doctor, "I have often thought how sad a thing it would be for you ever to part with her."

"Far more sad will it be for me to leave her unprotected, as it is but too likely that, in the ordinary course of nature I one day shall; and as any day in that same ordinary course, I so possibly may! Our best intentions, even when they have been most prudentially formed, fail often in their issue. I meant to train up Deborah in the way she should go, by fitting her for that state of life in which it had pleased God to place her; so that she might have made a good wife for some honest man in the humbler walks of life, and have been happy with him."

"And how was it possible," replied the Doctor, "that you could have succeeded better? Is she not qualified to be a good man's wife in any rank? Her manner would not do discredit to a mansion; her management would make a farm prosperous, or a cottage comfortable; and for her principles, and temper and cheerfulness, they would render any home a happy one."

"You have not spoken too highly in her praise, Doctor. But as she has from her childhood been all in all to me, there is a danger that I may have become too much so to her; and that, while her habits have properly been made conformable to our poor means and her poor prospects, she has been accustomed to a way of thinking, and a kind of conversation, which have given her a distaste for those whose talk is only of sheep and of oxen, and whose thoughts never get beyond the range of their every day employments. In her present circle, I do not think there is one man with whom she might otherwise have had a chance of settling in life, to whom she would not have the same intellectual objections as to Joseph Hebblethwaite: though I am glad that the moral objection was that which first instinctively occurred to her.

"I wish it were otherwise, both for her sake and my own: for hers, because the present separation would have more than enough to compensate it, and would in its consequences mitigate the evil of the final one, whenever that may be; for my own, because I should then have no cause whatever to render the prospect of dissolution otherwise than welcome, but be as willing to die as to sleep. It is not owing to any distrust in Providence, that I am not thus willing now, — God forbid! But if I gave heed to my own feelings, I should think that I am not long for this world; and surely it were wise to remove, if possible, the only cause that makes me fear to think so."

"Are you sensible of any symptons that can lead to such an apprehension?" said the Doctor.

"Of nothing that can be called a sympton. I am to all appearance in good health, of sound body and mind; and you know how unlikely my habits are to occasion any disturbance in either. But I have indefinable impressions, — sensations they might almost be called, — which, as I cannot but feel them, so I cannot but regard them."

"Can you not describe these sensations?"

"No better than by saying, that they hardly amount to sensations, and are indescribable."

"Do not," said the Doctor, "I entreat you, give way to any feelings of this kind. They may lead to consequences which, without shortening or endangering life, would render it anxious and burdensome, and destroy both your usefulness and your comfort."

"I have this feeling, Doctor; and you shall prescribe for it, if you think it requires either regimen or physic. But at present you will do me more good by assisting me to procure for Deborah such a situation as she must necessarily look for on the event of my death. What I have laid by, even if it should be most advantageously disposed of, would afford her only a bare subsistence; it is a resource in case of sickness, but while in health, it would never be her wish to eat the bread of idleness. You may have opportunities of learning whether any lady within the circle of your practice wants a young person in whom she might confide, either as an attendant upon herself, or to assist in the management of her children, or her household. You may be sure this is not the first time that I have thought upon the subject; but the circumstance which has this day occurred, and the feeling of which I have spoken, have pressed it upon my consideration. And the inquiry may better be made, and the step taken while it is a matter of foresight, than when it has become one of necessity."

"Let me feel your pulse!"

"You will detect no other disorder there," said Mr. Bacon, holding out his arm as he spake, "than what has been caused by this conversation, and the declaration of a purpose, which, though for some time perpended, I had never till now fully acknowledged to myself."

"You have never then mentioned it to Deborah?"

"In no other way than by sometimes incidentally speaking of the way of life which would be open to her, in case of her being unmarried at my death."

"And you have made up your mind to part with her?"

"Upon a clear conviction that I ought to do so; that it is best for herself and me."

"Well, then, you will allow me to converse with her first upon a different subject. — You will permit me to see whether I can speak more successfully for myself, than you have done for Joseph Hebblethwaite. — Have I your consent?"

Mr. Bacon rose in great emotion, and taking his friend's hand, pressed it fervently and tremulously. Presently they heard the wicket open, and Deborah came in.

"I dare say, Deborah," said her father, composing himself, "you have been telling Betsey Allison of the advantageous offer that you have this day refused."

"Yes," replied Deborah; "and what do you think she said? That little as she likes him, rather than that I should be thrown away upon such a man, she could almost make up her mind to marry him herself."

"And I," said the Doctor, "rather than such a man should have you, would marry you myself."

"Was not I right in refusing him, Doctor?"

"So right, that you never pleased me so well before; and never can please me better, — unless you will accept of me in his stead."

She gave a little start, and looked at him half incredulously, and half angrily withal; as if what he had said was too light in its manner to be serious, and yet too serious in its import to be spoken in jest. But when he took her by the hand, and said, "Will you, dear Deborah?" with a pressure, and in a tone that left no doubt of his earnest meaning, she cried, "Father, what am I to say? speak for me!" — "Take her, my friend!" said Mr. Bacon. "My blessing be upon you both. And, if it be not presumptuous to use the words, — let me say for myself, 'Lord, now lettest thou thy servant depart in peace!'"

CHAPTER XV.

THE WEDDING PEAL AT ST. GEORGE'S, AND THE BRIDE'S APPEARANCE AT CHURCH.

IN the month of April, 1761, the Doctor brought home his bride to Doncaster. Many eyes were turned upon her when she made her appearance at St. George's Church. The novelty of the place made her less regardful of this than she might otherwise have been. Hollis Pigot, who held the vicarage of Doncaster thirty years, and was then in the last year of his incumbency and his life, performed the service that day. I know not among what description of preachers he was to be classed; whether with those who obtain attention, and command respect, and win confidence, and strengthen belief, and inspire hope, or with the far more numerous race of Spintexts and of Martexts. But if he had preached that morning with the tongue of an angel, the bride would have had no ears for him. Her thoughts were neither upon those who on their way from church would talk over her instead of the sermon, nor of the service, nor of her husband, nor of herself in her new character, but of her father, — and with a feeling which might almost be called funereal, that she had passed from under his pastoral as well as his paternal care.

CHAPTER XVI.

SOMETHING SERIOUS.

If thou hast read all this book, and art never the better, yet catch this flower before thou go out of the garden, and peradventure the scent thereof will bring thee back to smell the rest.

HENRY SMITH.

DEBORAH found no one in Doncaster to supply the place of Betty Allison in the daily intercourse of familiar and perfect friendship. That indeed was impossible; no aftermath has the fragrance and the sweetness of the first crop. But why do I call her Deborah? She had never been known by that name to her new neighbors; and to her very father she was now spoken of as Mrs. Dove. Even the Allisons called her so in courteous and customary usage, but not without a melancholy reflection, that when Deborah Bacon became Mrs. Dove, she was in a great measure lost to them.

Friendship, although it ceases not
In marriage, is yet at less command
Than when a single freedom can dispose it.*

Doncaster has less of the *Rus in Urbe* now than it had in those days, and than Bath had when those words were

*Ford.

placed over the door of a lodging-house, on the North
Parade. And the house to which the Doctor brought home
his bride, had less of it than when Peter Hopkins set up
the gilt pestle and mortar there as the cognizance of his
vocation. It had no longer that air of quiet respectability
which belongs to such a dwelling in the best street of a
small country town. The Mansion House, by which it was
dwarfed and inconvenienced in many ways, occasioned a
stir and bustle about it, unlike the cheerful business of a market day. The back windows, however, still looked to the
fields, and there was still a garden. But neither fields nor
garden could prevail over the odor of the shop, in which, like

 Hot, cold, moist and dry, four champions fierce,

in Milton's Chaos, rhubarb and peppermint, and valerian, and
assafœtida, "strove for mastery," and to battle brought their
atoms. Happy was the day when peppermint predominated; though it always reminded Mrs. Dove of Thaxted
Grange, and the delight with which she used to assist Miss
Allison in her distillations. There is an Arabian proverb
which says, "The remembrance of youth is a sigh."
Southey has taken it for the text of one of those juvenile
poems in which he dwells with thoughtful forefeeling upon
the condition of declining life.

 Miss Allison had been to her, not indeed as a mother, but
as what a stepmother is, who is led by natural benevolence,
and a religious sense of duty, to perform as far as possible
a mother's part to her husband's children. There are more
such stepmothers than the world is willing to believe, and
they have their reward here as well as hereafter. It was
impossible that any new friend could fill up her place in
Mrs. Dove's affections, — impossible that she could ever feel
for another woman the respect, and reverence, and gratitude, which blended with her love for this excellent person.
Though she was born within four miles of Doncaster, and

had lived till her marriage in the humble vicarage in which she was born, she had never passed four-and-twenty hours in that town before she went to reside there; nor had she the slightest acquaintance with any of its inhabitants, except the few shopkeepers with whom her little dealings had lain, and the occasional visitants whom she had met at the Grange.

An Irish officer in the army, happening to be passenger in an armed vessel during the last war, used frequently to wish that they might fall in with an enemy's ship, because he said, he had been in many land battles, and there was nothing in the world which he desired more than to see what sort of a thing a sea-fight was. He had his wish, and when after a smart action, in which he bore his part bravely, an enemy of superior force had been beaten off, he declared with the customary emphasis of an Hibernian adjuration, that a sea-fight was a mighty *sairious* sort of thing.

The Doctor and Deborah, as soon as they were betrothed, had come to just the same conclusion upon a very different subject. Till the day of their engagement, nay, till the hour of proposal on his part, and the very instant of acceptance on hers, each had looked upon marriage, when the thought of it occurred, as a distant possibility, more or less desirable, according to the circumstances which introduced the thought, and the mood in which it was entertained. And when it was spoken of sportively, as might happen, in relation to either the one or the other, it was lightly treated as a subject in which they had no concern. But from the time of their engagement, it seemed to both the most serious event of their lives.

In the Dutch village of Broek, concerning which, singular as the habits of the inhabitants are, travellers have related more peculiarities than ever prevailed there, one remarkable custom shows with how serious a mind some of the Hollanders regard marriage. The great house-door is never opened but when the master of the house brings home his bride from the altar, and when husband and wife are borne out to the grave. Dr. Dove had seen that village of great baby-houses; but though much attached to Holland, and to the Dutch as a people, and disposed to think that we might learn many useful lessons from our prudent and thrifty neighbors, he thought this to be as preposterous, if not as shocking a custom, as it would be to have the bell toll at a marriage, and to wear a winding-sheet for a wedding garment.

We look with wonder at the transformations that take place in insects, and yet their physical metamorphoses are not greater than the changes which we ourselves undergo morally and intellectually, both in our relations to others and in our individual nature. *Chaque individu, considéré separément, differe encore de lui-même par l'effet du tems; il devient un autre, en quelque manière, aux diverses époques de sa vie. L'enfant, l'homme rait, le vieillard, sont comme autant d'étrangers unis dans une seule personne par le lien mystérieux du souvenir.** Of all changes in life, marriage is certainly the greatest, and though less change in every respect can very rarely be produced by it in any persons than in the Doctor and his wife, it was very great to both. On his part it was altogether an increase of happiness; or rather, from having been contented in his station he became happy in it, so happy as to be experimentally convinced that there can be no "single blessedness" for man. There were some drawbacks on her part, — in the removal from a quiet vicarage to a busy street; in the obstacle which four miles opposed to that daily and intimate intercourse with her friends at the Grange, which had been the chief delight of her maiden life; and above all, in the separation from her father, — for

---

* Necker.

even at a distance which may appear so inconsiderable, such it was; but there was the consolatory reflection, that those dear friends and that dear father concurred in approving her marriage, and in rejoicing in it for her sake; and the experience of every day and every year made her more and more thankful for her lot. In the full liturgic sense of the word, he worshipped her, that is, he loved and cherished and respected and honored her; and she would have obeyed him cheerfully as well as dutifully, if obedience could have been shown where there was ever but one will.

THE MYSTIC SUMMER.

By BAYARD TAYLOR.

'TIS not the dropping of the flower,
    The blush of fruit upon the tree,
Though Summer ripens, hour by hour,
    The garden's sweet maternity:

'T is not that birds have ceased to build,
    And wait their brood with tender care;
That corn is golden in the field,
    And clover balm is in the air;—

Not these the season's splendor bring,
    And crowd with life the happy year,
Nor yet, where yonder fountains sing,
    The blaze of sunshine, hot and clear.

In thy full womb, O Summer! lies
    A secret hope, a joy unsung,
Held in the hush of these calm skies,
    And trembling on the forest's tongue.

The lands of harvest throb anew
    In shining pulses, far away;
The Night distils a dearer dew,
    And sweeter eyelids has the Day.

And not in vain the peony burns
  In bursting globes, her crimson fire,
Her incense-dropping ivory urns
  The lily lifts in many a spire:

And not in vain the tulips clash
  In revelry the cups they hold
Of fiery wine, until they dash
  With ruby streaks the splendid gold!

Send down your roots the mystic charm
  That warms and flushes all your flowers,
And with the summer's touch disarm
  The thraldom of the under powers,

Until, in caverns, buried deep,
  Strange fragrance reach the diamond's home,
And murmurs of the garden sweep
  The houses of the frighted gnome!

For, piercing through their black repose,
  And shooting up beyond the sun,
I see that Tree of Life, which rose
  Before the eyes of Solomon:

Its boughs, that, in the light of God,
  Their bright, innumerous leaves display, —
Whose hum of life is borne abroad
  By winds that shake the dead away.

And, trembling on a branch afar,
  The topmost nursling of the skies,
I see my bud, the fairest star
  That ever dawned for watching eyes.

Unnoticed on the boundless tree,
   Its fragrant promise fills the air;
Its little bell expands, for me,
   A tent of silver, lily-fair.

All life to that one centre tends;
   All joy and beauty thence outflow;
Her sweetest gifts the summer spends,
   To teach that sweeter bud to blow.

So, compassed by the vision's gleam,
   In trembling hope, from day to day,
As in some bright, bewildering dream,
   The mystic summer wanes away.

TWO OF THE OLD MASTERS.

By MRS. JAMESON.

WITHIN a short period of about thirty years, that is, between 1490 and 1520, the greatest painters whom the world has yet seen were living and working together. On looking back, we cannot but feel that the excellence they attained was the result of the efforts and aspirations of a preceding age; and yet these men were so great in their vocation, and so individual in their greatness, that, losing sight of the linked chain of progress, they seemed at first to have had no precursors, as they have since had no peers. Though living at the same time, and most of them in personal relation with each other, the direction of each mind was different—was peculiar; though exercising in some sort a reciprocal influence, this influence never interfered with the most decided originality. These wonderful artists, who would have been remarkable men in their time, though they had never touched a pencil, were Lionardo da Vinci, Michael Angelo, Raphael, Correggio, Giorgione, Titian, in Italy; and in Germany, Albert Durer. Of these men, we might say, as of Homer and Shakespeare, that they belong to no particular age or country, but to all time, and to the universe. That they flourished together within one brief and brilliant period, and that each carried out to the highest degree of perfection his own peculiar aims, was no casualty; nor are we to seek for the causes of this surpassing excellence merely in the history of the art as such. The causes lay far deeper, and must be referred to the history of human culture. The fermenting activity of the fifteenth century found its results in the extraordinary development of human intelligence in the commencement of the sixteenth century. We often hear in these days of "the spirit of the age"; but in that wonderful age three mighty spirits were stirring society to its depths:— the spirit of bold investigation into truths of all kinds, which led to the Reformation; the spirit of daring adventure, which led men in search of new worlds beyond the eastern and the western oceans; and the spirit of art, through which men soared even to the "seventh heaven of invention."

LIONARDO DA VINCI.

LIONARDO DA VINCI seems to present in his own person a *résumé* of all the characteristics of the age in which he lived. He was *the* miracle of that age of miracles. Ardent and versatile as youth; patient and persevering as age; a most profound and original thinker; the greatest mathematician and most ingenious mechanic of his time; architect, chemist, engineer, musician, poet, painter! — we are not only astounded by the variety of his natural gifts and acquired knowledge, but by the practical direction of his amazing powers. The extracts which have been published from MSS. now existing in his own handwriting show him to have anticipated, by the force of his own intellect, some of the greatest discoveries made since his time. These fragments, says Mr. Hallam, "are, according to our common estimate of the age in which he lived, more like revelations of physical truths vouchsafed to a single mind, than the superstructure of its reasoning upon any established basis. The discoveries which made Galileo, Kepler, Castelli, and other names illustrious — the system of Copernicus — the very theories of recent geologists, are anticipated by Da Vinci within the compass

of a few pages, not perhaps in the most precise language, or on the most conclusive reasoning, but so as to strike us with something like the awe of preternatural knowledge. In an age of so much dogmatism, he first laid down the grand principle of Bacon, that experiment and observation must be the guides to just theory in the investigation of nature. If any doubt could be harbored, not as to the right of Lionardo da Vinci to stand as the first name of the fifteenth century, which is beyond all doubt, but as to his originality in so many discoveries which probably no one man, especially in such circumstances, has ever made, it must be by an hypothesis not very untenable, that some parts of physical science had already attained a height which mere books do not record."

It seems at first sight almost incomprehensible that, thus endowed as a philosopher, mechanic, inventor, discoverer, the fame of Lionardo should now rest on the works he has left as a painter. We cannot, within these limits, attempt to explain why and how it is that as the man of science he has been naturally and necessarily left behind by the onward march of intellectual progress, while as the poet-painter he still survives as a presence and a power. We must proceed at once to give some account of him in the character in which he exists to us and for us, — that of the great artist.

Lionardo was born at Vinci, near Florence, in the Lower Val d' Arno, on the borders of the territory of Pistoia. His father, Piero da Vinci, was an advocate of Florence, — not rich, but in independent circumstances, and possessed of estates in land. The singular talents of his son induced Piero to give him, from an early age, the advantage of the best instructors. As a child, he distinguished himself by his proficiency in arithmetic and mathematics. Music he studied early, as a science as well as an art. He invented a species of lyre for himself, and sung his own poetical compositions to his own music, — both being frequently extemporaneous. But his favorite pursuit was the art of design in all its branches; he modelled in clay or wax, or attempted to draw every object which struck his fancy. His father sent him to study under Andrea Verrocchio, famous as a sculptor, chaser in metal, and painter. Andrea, who was an excellent and correct designer, but a bad and hard colorist, was soon after engaged to paint a picture of the Baptism of our Saviour. He employed Lionardo, then a youth, to execute one of the angles. This he did with so much softness and richness of color that it far surpassed the rest of the picture; and Verrocchio from that time threw away his palette, and confined himself wholly to his works in sculpture and design; "enraged," says Vasari, "that a child should thus excel him."

The youth of Lionardo thus passed away in the pursuit of science and of art. Sometimes he was deeply engaged in astronomical calculations and investigations; sometimes ardent in the study of natural history, botany, and anatomy; sometimes intent on new effects of color, light, shadow, or expression, in representing objects animate or inanimate. Versatile, yet persevering, he varied his pursuits, but he never abandoned any. He was quite a young man when he conceived and demonstrated the practicability of two magnificent projects. One was, to lift the whole of the Church of San Lorenzo, by means of immense levers, some feet higher than it now stands, and thus supply the deficient elevation; the other project was, to form the Arno into a navigable canal, as far as Pisa, which would have added greatly to the commercial advantages of Florence.

It happened about this time that a peasant on the estate of Piero da Vinci brought him a circular piece of wood, cut horizontally from the trunk of a very large old fig-tree, which had been lately felled, and begged to have something painted on it as an ornament for his cottage. The man being an especial favorite, Piero desired his son Lionardo to gratify his request; and Lionardo, inspired by that wildness of fancy which was one of his characteristics, took the panel into his own room, and resolved to astonish his father by a most unlooked-for proof of his art. He determined to compose something which should have an effect similar to that of the Medusa on the shield of Perseus, and almost petrify beholders. Aided by his recent studies in natural history, he collected together from the neighboring swamps and the river-mud all kinds of hideous reptiles, as adders, lizards, toads, serpents; insects, as moths, locusts; and other crawling and flying, obscene and obnoxious things; and out of these he compounded a sort of monster, or chimera, which he represented as about to issue from the shield, with eyes flashing fire, and of an aspect so fearful and abominable that it seemed to infect the very air around. When finished, he led his father into the room in which it was placed, and the terror and horror of Piero proved the success of his attempt. This production, afterwards known as the Rotello del Fico, from the material on which it was painted, was sold by Piero secretly for one hundred ducats, to a merchant, who carried it to Milan, and sold it to the duke for three hundred. To the poor peasant thus cheated of his Rotello, Piero gave a wooden shield, on which was painted a heart transfixed by a dart; a device better suited to his taste and comprehension. In the subsequent troubles of Milan, Lionardo's picture disappeared, and was probably destroyed, as an object of horror, by those who did not understand its value as a work of art.

The anomalous monster represented on the Rotello was wholly different from the Medusa, afterwards painted by Lionardo, and now existing in the Florence Gallery. It represents the severed head of Medusa, seen foreshortened, lying on a fragment of rock. The features are beautiful and regular; the hair already metamorphosed into serpents,

"which curl and flow,
And their long tangles in each other lock,
And with unending involutions show
Their mailéd radiance."

Those who have once seen this terrible and fascinating picture can never forget it. The ghastly head seems to expire, and the serpents to crawl into glittering life, as we look upon it.

During this first period of his life, which was wholly passed in Florence and its neighborhood, Lionardo painted several other pictures, of a very different character, and designed some beautiful cartoons of sacred and mythological subjects, which showed that his sense of the beautiful, the elevated, and the graceful, was not less a part of his mind, than that eccentricity and almost perversion of fancy which made him delight in sketching ugly, exaggerated caricatures, and representing the deformed and the terrible.

Lionardo da Vinci was now about thirty years old, in the prime of his life and talents. His taste for pleasure and expense was, however, equal to his genius and indefatigable industry; and, anxious to secure a certain provision for the future, as well as a wider field for the exercise of his various talents, he accepted the invitation of Ludovico Sforza il Moro, then regent, afterwards Duke of Milan, to reside in his court, and to execute a colossal equestrian statue of his ancestor Francesco Sforza. Here begins the second period of his artistic career, which includes his sojourn at Milan, that is, from 1483 to 1499.

Vasari says that Lionardo was invited to the court of Milan for the Duke Ludovico's amusement, "as a musician and performer on the lyre, and as the greatest singer and *improvisatore* of his time"; but this is improbable. Lionardo, in his long letter to that prince, in which he recites his own qualifications for employment, dwells chiefly on his skill in engineering and fortification, and sums up his pretensions as an artist in these few brief words: "I understand the different modes of sculpture in marble, bronze, and terra-cotta. In painting, also, I may esteem myself equal to any one, let him be who he may." Of his musical talents he makes no mention whatever, though undoubtedly these, as well as his other social accomplishments, his handsome person, his winning address, his wit and eloquence, recommended him to the notice of the prince, by whom he was greatly beloved, and in whose service he remained for about seventeen years. It is not necessary, nor would it be possible here, to give a particular account of all the works in which Lionardo was engaged for his patron, nor of the great political events in which he was involved, more by his position than by his inclination; for instance, the invasion of Italy by Charles VIII. of France, and the subsequent invasion of Milan by Louis XII., which ended in the destruction of the Duke Ludovico. We shall only mention a few of the pictures he executed. One of these, the portrait of Lucrezia Crivelli, is now in the Louvre (No. 1091). Another was the Nativity of our Saviour, in the imperial collection at Vienna; but the greatest work of all, and by far the grandest picture which, up to that time, had been executed in Italy, was the Last Supper, painted on the wall of the refectory, or dining-room, of the Dominican convent of the Madonna delle Grazie. It occupied the painter about two years. Of this magnificent creation of art only the mouldering remains are now visible. It has been so often repaired, that almost every vestige of the original painting is annihilated; but, from the multiplicity of descriptions, engravings, and copies that exist, no picture is more universally known and celebrated.

The moment selected by the painter is described in the twenty-sixth chapter of St. Matthew, twenty-first and twenty-second verses: "And as they did eat, he said, Verily, I say unto you, that one of you shall betray me:

and they were exceedingly sorrowful, and began every one of them to say unto him, Lord, is it I?" The knowledge of character displayed in the heads of the different apostles is even more wonderful than the skilful arrangement of the figures and the amazing beauty of the workmanship. The space occupied by the picture is a wall twenty-eight feet in length, and the figures are larger than life. The best judgment we can now form of its merits is from the fine copy executed by one of Lionardo's best pupils, Marco Uggione, for the Certosa at Pavia, and now in London, in the collection of the Royal Academy. Eleven other copies, by various pupils of Lionardo, painted either during his lifetime or within a few years after his death, while the picture was in perfect preservation, exist in different churches and collections.

Of the grand equestrian statue of Francesco Sforza, Lionardo never finished more than the model in clay, which was considered a masterpiece. Some years afterwards, (in 1499,) when Milan was invaded by the French, it was used as a target by the Gascon bowmen, and completely destroyed. The profound anatomical studies which Lionardo made for this work still exist.

In the year 1500, the French being in possession of Milan, his patron Ludovico in captivity, and the affairs of the state in utter confusion, Lionardo returned to his native Florence, where he hoped to re-establish his broken fortunes, and to find employment. Here begins the third period of his artistic life, from 1500 to 1513, that is, from his forty-eighth to his sixtieth year. He found the Medici family in exile, but was received by Pietro Soderini (who governed the city as "*Gonfaloniere perpetuo*") with great distinction, and a pension was assigned to him as painter in the service of the republic.

Then began the rivalry between Lionardo and Michael Angelo, which lasted during the remainder of Lionardo's life. The difference of age (for Michael Angelo was twenty-two years younger) ought to have prevented all unseemly jealousy. But Michael Angelo was haughty, and impatient of all superiority, or even equality; Lionardo, sensitive, capricious, and naturally disinclined to admit the pretensions of a rival, to whom he could say, and *did* say, "I was famous before you were born!" With all their admiration of each other's genius, their mutual frailties prevented any real good-will on either side. The two painters competed for the honor of painting in fresco one side of the great Council-hall in the Palazzo Vecchio at Florence. Each prepared his cartoon; each, emulous of the fame and conscious of the abilities of his rival, threw all his best powers into his work. Lionardo chose for his subject the Defeat of the Milanese general, Niccolò Piccinino, by the Florentine army in 1440. One of the finest groups represented a combat of cavalry disputing the possession of a standard. "It was so wonderfully executed, that the horses themselves seemed animated by the same fury as their riders; nor is it possible to describe the variety of attitudes, the splendor of the dresses and armor of the warriors, nor the incredible skill displayed in the forms and actions of the horses."

Michael Angelo chose for his subject the moment before the same battle, when a party of Florentine soldiers bathing in the Arno are surprised by the sound of the trumpet calling them to arms. Of this cartoon we shall have more to say in treating of his life. The preference was given to Lionardo da Vinci. But, as Vasari relates, he spent so much time in trying experiments, and in preparing the wall to receive oil painting, which he preferred to fresco, that in the interval some changes in the government intervened, and the design was abandoned. The two cartoons remained for several years open to the public, and artists flocked from every part of Italy to study them. Subsequently they were cut up into separate parts, dispersed, and lost. It is curious that of Michael Angelo's composition only one small copy exists; of Lionardo's, not one. From a fragment which existed in his time, but which has since disappeared, Rubens made a fine drawing, which was engraved by Edelinck, and is known as the Battle of the Standard.

It was a reproach against Lionardo, in his own time, that he began many things and finished few; that his magnificent designs and projects, whether it art or mechanics, were seldom completed. This may be a subject of regret, but it is unjust to make it a reproach. It was in the nature of the man. The grasp of his mind was so nearly superhuman, that he never, in anything he effected, satisfied himself or realized his own vast conceptions. The most exquisitely finished of his works, those that in the perfection of the execution have excited the wonder and despair of succeeding artists, were put aside by him as unfinished sketches. Most of the pictures now attributed to him were wholly or in part painted by his scholars and imitators from his cartoons. One of the most famous of these was designed for the altarpiece of the church of the convent called the Nunziata. It represented the Virgin Mary seated in the lap of her mother, St. Anna, having in her arms the infant Christ, while St. John is playing with a lamb at their feet; St. Anna, looking on with a tender smile, rejoices in her divine offspring. The figures were drawn with such skill, and the various expressions proper to each conveyed with such inimitable truth and grace, that, when exhibited in a chamber of the convent, the inhabitants of the city flocked to see it, and for two days the streets were crowded with people, " as if it had been some solemn festival"; but the picture was never painted, and the monks of the Nunziata, after waiting long and in vain for their altar-piece, were obliged to employ other artists. The cartoon, or a very fine repetition of it, is now in the possession of the Royal Academy, and it must not be confounded with the St. Anna in the Louvre, a more fantastic and apparently an earlier composition.

Lionardo, during his stay at Florence, painted the portrait of Ginevra Benci, already mentioned, in the memoir of Ghirlandajo, as the reigning beauty of her time; and also the portrait of Mona Lisa del Giocondo, sometimes called La Joconde. On this last picture he worked at intervals for four years, but was still unsatisfied. It was purchased by Francis I. for four thousand golden crowns, and is now in the Louvre. We find Lionardo also engaged by Cæsar Borgia to visit and report on the fortifications of his territories, and in this office he was employed for two years. In 1514 he was invited to Rome by Leo X., but more in his character of philosopher, mechanic, and alchemist, than as a painter. Here he found Raphael at the height of his fame, and then engaged in his greatest works, — the frescos of the Vatican. Two pictures which Lionardo painted while at Rome — the Madonna of St. Onofrio, and the Holy Family, painted for Filiberta of Savoy, the Pope's sister-in-law (which is now at St. Petersburg) — show that even this veteran in art felt the irresistible influence of the genius of his young rival. They were both *Raffaellesque* in the subject and treatment.

It appears that Lionardo was ill-satisfied with his sojourn at Rome. He had long been accustomed to hold the first rank as an artist wherever he resided; whereas at Rome he found himself only one among many who, if they acknowledged his greatness, affected to consider his day as past. He was conscious that many of the improvements in the arts which were now brought into use, and which enabled the painters of the day to produce such extraordinary effects, were invented or introduced by himself. If he could no longer assert that measureless superiority over all others which he had done in his younger days, it was because he himself had opened to them new paths to excellence. The arrival of his old competitor Michael Angelo, and some slight on the part of Leo X., who was annoyed by his speculative and dilatory habits in executing the works intrusted to him, all added to his irritation and disgust. He left Rome, and set out for Pavia, where the French king Francis I. then held his court. He was received by the young monarch with every mark of respect, loaded with favors, and a pension of seven hundred gold crowns settled on him for life. At the famous conference between Francis I. and Leo X. at Bologna, Lionardo attended his new patron, and was of essential service to him on that occasion. In the following year, 1516, he returned with Francis I. to France, and was attached to the French court as principal painter. It appears, however, that during his residence in France he did not paint a single picture. His health had begun to decline from the time he left Italy; and, feeling his end approach, he prepared himself for it by religious meditation, by acts of charity, and by a most conscientious distribution by will of all his worldly possessions to his relatives and friends. At length, after protracted suffering, this great and most extraordinary man died at Cloux, near Amboise, on the 2d of May, 1519, being then in his sixty-seventh year. It is to be regretted that we cannot wholly credit the beautiful story of his dying in the arms of Francis I., who, as it is said, had come to visit him on his death-bed. It would, indeed, have been, as Fuseli expressed it, "an honor to the king, by which Destiny would have atoned to that monarch for his future disaster at Pavia," had the incident really happened, as it has been so often related by biographers, celebrated by poets, represented with a just pride by painters, and willingly believed by all the world; but the well-authenticated fact that the court was *on that day* at St. Germain-en-Laye, whence the royal ordinances are dated, renders the story, unhappily, very doubtful.

TITIAN.

TIZIANO VECELLI was born at Cadore in the Friuli, a district to the north of Venice, where the ancient family of the Vecelli had been long settled. There is something very amusing and characteristic in the first indication of his love of art; for while it is recorded of other young artists that they took a piece of charcoal or a piece of slate to trace the images in their fancy, we are told that the infant Titian, with an instinctive feeling prophetic of his future excellence as a colorist, used the expressed juice of certain flowers to paint a figure of a Madonna. When he was a boy of nine years old his father, Gregorio, carried him to Venice and placed him under the tuition of Sebastian Zuccato, a painter and worker in mosaic. He left this school for that of the Bellini, where the friendship and fellowship of Giorgione seems early to have awakened his mind to new ideas of art and color. Albert Durer, who was at Venice in 1494, and again in 1507, also influenced him. At this time, when Titian and Giorgione were youths of eighteen and nineteen, they lived and worked together. It has been related that they were employed in painting the frescos of the Fondaco dei Tedeschi. The preference being given to Titian's performance, which represented the story of Judith, caused such a jealousy between the two friends, that they ceased to reside together; but at this time, and for some years afterwards, the influence of Giorgione on the mind and the style of Titian was such that it became difficult to distinguish their works; and on the death of Giorgione, Titian was required to complete his unfinished pictures. This great loss to Venice and the world left him in the prime of youth without a rival. We find him for a few years chiefly employed in decorating the palaces of the Venetian nobles, both in the city and on the mainland.

The first of his historical compositions which is celebrated by his biographers is the Presentation of the Virgin in the Temple, a large picture, now in the Academy of Arts at Venice; and the first portrait recorded is that of Catherine, Queen of Cyprus, of which numerous repetitions and copies were scattered over all Italy. There is a fine original in the Dresden Gallery. This unhappy Catherine Cornaro, the "daughter of St. Mark," having been forced to abdicate her crown in favor of the Venetian state, was at this time living in a sort of honorable captivity at Venice. She had been a widow for forty years, and he has represented her in deep mourning, holding a rosary in her hand, — the face still bearing traces of that beauty for which she was celebrated.

It appears that Titian was married about 1512, but of his wife we do not hear anything more. It is said that her name was Lucia, and we know that she bore him three children, — two sons, and a daughter called Lavinia. It seems probable, on a comparison of dates, that she died about the year 1530.

One of the earliest works on which Titian was engaged was the decoration of the convent of St. Antony, at Padua, in which he executed a series of frescos from the life of St. Antony. He was next summoned to Ferrara by the Duke Alphonso I., and was employed in his service for at least two years. He painted for this prince the beautiful picture of Bacchus and Ariadne, which is now in the National Gallery, and which represents on a small scale an epitome of all the beauties which characterize Titian, in the rich, picturesque, animated composition, in the ardor of Bacchus, who flings himself from his car to pursue Ariadne; the dancing bacchanals, the frantic grace of the bacchante, and the little joyous satyr in front, trailing the head of the sacrifice. He painted for the same prince two other festive subjects: one in which a nymph and two men are dancing, while another nymph lies asleep; and a third, in which a number of children and cupids are sporting round a statue of Venus. There are here upwards of sixty figures in every variety of attitude, some fluttering in the air, some climbing the fruit-trees, some shooting arrows, or embracing each other. This picture is known as the Sacrifice to the Goddess of Fertility. While it remained in Italy, it was a study for the first painters, — for Poussin, the Carracci, Albano, and Fiamingo the sculptor, so famous for his models of children. At Ferrara, Titian also painted the portrait of the first wife of Alphonso, the famous and infamous Lucrezia Borgia; and here also he formed a friendship with the poet Ariosto, whose portrait he painted.

At this time he was invited to Rome by Leo X., for whom Raphael, then in the zenith of his powers, was executing some of his finest works. It is curious to speculate what influence these two distinguished men might have exercised on each other had they met; but it was not so decreed. Titian was strongly attached to his home and his friends at Venice; and to his birthplace, the little town of Cadore, he paid an annual summer visit. His long absence at Ferrara had wearied him of courts and princes; and, instead of going to Rome to swell the luxurious state of Leo X., he returned to Venice and remained there stationary for the next few years, enriching its palaces and churches with his magnificent works. These were so numerous that it would be in vain to attempt to give an account even of those considered as the finest among them. Two, however, must be pointed out as pre-eminent in beauty and celebrity. First, the Assumption of the Virgin, painted for the Church of Santa Maria de' Frari, and now in the Academy of the Fine Arts at Venice, and well known from the magnificent engraving of Schiavone — the Virgin is soaring to heaven amid groups of angels, while the apostles gaze upwards; and, secondly, the Death of St. Peter Martyr when attacked by assassins at the entrance of a wood; the resignation of the prostrate victim and the ferocity of the murderer, the attendant flying "in the agonies of cowardice," with the trees waving their distracted boughs amid the violence of the tempest, have rendered this picture famous as a piece of scenic poetry as well as of dramatic expression.

The next event of Titian's life was his journey to Bologna in 1530. In that year the Emperor Charles V. and Pope Clement VII. met at Bologna, each surrounded by a brilliant retinue of the most distinguished soldiers, statesmen, and scholars, of Germany and Italy. Through the influence of his friend Aretino, Titian was recommended to the Cardinal Ippolito de' Medici, the Pope's nephew, through whose patronage he was introduced to the two potentates who sat to him. One of the portraits of Clement VII., painted at this time, is now in the Bridgewater Gallery. Charles V. was so satisfied with his portrait, that he became the zealous friend and patron of the painter. It is not precisely known which of several portraits of the Emperor painted by Titian was the one executed at Bologna on this memorable occasion, but it is supposed to be that which represents him on horseback charging with his lance, now in the Royal Gallery at Madrid, and of which Mr. Rogers possesses the original study. The two portraits of Ippolito de' Medici in the Pitti Palace and the Louvre were also painted at this period.

After a sojourn of some months at Bologna, Titian returned to Venice loaded with honors and rewards. There was no potentate, prince, or poet, or reigning beauty, who did not covet the honor of being immortalized by his pencil. He had, up to this time, managed his worldly affairs with great economy; but now he purchased for himself a house opposite to Murano, and lived splendidly, combining with the most indefatigable industry the liveliest enjoyment of existence; his favorite companions were the architect Sansovino and the witty profligate Pietro Aretino. Titian has often been reproached with his friendship for Aretino, and nothing can be said in his excuse, except that the proudest princes in Europe condescended to flatter and caress this unprincipled literary ruffian, who was pleased to designate himself as the "friend of Titian, and the scourge of princes." One of the finest of Titian's portraits is that of Aretino, in the Munich Gallery.

Thus in the practice of his art, in the society of his friends, and in the enjoyment of the pleasures of life, did Titian pass several years. The only painter of his time who was deemed worthy of competing with him was Licinio Regillo, better known as Pordenone. Between Titian and Pordenone there existed not merely rivalry, but a personal hatred, so bitter that Pordenone affected to think his life in danger, and when at Venice painted with his shield and poniard lying beside him. As long as Pordenone lived, Titian had a spur to exertion, to emulation. All the other good painters of the time, Palma, Bonifazio, Tintoretto, were his pupils or his creatures; Pordenone would never owe anything to him; and the picture called the St. Justina, at Vienna, shows that he could equal Titian on his own ground.

After the death of Pordenone at Ferrara, in 1539, Titian was left without a rival. Everywhere in Italy art was on the decline: Lionardo, Raphael, Correggio, had all passed away. Titian himself, at the age of sixty, was no longer young, but he still retained all the vigor and the freshness of youth ; neither eye nor hand, nor creative energy of mind had failed him yet. He was again invited to Ferrara, and painted there the portrait of the old Pope Paul III. He then visited Urbino, where he painted for the Duke the famous Venus which hangs in the Tribune of the Florence Gallery, and many other pictures. He again, by order of Charles V., repaired to Bologna, and painted the Emperor, standing, and by his side a favorite Irish wolf-dog. This picture was given by Philip IV. to Charles I. of England, but after his death was sold into Spain, and is now at Madrid.

Pope Paul III. invited him to Rome, whither he repaired in 1548. There he painted that wonderful picture of the old Pope with his two nephews, the Duke Ottavio and Cardinal Farnese, which is now at Vienna. The head of the Pope is a miracle of character and expression. A keen-visaged, thin little man, with meagre fingers like birds' claws, and an eager cunning look, riveting the gazer like the eye of a snake, — nature itself! — and the Pope had either so little or so much vanity as to be perfectly satisfied. He rewarded the painter munificently; he even offered to make his son Pomponio Bishop of Ceneda, which Titian had the good sense to refuse. While at Rome he painted several pictures for the Farnese family, among them the Venus and Adonis, of which a repetition is in the National Gallery, and a Danaë which excited the admiration of Michael Angelo. At this time Titian was seventy-two.

He next, by command of Charles V., repaired to Augsburg, where the Emperor held his court: eighteen years had elapsed since he first sat to Titian, and he was now broken by the cares of government, — far older at fifty than the painter at seventy-two. It was at Augsburg that the incident occurred which has been so often related: Titian dropped his pencil, and Charles, taking it up and presenting it, replied to the artist's excuses that "Titian was worthy of being served by Cæsar." This pretty anecdote is not without its parallel in modern times. When Sir Thomas Lawrence was painting at Aix-la-Chapelle, as he stooped to place a picture on his easel, the Emperor of Russia anticipated him, and, taking it up, adjusted it himself; but we do not hear that he made any speech on the occasion. When at Augsburg, Titian was ennobled and created a count of the empire, with a pension of two hundred gold ducats, and his son Pomponio was appointed canon of the cathedral of Milan.

After the abdication and death of Charles V., Titian continued in great favor with his successor Philip II., for whom he painted several pictures. It is not true, however, that Titian visited Spain. The assertion that he did so rests on the sole authority of Palomino, a Spanish writer on art, and, though wholly unsupported by evidence, has been copied from one book into another. Later researches have proved that Titian returned from Augsburg to Venice; and an uninterrupted series of letters and documents, with dates of time and place, remain to show that, with the exception of this visit to Augsburg and another to Vienna, he resided constantly in Italy, and principally at Venice, from 1530 to his death. Notwithstanding the compliments and patronage and nominal rewards he received from the Spanish court, Titian was worse off under Philip II. than he had been under Charles V.: his pension was constantly in arrears; the payments for his pictures evaded by the officials; and we find the great painter constantly presenting petitions and complaints in moving terms, which always obtained gracious but illusive answers. Philip II., who commanded the riches of the Indies, was for many years a debtor to Titian for at least two thousand gold crowns; and his accounts were not settled at the time of his death. For Queen Mary of England, who wished to patronize one favored by her husband, Titian painted several pictures, some of which were in the possession of Charles I.; others had been carried to Spain after the death of Mary, and are now in the Royal Gallery at Madrid.

Besides the pictures painted by command for royal and noble patrons, Titian, who was unceasingly occupied, had always a great number of pictures in his house which he presented to his friends, or to the officers and attendants of the court, as a means of procuring their favor. There is extant a letter of Aretino, in which he describes the scene which took place when the Emperor summoned his favorite painter to attend the court at Augsburg. "It was," he says, "the most flattering testimony to his excellence to behold, as soon as it was known that the divine painter was sent for, the crowds of people running to obtain, if possible, the productions of his art; and how they endeavored to purchase the pictures, great and small, and everything that was in the house, at any price; for everybody seems assured that his august majesty will so treat his Apelles that he will no longer condescend to exercise his pencil except to oblige him."

Years passed on, and seemed to have no power to quench the ardor of this wonderful old man. He was eighty-one when he painted the Martyrdom of St. Laurence, one of his largest and grandest compositions. The Magdalen, the half-length figure with uplifted streaming eyes, which he sent to Philip II., was executed even later; and it was not till he was approaching his ninetieth year that he showed in his works symptoms of enfeebled powers; and then it seemed as if sorrow rather than time had reached him and conquered him at last. The death of many friends, the companions of his convivial hours, left him "alone in his glory." He found in his beloved art the only refuge from grief. His son Pomponio was still the same worthless profligate in age that he had been in youth. His son Orazio attended upon him with truly filial duty and affection, and under his father's tuition had become an accomplished artist; but as they always worked together, and on the same canvas, his works are not to be distinguished from his father's. Titian was likewise surrounded by painters who, without being precisely his scholars, had assembled from every part of Europe to profit by his instructions. The early morning and the evening hour found him at his easel; or lingering in his little garden (where he had feasted with Aretino and Sansovino, and Bembo and Ariosto, and "the most gracious Virginia," and "the most beautiful Violante"), and gazing on the setting sun, with a thought perhaps of his own long and bright career fast hastening to its close; — not that such anticipations clouded his cheerful spirit, — buoyant to the last! In 1574, when he was in his ninety-seventh year, Henry III. of France landed at Venice on his way from Poland, and was magnificently entertained by the Republic. On this occasion the King visited Titian at his own house, attended by a numerous suite of princes and nobles. Titian entertained them with splendid hospitality; and when the King asked the price of some pictures which pleased him, he presented them as a gift to his Majesty, and every one praised his easy and noble manners and his generous bearing.

Two years more passed away, and the hand did not yet tremble nor was the eye dim. When the plague broke out in Venice, the nature of the distemper was at first mistaken, and the most common precautions neglected; the contagion spread, and Titian and his son were among those who perished. Every one had fled, and before life was extinct some ruffians entered his chamber and carried off, before his eyes, his money, jewels, and some of his pictures. His death took place on the 9th of September, 1575. A law had been made during the plague that none should be buried in the churches, but that all the dead bodies should be carried beyond the precincts of the city; an exception, however, even in that hour of terror and anguish, was made in favor of Titian. His remains were borne with honor to the tomb, and deposited in the Church of Santa Maria de' Frari, for which he had painted his famous Assumption. There he lies beneath a plain black marble slab, on which is simply inscribed,

"TIZIANO VECELLIO."

In the year 1794 the citizens of Venice resolved to erect a noble and befitting monument to his memory. Canova made the design; — but the troubles which intervened, and the extinction of the Republic, prevented the execution of this project. Canova's magnificent model was appropriated to another purpose, and now forms the cenotaph of the Archduchess Christina, in the Church of the Augustines at Vienna.

This was the life and death of the famous Titian. He was pre-eminently the painter of nature; but to him nature was clothed in a perpetual garb of beauty, or rather to him nature and beauty were one. In historical compositions and sacred subjects he has been rivalled and surpassed, but as a portrait painter never; and his portraits of celebrated persons have at once the truth and the dignity of history.

THE POET'S HEART.

By FREDERICK TENNYSON.

I.

WHEN the Poet's heart is dead,
   That with fragrance, light, and sound,
Like a Summer-day was fed,
   Where, O, where shall it be found, —
In Sea, or Air, or underground?

II.

It shall be a sunny place;
   An urn of odors; a still well,
Upon whose undisturbed face
   The lights of Heaven shall love to dwell,
   And its far depths make visible.

III.

It shall be a crimson flower
   That in Fairyland hath thriven;
For dew a gentle Sprite shall pour
   Tears of Angels down from Heaven,
   And hush the winds at morn and even.

IV.

It shall be on some fair morn
  A swift and many-voiced wind,
Singing down the skies of June,
And with its breath and gladsome tune
  Send joy into the heart and mind.

V.

It shall be a fountain springing,
  Far up into the happy light,
With a silver carol ringing,
With a magic motion flinging
  Its jocund waters, starry-bright.

VI.

It shall be a tiny thing
  Whose breath is in it for a day,
To fold at Eve its weary wing,
  And at the dewfall die away
  On some pure air, or golden ray,

VII.

Falling in a violet-bloom;
  Tombed in a sphere of pearly rain;
Its blissful ghost a wild perfume
  To come forth with the Morn again,
  And wander through an infant's brain;

VIII.

And the pictures it should set
  In that temple of Delight
Would make the tearless cherub fret
  With its first longing for a sight
  Of things beyond the Day and Night.

IX.

But one moment of its span
  Should thicker grow with blissful things
Than any days of mortal Man,
Or his years of Sorrow can,
  Though beggars should be crowned kings.

X.

It shall be a tuneful voice
  Falling on a Lover's ear,
Enough to make his heart rejoice
  For evermore, or far, or near,
  In dreams that swallow hope and fear.

XI.

It shall be a chord divine
  By Mercy out of Heaven hung forth,
Along whose trembling, airy line
  A dying Saint shall hear on earth
  Triumphant songs, and harped mirth!

XII.

It shall be a wave forlorn
  That o'er the vast and fearful Sea
In troubled pride and beauty borne
  From winged storms shall vainly flee
  And seek for rest where none shall be.

XIII.

It shall be a mountain Tree,
  Thro' whose great arms the winds shall blow
Louder than the roaring Sea,
  And toss its plumed head to and fro;
  But a thousand flowers shall live below.

XIV.

It shall be a kingly Star
   That o'er a thousand Suns shall burn
Where the high Sabaoth are,
   And round its glory flung afar
   A mighty host shall swiftly turn.

XV.

All things of beauty it shall be —
   All things of power — of joy — of fear;
But out of bliss and agony
   It shall come forth more pure and free,
   . And sing a song more sweet to hear.

XVI.

For methinks, when it hath passed
   Thro' wondrous Nature's world-wide reign,
Perchance it may come home at last,
   And the old Earth may hear again
   Its lofty voice of Joy and Pain.

CHARACTER OF FRA ANGELICO.

By GIORGIO VASARI.

FRA ANGELICO was a man of the utmost simplicity of intention, and was most holy in every act of his life. It is related of him, and it is a good evidence of his simple earnestness of purpose, that being one morning invited to breakfeast by Pope Nicholas V., he had scruples of conscience as to eating meat without the permission of his prior, not considering that the authority of the pontiff was superseding that of the prior. He disregarded all earthly advantages; and, living in pure holiness, was as much the friend of the poor in life as I believe his soul now is in heaven. He labored continually at his paintings, but would do nothing that was not connected with things holy. He might have been rich, but for riches he took no care ; on the contrary he was accustomed to say, that the only true riches was contentment with little. He might have commanded many, but would not do so, declaring that there was less fatigue and less danger of error in obeying others, than in commanding others. It was at his option to hold places of dignity in the brotherhood of his order, and also in the world ; but he regarded them not, affirming that he sought no dignity and took no care but that of escaping hell and drawing near to Paradise. And of a truth what dignity can be compared to that which should be most coveted by all Churchmen, nay, by every man living, that, namely, which is found in God alone, and in a life of virtuous labor?

Fra Angelico was kindly to all, and moderate in all his habits, living temperately, and holding himself entirely apart from the snares of the world. He used frequently to say, that he who practised the art of painting had need of quiet, and should live without cares or anxious thoughts; adding, that he who would do the work of Christ should perpetually remain with Christ. He was never seen to display anger among the brethren of his order; a thing which appears to me most extraordinary, nay, almost incredible; if he admonished his friends, it was with gentleness and a quiet smile; and to those who sought his works, he would reply with the utmost cordiality, that they had but to obtain the assent of the prior, when he would assuredly not fail to do what they desired. In fine, this never sufficiently to be lauded father was most humble, modest, and excellent in all his words and works; in his painting he gave evidence of piety and devotion, as well as of ability, and the saints that he painted have more of the air and expression of sanctity than have those of any other master.

It was the custom of Fra Angelico to abstain from retouching or improving any painting once finished. He altered nothing, but left all as it was done the first time, believing, as he said, that such was the will of God. It is also affirmed that he would never take the pencil in hand until he had first offered a prayer. He is said never to have painted a Crucifix without tears streaming from his eyes, and in the countenances and attitudes of his figures it is easy to perceive proof of his sincerity, his goodness, and the depth of his devotion to the religion of Christ.

He died in 1455, at the age of sixty-eight.

SONGS.

By WILLIAM BLAKE.

I give you the end of a golden string·
  Only wind it into a ball,
It will lead you in at Heaven's gate,
  Built in Jerusalem wall.

I.

MY SILKS AND FINE ARRAY:

MY silks and fine array,
  My smiles and languished air,
By love are driven away.
  And mournful, lean Despair
Brings me yew to deck my grave:
Such end true lovers have.

His face is fair as heaven
  When springing buds unfold;
O, why to *him* was 't given,
  Whose heart is wintry cold?
His breast is Love's all-worshipped tomb
Where all love's pilgrims come.

Bring me an axe and spade,
  Bring me a winding-sheet;

When I my grave have made,
  Let winds and tempests beat:
Then down I'll lie, as cold as clay.
  True love doth pass away!

II.

THE FIRST SONG OF INNOCENCE.

PIPING down the valleys wild,
  Piping songs of pleasant glee,
On a cloud I saw a child,
  And he, laughing, said to me:

"Pipe a song about a Lamb!"
  So I piped with merry cheer
"Piper, pipe that song again";
  So I piped: he wept to hear

"Drop thy pipe, thy happy pipe:
  Sing thy songs of happy cheer!"
So I sang the same again,
  While he wept with joy to hear.

"Piper, sit thee down and write
  In a book, that all may read."
So he vanished from my sight,
  And I plucked a hollow reed,

And I made a rural pen,
  And I stained the water clear,
And I wrote my happy songs
  Every child may joy to hear.

III.

THE LITTLE BLACK BOY.

My mother bore me in the southern wild,
    And I am black, but O, my soul is white.
White as an angel is the English child,
    But I am black, as if bereaved of light.

My mother taught me underneath a tree,
    And, sitting down before the heat of day,
She took me on her lap and kissèd me,
    And, pointing to the East, began to say:

" Look on the rising sun : there God does live,
    And gives this light, and gives His heat away;
And flowers and trees and beasts and men receive
    Comfort in morning, joy in the noonday.

" And we are put on earth a little space,
    That we may learn to bear the beams of love;
And these black bodies and this sunburnt face
    Are but a cloud, and like a shady grove.

" For when our souls have learned the heat to bear,
    The cloud will vanish, we shall hear His voice,
Saying, ' Come out from the grove, my love and care,
    And round my golden tent like lambs rejoice.' "

Thus did my mother say, and kissèd me,
    And thus I say to little English boy:
When I from black, and he from white cloud free,
    And round the tent of God like lambs we joy;

I'll shade him from the heat till he can bear
To lean in joy upon our Father's knee;
And then I'll stand and stroke his silver hair,
And be like him, and he will then love me.

IV.

THE CHIMNEY-SWEEPER.

WHEN my mother died I was very young,
And my father sold me while yet my tongue
Could scarcely cry, "Weep! weep! weep! weep!"
So your chimneys I sweep and in soot I sleep.

There's little Tom Dacre, who cried when his head,
That curled like a lamb's back, was shaved; so I said,
"Hush, Tom! never mind it, for when your head's bare,
You know that the soot cannot spoil your white hair."

And so he was quiet, and that very night,
As Tom was a-sleeping, he had such a sight;
That thousands of sweepers, Dick, Joe, Ned, and Jack,
Were all of them locked up in coffins of black.

And by came an angel, who had a bright key,
And he opened the coffins, and set them all free;
Then down a green plain, leaping, laughing they run,
And wash in a river, and shine in the sun.

Then naked and white, all their bags left behind,
They rise upon clouds, and sport in the wind;
And the angel told Tom, if he'd be a good boy,
He'd have God for his father, and never want joy.

And so Tom awoke, and we rose in the dark,
And got with our bags and our brushes to work:
Though the morning was cold, Tom was happy and warm:
So, if all do their duty, they need not fear harm.

V.

THE DIVINE IMAGE.

To mercy, pity, peace, and love,
    All pray in their distress,
And to these virtues of delight
    Return their thankfulness.

For mercy, pity, peace, and love,
    Is God our Father dear;
And mercy, pity, peace, and love,
    Is man, His child and care.

For Mercy has a human heart;
    Pity, a human face;
And Love, the human form divine;
    And Peace, the human dress.

Then every man, of every clime,
    That prays in his distress,
Prays to the human form divine:
    Love, Mercy, Pity, Peace.

And all must love the human form,
    In heathen, Turk, or Jew;
Where mercy, love, and pity dwell,
    There God is dwelling too.

VI.

ON ANOTHER'S SORROW.

CAN I see another's woe,
And not be in sorrow too?
Can I see another's grief,
And not seek for kind relief?

Can I see a falling tear,
And not feel my sorrow's share?
Can a father see his child
Weep, nor be with sorrow filled?

Can a mother sit and hear
An infant groan, an infant fear?
No! no! never can it be!
Never, never can it be!

And can He, who smiles on all,
Hear the wren, with sorrows small,
Hear the small bird's grief and care,
Hear the woes that infants bear?

And not sit beside the nest,
Pouring Pity in their breast?
And not sit the cradle near,
Weeping tear on infant's tear?

And not sit both night and day,
Wiping all our tears away?
O, no! never can it be!
Never, never can it be!

He doth give his joy to all:
He becomes an infant small,
He becomes a man of woe,
He doth feel the sorrow too.

Think not thou canst sigh a sigh,
And thy Maker is not by:
Think not thou canst weep a tear,
And thy Maker is not near.

O, He gives to us his joy,
That our griefs He may destroy:
Till our grief is fled and gone,
He doth sit by us and moan.

VII.

THE TIGER.

TIGER, Tiger, burning bright
In the forests of the night,
What immortal hand or eye
Framed thy fearful symmetry?

In what distant deeps or skies
Burned that fire within thine eyes?
On what wings dared he aspire?
What the hand dared seize the fire?

And what shoulder, and what art,
Could twist the sinews of thy heart?
When thy heart began to beat,
What dread hand formed thy dread feet?

What the hammer, what the chain,
Knit thy strength and forged thy brain?
What the anvil? What dread grasp
Dared thy deadly terrors clasp?

When the stars threw down their spears,
And watered heaven with their tears,
Did he smile his work to see?
Did He who made the lamb make thee?

VIII.

A LITTLE BOY LOST.

"Nought loves another as itself,
  Nor venerates another so,
Nor is it possible to thought
  A greater than itself to know.

"And, Father, how can I love you
  Or any of my brothers more?
I love you like the little bird
  That picks up crumbs around the door."

The Priest sat by and heard the child;
  In trembling zeal he seized his hair,
He led him by his little coat,
  And all admired the priestly care.

And standing on the altar high,
  "Lo! what a fiend is here," said he,
"One who sets reason up for judge
  Of our most holy Mystery."

The weeping child could not be heard,
  The weeping parents wept in vain,
They stripped him to his little shirt,
  And bound him in an iron chain,

And burned him in a holy place
  Where many had been burned before;
The weeping parents wept in vain.
  Are such things done on Albion's shore?

IX

SMILE AND FROWN.

THERE is a smile of Love,
  And there is a smile of Deceit,
And there is a smile of smiles
  In which the two smiles meet.

And there is a frown of Hate,
  And there is a frown of Disdain,
And there is a frown of frowns
  Which you strive to forget in vain;

For it sticks in the heart's deep core,
  And it sticks in the deep backbone.
And no smile ever was smiled
  But only one smile alone.

(And betwixt the cradle and grave
  It only once smiled can be,)
That when it once is smiled
  There's an end to all misery.

X.

OPPORTUNITY.

He who bends to himself a joy
Does the wingèd life destroy;
But he who kisses the joy as it flies
Lives in eternity's sunrise.

UPON GROWING OLD.

By J. HAIN FRISWELL.

JOHN FOSTER, (he who sprung into celebrity from one essay, *Popular Ignorance*,) had a diseased feeling against growing old, which seems to us to be very prevalent. He was sorry to lose every parting hour. "I have seen a fearful sight to-day," he would say, — "I have seen a buttercup." To others the sight would only give visions of the coming spring and future summer; to him it told of the past year, the last Christmas, the days which would never come again, — the so many days nearer the grave. Thackeray continually expressed the same feeling. He reverts to the merry old time when George the Third was king. He looks back with a regretful mind to his own youth. The black Care constantly rides behind his chariot. "Ah, my friends," he says, "how beautiful was youth! We are growing old. Spring-time and summer are past. We near the winter of our days. We shall never feel as we have felt. We approach the inevitable grave." Few men, indeed, know how to grow old gracefully as Madame de Staël very truly observed. There is an unmanly sadness at leaving off the old follies and the old games. We all hate fogeyism. Dr. Johnson, great and good as he was, had a touch of this regret, and we may pardon him for the feeling. A youth spent in poverty and neglect, a manhood consumed in unceasing struggle, are not preparatives to growing old in peace. We fancy that, after a stormy morning and a lowering day, the evening should have a sunset glow, and, when the night sets in, look back with regret at the " gusty, babbling, and remorseless day"; but if we do so, we miss the supporting faith of the Christian and the manly cheerfulness of the heathen. To grow old is quite natural; being natural, it is beautiful; and if we grumble at it, we miss the lesson, and lose all the beauty.

Half of our life is spent in vain regrets. When we are boys we ardently wish to be men; when men we wish as ardently to be boys. We sing sad songs of the lapse of time. We talk of "auld lang syne," of the days when we were young, of gathering shells on the sea-shore and throwing them carelessly away. We never cease to be sentimental upon past youth and lost manhood and beauty. Yet there are no regrets so false, and few half so silly. Perhaps the saddest sight in the world is to see an old lady, wrinkled and withered, dressing, talking, and acting like a very young one, and forgetting all the time, as she clings to the feeble remnant of the past, that there is no sham so transparent as her own, and that people, instead of feeling with her, are laughing at her. Old boys disguise their foibles a little better; but they are equally ridiculous. The feeble protests which they make against the flying chariot of Time are equally futile. The great Mower enters the field, and all must come down. To stay him would be impossible. We might as well try with a finger to stop Ixion's wheel, or to dam up the current of the Thames with a child's foot.

Since the matter is inevitable, we may as well sit down and reason it out. Is it so dreadful to grow old? Does old age need its apologies and its defenders? Is it a benefit or a calamity? Why should it be odious and ridiculous? An old tree is picturesque, an old castle venerable, an old cathedral inspires awe, — why should man be worse than his works?

Let us, in the first place, see what youth is. Is it so blessed and happy and flourishing as it seems to us? Schoolboys do not think so. They always wish to be older. You cannot insult one of them more than by telling him that he is a year or two younger than he is. He fires up at once: "Twelve, did you say, sir? No, I'm fourteen." But men and women who have reached twenty-eight do not thus add to their years. Amongst schoolboys, notwithstanding the general tenor of those romancists who see that everything young bears a rose-colored blush, misery is prevalent enough. Emerson, Coleridge, Wordsworth, were each and all unhappy boys. They all had their rebuffs, and bitter, bitter troubles; all the more bitter because their sensitiveness was so acute. Suicide is not unknown amongst the young; fears prey upon them and terrify them; ignorances and follies surround them. Arriving at manhood, we are little better off. If we are poor, we mark the difference between the rich and us; we see position gains all the day. If we are as clever as Hamlet, we grow just as philosophically disappointed. If we love, we can only be sure of a brief pleasure, — an April day. Love has its bitterness. "It is," says Ovid, an adept in the matter, "full of anxious fear." We fret and fume at the authority of the wise heads; we have an intense idea of our own talent. We believe calves of our own age to be as big and as valuable as full-grown bulls; we envy whilst we jest at the old. We cry, with the puffed-up hero of the *Patrician's Daughter* —

"It may be by the calendar of years
You are the elder man; but 't is the sun
Of knowledge on the mind's dial shining bright,
And chronicling deeds and thoughts, that makes true time."

And yet life is withal very unhappy, whether we live amongst the grumbling captains of the clubs, who are ever seeking and not finding promotion; amongst ths struggling authors and rising artists who never rise; or among the young men who are full of riches, titles, places, and honor, who have every wish fulfilled, and are miserable because they have nothing to wish for. Thus the young Romans killed themselves after the death of their emperor, not for grief, not for affection, not even for the fashion of suicide, which grew afterwards prevalent enough, but from the simple weariness of doing everything over and over again. Old age has passed such stages as these, landed on a safer shore, and matriculated in a higher college, in a purer air. We do not sigh for impossibilities; we cry not —

> "Bring these anew, and set me once again
> In the delusion of life's infancy;
> I was not happy, but I knew not then
> That happy I was never doomed to be."

We know that we are not happy. We know that life perhaps was not given us to be continuously comfortable and happy. We have been behind the scenes, and know all the illusions; but when we are old we are far too wise to throw life away for mere *ennui*. With Dandolo, refusing a crown at ninety-six, winning battles at ninety-four; with Wellington, planning and superintending fortifications at eighty; with Bacon and Humboldt, students to the last gasp; with wise old Montaigne, shrewd in his gray-beard wisdom and loving life, even in the midst of his fits of gout and colic, — Age knows far too much to act like a sulky child. It knows too well the results and the value of things to care about them; that the ache will subside, the pain be lulled, the estate we coveted be worth little; the titles, ribbons, gewgaws, honors, be all more or less worthless. "Who has honor? He that died o' Wednesday!" Such a one passed us in the race, and gained it but to fall. We are still up and doing; we may be frosty and shrewd, but kindly. We can wish all men well; like them, too, so far as they may be liked, and smile at the fuss, bother, hurry, and turmoil, which they make about matters which to us are worthless dross. The greatest prize in the whole market — in any and in every market — success, is to the old man nothing. He little cares who is up and who is down; the present he lives in and delights in. Thus, in one of those admirable comedies in which Robson acted, we find the son a wanderer, the mother's heart nearly broken, the father torn and broken by a suspicion of his son's dishonesty, but the grandfather all the while concerned only about his gruel and his handkerchief. Even the pains and troubles incident to his state visit the old man lightly. Because Southey sat for months in his library, unable to read or touch the books he loved, we are not to infer that he was unhappy. If the stage darkens as the curtain falls, certain it also is that the senses grow duller and more blunted. "Don't cry for me, my dear," said an old lady undergoing an operation; "I do not feel it."

It seems to us, therefore, that a great deal of unnecessary pity has been thrown away upon old age. We begin at school reading Cicero's treatise, hearing him talk with Scipio and Lælius; we hear much about poor old men; we are taught to admire the vigor, quickness, and capacity of youth and manhood. We lose sight of the wisdom which age brings even to the most foolish. We think that a circumscribed sphere must necessarily be an unhappy one. It is not always so. What one abandons in growing old is perhaps after all not worth having. The chief part of youth is but excitement; often both unwise and unhealthy. The same pen which has written, with a morbid feeling, that "there is a class of beings who do grow old in their youth and die ere middle age," tells us also that "the best of life is but intoxication." That passes away. The man who has grown old does not care about it. The author at that period has no feverish excitement about seeing himself in print;

he does not hunt newspapers for reviews and notices. He is content to wait; he knows what fame is worth. The obscure man of science, who has been wishing to make the world better and wiser; the struggling curate, the poor and hard-tried man of God; the enthusiastic reformer, who has watched the sadly slow dawning of progress and liberty; the artist, whose dream of beauty slowly fades before his dim eyes — all lay down their feverish wishes as they advance in life, forget the bright ideal which they cannot reach, and embrace the more imperfect real. We speak not here of the assured Christian. He, from the noblest pinnacle of faith, beholds a promised land, and is eager to reach it; he prays "to be delivered from the body of this death"; but we write of those humbler, perhaps more human souls, with whom increasing age each day treads down an illusion. All feverish wishes, raw and inconclusive desires, have died down, and a calm beauty and peace survive; passions are dead, temptations weakened or conquered; experience has been won; selfish interests are widened into universal ones; vain, idle hopes, have merged into a firmer faith or a complete knowledge; and more light has broken in upon the soul's dark cottage, battered and decayed, "through chinks which Time has made."

Again, old men are valuable, not only as relics of the past, but as guides and prophets for the future. They know the pattern of every turn of life's kaleidoscope. The colors merely fall into new shapes; the groundwork is just the same. The good which a calm, kind, and cheerful old man can do is incalculable. And whilst he does good to others, he enjoys himself. He looks not unnaturally to that which should accompany old age — honor, love, obedience, troops of friends; and he plays his part in the comedy or tragedy of life with as much gusto as any one else. Old Montague or Capulet, and old Polonius, that wise maxim-man, enjoy themselves quite as well as the moody Hamlet, the perturbed

Laertes, or even gallant Mercutio or love-sick Romeo. Friar Lawrence, who is a good old man, is perhaps the happiest of all in the *dramatis personæ*, — unless we take the gossiping, garrulous old nurse, with her sunny recollections of maturity and youth. The great thing is to have the mind well employed, to work whilst it is yet day. The precise Duke of Wellington, answering every letter with " F. M. presents his compliments"; the wondrous worker Humboldt, with his orders of knighthood, stars, and ribbons, lying dusty in his drawer, still contemplating *Cosmos*, and answering his thirty letters a day, — were both men in exceedingly enviable, happy positions; they had reached the top of the hill, and could look back quietly over the rough road which they had travelled. We are not all Humboldts or Wellingtons; but we can all be busy and good. Experience must teach us all a great deal; and if it only teaches us not to fear the future, not to cast a maundering regret over the past, we can be as happy in old age — ay, and far more so — than we were in youth. We are no longer the fools of time and error. We are leaving by slow degrees the old world; we stand upon the threshold of the new; not without hope, but without fear, in an exceedingly natural position, with nothing strange or dreadful about it; with our domain drawn within a narrow circle, but equal to our power. Muscular strength, organic instincts, are all gone; but what then? We do not want them; we are getting ready for the great change, one which is just as necessary as it was to be born; and to a little child perhaps one is not a whit more painful, — perhaps not so painful as the other. The wheels of Time have brought us to the goal; we are about to rest while others labor, to stay at home while others wander. We touch at last the mysterious door, — are we to be pitied or to be envied?

THE TITMOUSE.

By R. W. EMERSON.

YOU shall not be over-bold
When you deal with arctic cold,
As late I found my lukewarm blood
Chilled wading in the snow-choked wood.
How should I fight? my foeman fine
Has million arms to one of mine.
East, west, for aid I looked in vain;
East, west, north, south, are his domain.
Miles off, three dangerous miles, is home;
Must borrow his winds who there would come.
Up and away for life! be fleet!
The frost-king ties my fumbling feet,
Sings in my ears, my hands are stones,
Curdles the blood to the marble bones,
Tugs at the heartstrings, numbs the sense,
Hems in the life with narrowing fence.

Well, in this broad bed lie and sleep,
The punctual stars will vigil keep,
Enbalmed by purifying cold,
The winds shall sing their dead-march old,
The snow is no ignoble shroud,
The moon thy mourner, and the cloud.

Softly, — but this way fate was pointing,
'T was coming fast to such anointing,

THE TITMOUSE.

When piped a tiny voice hard by,
Gay and polite, a cheerful cry,
" *Chic-chic-a-dee-dee!* " saucy note,
Out of sound heart and merry throat,
As if it said, " Good day, good sir !
Fine afternoon, old passenger !
Happy to meet you in these places,
Where January brings few men's faces."

This poet, though he live apart,
Moved by a hospitable heart,
Sped, when I passed his sylvan fort,
To do the honors of his court,
As fits a feathered lord of land,
Flew near, with soft wing grazed my hand,
Hopped on the bough, then, darting low,
Prints his small impress on the snow,
Shows feats of his gymnastic play,
Head downward, clinging to the spray.
Here was this atom in full breath
Hurling defiance at vast death,
This scrap of valor just for play
Fronts the north-wind in waistcoat gray,
As if to shame my weak behavior.
I greeted loud my little saviour :
" Thou pet ! what dost here ? and what for ?
In these woods, thy small Labrador
At this pinch, wee San Salvador !
What fire burns in that little chest,
So frolic, stout, and self-possest ?
Didst steal the glow that lights the West ?
Henceforth I wear no stripe but thine :
Ashes and black all hues outshine.
Why are not diamonds black and gray,
To ape thy dare-devil array ?

And I affirm the spacious North
Exists to draw thy virtue forth.
I think no virtue goes with size:
The reason of all cowardice
Is, that men are overgrown,
And, to be valiant, must come down
To the titmouse dimension."

'T is good-will makes intelligence,
And I began to catch the sense
Of my bird's song: " Live out of doors,
In the great woods, and prairie floors.
I dine in the sun; when he sinks in the sea,
I, too, have a hole in a hollow tree.
And I like less when summer beats
With stifling beams on these retreats
Than noontide twilight which snow makes
With tempest of the blinding flakes:
For well the soul, if stout within,
Can arm impregnably the skin;
And polar frost my frame defied,
Made of the air that blows outside."

With glad remembrance of my debt,
I homeward turn. Farewell, my pet!
When here again thy pilgrim comes,
He shall bring store of seeds and crumbs.
Henceforth I prize thy wiry chant
O'er all that mass and minster vaunt:
For men mishear thy call in spring,
As 't would accost some frivolous wing,
Crying out of the hazel copse, " *Phe—be!* "
And in winter " *Chic-a-dee-dee!* "
I think old Cæsar must have heard
In Northern Gaul my dauntless bird,

And, echoed in some frosty wold,
Borrowed thy battle-numbers bold.
And I shall write our annals new,
And thank thee for a better clew:
I, who dreamed not, when I came here,
To find the antidote of fear,
Now hear thee say in Roman key,
" *Pæan! Ve-ni, Vi-di, Vi-ci.*"

LITTLE PANSIE.

A FRAGMENT.

By NATHANIEL HAWTHORNE

DOCTOR DOLLIVER, a worthy personage of extreme antiquity, was aroused rather prematurely, one summer morning, by the shouts of the child Pansie, in an adjoining chamber, summoning Old Martha (who performed the duties of nurse, housekeeper, and kitchen-maid, in the Doctor's establishment) to take up her little ladyship and dress her. The old gentleman woke with more than his customary alacrity, and, after taking a moment to gather his wits about him, pulled aside the faded moreen curtains of his ancient bed, and thurst his head into a beam of sunshine that caused him to wink and withdraw it again. This transitory glimpse of good Dr. Dolliver showed a flannel nightcap, fringed round with stray locks of silvery white hair, and surmounting a meagre and duskily yellow visage, which was crossed and criss-crossed with a record of his long life in wrinkles, faithfully written, no doubt, but with such cramped chirography of Father Time that the purport was illegible. It seemed hardly worth while for the patriarch to get out of bed any more, and bring his forlorn shadow into the summer day that was made for younger folks. The Doctor, however, was by no means of that opinion, being considerably encouraged towards the toil of living twenty-four hours longer by the comparative ease with which he found

himself going through the usually painful process of bestirring his rusty joints, (stiffened by the very rest and sleep that should have made them pliable,) and putting them in a condition to bear his weight upon the floor. Nor was he absolutely disheartened by the idea of those tonsorial, ablutionary, and personally decorative labors which are apt to become so intolerably irksome to an old gentleman, after performing them daily and daily for fifty, sixty, or seventy years, and finding them still as immitigably recurrent as at first. Dr. Dolliver could nowise account for this happy condition of his spirits and physical energies, until he remembered taking an experimental sip of a certain cordial which was long ago prepared by his grandson and carefully sealed up in a bottle, and had been reposited in a dark closet among a parcel of effete medicines ever since that gifted young man's death.

"It may have wrought effect upon me," thought the Doctor, shaking his head as he lifted it again from the pillow. "It may be so; for poor Cornelius oftentimes instilled a strange efficacy into his perilous drugs. But I will rather believe it to be the operation of God's mercy, which may have temporarily invigorated my feeble age for little Pansie's sake."

A twinge of his familiar rheumatism, as he put his foot out of bed, taught him that he must not reckon too confidently upon even a day's respite from the intrusive family of aches and infirmities which, with their proverbial fidelity to attachments once formed, had long been the closest acquaintances that the poor old gentleman had in the world. Nevertheless, he fancied the twinge a little less poignant than those of yesterday; and, moreover, after stinging him pretty smartly, it passed gradually off with a thrill, which, in its latter stages, grew to be almost agreeable. Pain is but pleasure too strongly emphasized. With cautious movements, and only a groan or two, the good Doctor transferred himself from the bed to the floor, where he stood awhile, gazing from one piece of quaint furniture to another, (such as stiff-backed Mayflower chairs, an oaken chest-of-drawers carved cunningly with shapes of animals and wreaths of foliage, a table with multitudinous legs, a family-record in faded embroidery, a shelf of black-bound books, a dirty heap of gallipots and phials in a dim corner,) — gazing at these things and steadying himself by the bedpost, while his inert brain, still partially benumbed with sleep, came slowly into accordance with the realities about him. The object which most helped to bring Dr. Dolliver completely to his waking perceptions was one that common observers might suppose to have been snatched bodily out of his dreams. The same sunbeam that had dazzled the Doctor between the bed-curtains gleamed on the weather-beaten gilding which had once adorned this mysterious symbol, and showed it to be an enormous serpent, twining round a wooden post, and reaching quite from the floor of the chamber to its ceiling.

It was evidently a thing that could boast of considerable antiquity, the dry-rot having eaten out its eyes and gnawed away the tip of its tail; and it must have stood long exposed to the atmosphere, for a kind of gray moss had partially overspread its tarnished gilt surface, and a swallow, or other familiar little bird, in some by-gone summer, seemed to have built its nest in the yawning and exaggerated mouth. It looked like a kind of Manichean idol, which might have been elevated on a pedestal for a century or so, enjoying the worship of its votaries in the open air, until the impious sect perished from among men, — all save old Dr. Dolliver, who had set up the monster in his bedchamber. for the convenience of private devotion. But we are unpardonable in suggesting such a fantasy to the prejudice of our venerable friend, knowing him to have been as pious and upright a Christian, and with as little of the serpent in his character, as ever came of Puritan lineage. Not to make a further mystery about a very simple matter, this bedimmed and rotten reptile was once the medical emblem or apothecary's sign of the famous Dr. Swinnerton, who practised physic in the earlier days of New England, when a head of Æsculapius or Hippocrates would have vexed the souls of the righteous as savoring of heathendom. The ancient dispenser of drugs had therefore set up an image of the Brazen Serpent, and followed his business for many years, with great credit under this Scriptural device; and Dr. Dolliver, being the apprentice, pupil, and humble friend of the learned Swinnerton's old age, had inherited the symbolic snake, and much other valuable property, by his bequest.

While the patriarch was putting on his small-clothes, he took care to stand in the parallelogram of bright sunshine that fell upon the uncarpeted floor. The summer warmth was very genial to his system, and yet made him shiver; his wintry veins rejoiced at it, though the reviving blood tingled through them with a half painful and only half pleasurable titillation. For the first few moments after creeping out of bed, he kept his back to the sunny window and seemed mysteriously shy of glancing thitherward; but as the June fervor pervaded him more and more thoroughly, he turned bravely about, and looked forth at a burial-ground on the corner of which he dwelt. There lay many an old acquaintance, who had gone to sleep with the flavor of Dr. Dolliver's tinctures and powders upon his tongue; it was the patient's final bitter taste of this world, and perhaps doomed to be a recollected nauseousness in the next. Yesterday, in the chill of his forlorn old age, the Doctor expected soon to stretch out his weary bones among that quiet community, and might scarcely have shrunk from the prospect on his own account, except, indeed, that he dreamily mixed up the infirmities of his present condition with the repose of the approaching one, being haunted by a notion that the damp earth, under the grass and dandelions, must needs be pernicious for his cough and his rheumatism. But, this morning, the cheerful sunbeams, or the mere taste of his grandson's cordial that he had taken at bedtime, or the fitful vigor that often sports irreverently with aged people, had caused an unfrozen drop of youthfulness, somewhere within him, to expand.

"Hem! ahem!" quoth the Doctor, hoping with one effort to clear his throat of the dregs of a ten years' cough. "Matters are not so far gone with me as I thought. I have known mighty sensible men, when only a little age-stricken or otherwise out of sorts, to die of mere faintheartedness, a great deal sooner than they need."

He shook his silvery head at his own image in the looking-glass, as if to impress the apophthegm on that shadowy representative of himself; and for his part, he determined to pluck up a spirit and live as long as he possibly could, if it were only for the sake of little Pansie, who stood as close to one extremity of human life as her great-grandfather to the other. This child of three years old occupied all the unfossilized portion of good Dr. Dolliver's heart. Every other interest that he formerly had, and the entire confraternity of persons whom he once loved, had long ago departed, and the poor Doctor could not follow them, because the grasp of Pansie's baby-fingers held him back.

So he crammed a great silver watch into his fob, and drew on a patchwork morning-gown of an ancient fashion. Its original material was said to have been the embroidered front of his own wedding-waistcoat and the silken skirt of his wife's bridal attire, which his eldest granddaughter had taken from the carved chest-of-drawers, after poor Bessie, the beloved of his youth, had been half a century in the grave. Throughout many of the intervening years, as the garment got ragged, the spinsters of the old man's family had quilted their duty and affection into it in the shape of patches upon patches, rose-color, crimson, blue, violet, and green, and·then (as their hopes faded, and their life kept growing shadier, and their attire took a sombre hue) sober gray and great fragments of funereal black, until the Doctor could revive the memory of most things that had befallen him by looking at his patchwork-gown, as it hung upon a chair. And now it was ragged again, and all the fingers that should have mended it were cold. It had an Eastern fragrance, too, a smell of drugs, strong-scented herbs, and spicy gums, gathered from the many potent infusions that had from time to time been spilt over it; so that, snuffing him afar off, you might have taken Dr. Dolliver for a mummy, and could hardly have been undeceived by his shrunken and torpid aspect, as he crept nearer.

Wrapt in his odorous and many-colored robe, he took staff in hand and moved pretty vigorously to the head of the staircase. As it was somewhat steep, and but dimly lighted, he began cautiously to descend, putting his left hand on the banister, and poking down his long stick to assist him in making sure of the successive steps; and thus he became a living illustration of the accuracy of Scripture, where it describes the aged as being "afraid of that which is high," — a truth that is often found to have a sadder purport than its external one. Half-way to the bottom, however, the Doctor heard the impatient and authoritative tones of little Pansie, — Queen Pansie, as she might fairly have been styled, in reference to her position in the household, — calling amain for grandpapa and breakfast. He was startled into such perilous activity by the summons, that his heels slid on the stairs, the slippers were shuffled off his feet, and he saved himself from a tumble only by quickening his pace, and coming down at almost a run.

"Mercy on my poor old bones!" mentally exclaimed the Doctor, fancying himself fractured in fifty places. "Some of them are broken, surely, and methinks my heart has leaped out of my mouth! What! all right? Well, well! but Providence is kinder to me than I deserve, prancing down this steep staircase like a kid of three months old!"

He bent stiffly to gather up his slippers and fallen staff; and meanwhile Pansie had heard the tumult of her great-grandfather's descent, and was pounding against the door of the breakfast-room in her haste to come at him. The Doctor opened it, and there she stood, a rather pale and large-eyed little thing, quaint in her aspect, as might well be the case with a motherless child, dwelling in an uncheerful house, with no other playmates than a decrepit old man and a kitten, and no better atmosphere within-doors than the odor of decayed apothecary's stuff, nor gayer neighborhood than that of the adjacent burial-ground, where all her relatives, from her great-grandmother downward, lay calling to her, "Pansie, Pansie, it is bedtime!" even in the prime of the summer morning. For those dead women-folk, especially her mother and the whole row of maiden aunts and grand-aunts, could not but be anxious about the child, knowing that little Pansie would be far safer under a tuft of dandelions than if left alone, as she soon must be, in this difficult and deceitful world.

Yet, in spite of the lack of damask roses in her cheeks, she seemed a healthy child, and certainly showed great capacity of energetic movement in the impulsive capers with which she welcomed her venerable progenitor. She shouted out her satisfaction, moreover, (as her custom was, having never had any over-sensitive auditors about her to tame down her voice,) till even the Doctor's dull ears were full of the clamor.

"Pansie, darling," said Dr. Dolliver cheerily, patting her brown hair with his tremulous fingers, "thou hast put some of thine own friskiness into poor old grandfather, this fine morning! Dost know, child, that he came near breaking his neck down-stairs at the sound of thy voice? What wouldst thou have done then, little Pansie?"

"Kiss poor grandpapa and make him well!" answered the child, remembering the Doctor's own mode of cure in similar mishaps to herself. "It shall do poor grandpapa good!" she added, putting up her mouth to apply the remedy.

"Ah, little one, thou hast greater faith in thy medicines than ever I had in my drugs," replied the patriarch with a giggle, surprised and delighted at his own readiness of response. "But the kiss is good for my feeble old heart, Pansie, though it might do little to mend a broken neck; so give grandpapa another dose, and let us to breakfast."

In this merry humor they sat down to the table, great-grandpapa and Pansie side by side, and the kitten, as soon appeared, making a third in the party. First, she showed her mottled head out of Pansie's lap, delicately sipping milk from the child's basin without rebuke; then she took post on the old gentleman's shoulder, purring like a spinning-wheel, trying her claws in the wadding of his dressing-gown, and still more impressively reminding him of her presence by putting out a paw to intercept a warmed-over morsel of yesterday's chicken on its way to the Doctor's mouth. After skilfully achieving this feat, she scrambled down upon the breakfast-table and began to wash her face and hands. Evidently, these companions were all three on intimate terms, as was natural enough, since a great many childish impulses were softly creeping back on the simple-minded old man; insomuch that, if no worldly necessities nor painful infirmity had disturbed him, his remnant of life might have been as cheaply and cheerily enjoyed as the early playtime of the kitten and the child. Old Dr. Dolliver and his great-granddaughter (a ponderous title, which seemed quite to overwhelm the tiny figure of Pansie) had met one another at the two extremities of the life-circle:

her sunrise served him for a sunset, illuminating his locks of silver and hers of golden brown with a homogeneous shimmer of twinkling light.

Little Pansie was the one earthly creature that inherited a drop of the Dolliver blood. The Doctor's only child, poor Bessie's offspring, had died the better part of a hundred years before, and his grandchildren, a numerous and dimly remembered brood, had vanished along his weary track in their youth, maturity, or incipient age, till, hardly knowing how it had all happened, he found himself tottering onward with an infant's small fingers in his nerveless grasp. So mistily did his dead progeny come and go in the patriarch's decayed recollection, that this solitary child represented for him the successive babyhoods of the many that had gone before. The emotions of his early paternity came back to him. She seemed the baby of a past age oftener than she seemed Pansie. A whole family of grand-aunts, (one of whom had perished in her cradle, never so mature as Pansie now, another in her virgin bloom, another in autumnal maidenhood, yellow and shrivelled, with vinegar in her blood, and still another, a forlorn widow, whose grief outlasted even its vitality, and grew to be merely a torpid habit, and was saddest then,) — all their hitherto forgotten features peeped through the face of the great-grandchild, and their long inaudible voices sobbed, shouted, or laughed, in her familiar tones. But it often happened to Dr. Dolliver, while frolicking amid this throng of ghosts, where the one reality looked no more vivid than its shadowy sisters, — it often happened that his eyes filled with tears at a sudden perception of what a sad and poverty-stricken old man he was, already remote from his own generation, and bound to stray farther onward as the sole playmate and protector of a child!

As Dr. Dolliver, in spite of his advanced epoch of life, is likely to remain a considerable time longer upon our hands, we deem it expedient to give a brief sketch of his position, in order that the story may get onward with the greater freedom when he rises from the breakfast-table. Deeming it a matter of courtesy, we have allowed him the honorary title of Doctor, as did all his townspeople and contemporaries, except, perhaps, one or two formal old physicians, stingy of civil phrases and over-jealous of their own professional dignity. Nevertheless, these crusty graduates were technically right in excluding Dr. Dolliver from their fraternity. He had never received the degree of any medical school, nor (save it might be for the cure of a toothache, or a child's rash, or a whitlow on a seamstress's finger, or some such trifling malady) had he ever been even a practitioner of the awful science with which his popular designation connected him. Our old friend, in short, even at his highest social elevation, claimed to be nothing more than an apothecary, and, in these later and far less prosperous days, scarcely so much. Since the death of his last surviving grandson, (Pansie's father, whom he had instructed in all the mysteries of his science, and who, being distinguished by an experimental and inventive tendency, was generally believed to have poisoned himself with an infallible panacea of his own distillation,) — since that final bereavement, Dr. Dolliver's once pretty flourishing business had lamentably declined. After a few months of unavailing struggle, he found it expedient to take down the Brazen Serpent from the position to which Dr. Swinnerton had originally elevated it, in front of his shop in the main street, and to retire to his private dwelling, situated in a by-lane and on the edge of a burial-ground.

This house, as well as the Brazen Serpent, some old medical books, and a drawer full of manuscripts, had come to him by the legacy of Dr. Swinnerton. The dreariness of the locality had been of small importance to our friend in his young manhood, when he first led his fair wife over the threshold, and so long as neither of them had any kinship with the human dust that rose into little hillocks, and still kept accumulating beneath their window. But, too soon afterwards, when poor Bessie herself had gone early to rest there, it is probable that an influence from her grave may have prematurely calmed and depressed her widowed husband, taking away much of the energy from what should have been the most active portion of his life. Thus he never grew rich. His thrifty townsmen used to tell him, that, in any other man's hands, Dr. Swinnerton's Brazen Serpent (meaning, I presume, the inherited credit and goodwill of that old worthy's trade) would need but ten years' time to transmute its brass into gold. In Dr. Dolliver's keeping, as we have seen, the inauspicious symbol lost the greater part of what superficial gilding it originally had. Matters had not mended with him in more advanced life, after he had deposited a further and further portion of his heart and its affections in each successive one of a long row of kindred graves; and as he stood over the last of them, holding Pansie by the hand and looking down upon the coffin of his grandson, it is no wonder that the old man wept, partly for those gone before, but not so bitterly as for the little one that stayed behind. Why had not God taken her with the rest? And then, so hopeless as he was, so destitute of possibilities of good, his weary frame, his decrepit bones, his dried-up heart, might have crumbled into dust at once, and have been scattered by the next wind over all the heaps of earth that were akin to him.

This intensity of desolation, however, was of too positive a character to be long sustained by a person of Dr. Dolliver's original gentleness and simplicity, and now so completely tamed by age and misfortune. Even before he turned away from the grave, he grew conscious of a slightly cheering and invigorating effect from the tight grasp of the child's warm little hand. Feeble as he was, she seemed to adopt him willingly for her protector. And the Doctor never afterwards shrank from his duty nor quailed beneath it, but bore himself like a man, striving, amid the sloth of age and the breaking-up of intellect, to earn the competency which he had failed to accumulate even in his most vigorous days.

To the extent of securing a present subsistence for Pansie and himself, he was successful. After his son's death, when the Brazen Serpent fell into popular disrepute, a small share of tenacious patronage followed the old man into his retirement. In his prime, he had been allowed to possess more skill than usually fell to the share of a Colonial apothecary, having been regularly apprenticed to Dr. Swinnerton, who, throughout his long practice, was accustomed personally to concoct the medicines which he prescribed and dispensed. It was believed, indeed, that the ancient physician had learned the art at the world-famous drug-manufactory of Apothecary's Hall, in London, and, as some people half-malignly whispered, had perfected himself under masters more subtle than were to be found even there. Unquestionably, in many critical cases he was known to have employed remedies of mysterious composition and dangerous potency, which in less skilful hands would have been more likely to kill than cure. He would willingly, it is said, have taught his apprentice the secrets of these prescriptions, but the latter, being of a timid character and delicate conscience, had shrunk from acquaintance with them. It was probably as the result of the same scrupulosity that Dr. Dolliver had always declined to enter the medical profession, in which his old instructor had set him such heroic examples of adventurous dealing with matters of life and death. Nevertheless, the aromatic fragrance, so to speak, of the learned Swinnerton's reputation had clung to our friend through life; and there were elaborate preparations in the pharmacopœia of that day, requiring such minute skill and conscientious fidelity in the concocter that the physicians were still glad to confide them to one in whom these qualities were so evident.

Moreover, the grandmothers of the community were kind to him, and mindful of his perfumes, his rose-water, his cosmetics, tooth-powders, pomanders, and pomades, the scented memory of which lingered about their toilet-tables, or came faintly back from the days when they were beautiful. Among this class of customers there was still a demand for certain comfortable little nostrums, (delicately sweet and pungent to the taste, cheering to the spirits, and fragrant in the breath,) the proper distillation of which was the airiest secret that the mystic Swinnerton had left behind him. And, besides, these old ladies had always liked the manners of Dr. Dolliver, and used to speak of his gentle courtesy behind the counter as having positively been something to admire; though, of later years, an unrefined, an almost rustic simplicity, such as belonged to his humble ancestors, appeared to have taken possession of him, as it often does of prettily mannered men in their late decay.

But it resulted from all these favorable circumstances that the Doctor's marble mortar, though worn with long service and considerably damaged by a crack that pervaded it, continued to keep up an occasional intimacy with the pestle; and he still weighed drachms and scruples in his delicate scales, though it seemed impossible, dealing with such minute quantities, that his tremulous fingers should not put in too little or too much, leaving out life with the deficiency or spilling in death with the surplus. To say the truth, his stanchest friends were beginning to think that Dr. Dolliver's fits of absence (when his mind appeared absolutely to depart from him, while his frail old body worked on mechanically) rendered him not quite trustworthy without a close supervision of his proceedings. It was impossible, however, to convince the aged apothecary of the necessity for such vigilance; and if anything could stir up his gentle temper to wrath, or, as oftener happened, to tears, it was the attempt (which he was marvellously quick to detect) thus to interfere with his long-familiar business.

The public, meanwhile, ceasing to regard Dr. Dolliver in his professional aspect, had begun to take an interest in him as perhaps their oldest fellow-citizen. It was he that remembered the Great Fire and the Great Snow, and that had been a grown-up stripling at the terrible epoch of Witch-Times, and a child just breeched at the breaking-out of King Philip's Indian War. He, too, in his school-boy days, had received a benediction from the patriarchal Governor Bradstreet, and thus could boast (somewhat as Bishops do of their unbroken succession from the Apostles) of a transmitted blessing from the whole company of sainted Pilgrims, among whom the venerable magistrate had been an honored companion. Viewing their townsman in this aspect, the people revoked the courteous Doctorate with which they had heretofore decorated him, and now knew him most familiarly as Grandsir Dolliver. His white head, his Puritan band, his threadbare garb, (the fashion of which he had ceased to change, half a century ago,) his gold-headed staff, that had been Dr. Swinnerton's, his shrunken, frosty figure, and its feeble movement, — all these characteristics had a wholeness and permanence in the public recognition, like the meeting-house steeple or the town-pump. All the younger portion of the inhabitants unconsciously ascribed a sort of aged immortality to Grandsir Dolliver's infirm and reverend presence. They fancied that he had been born old, (at least, I remember entertaining some such notions about age-stricken people, when I myself was young,) and that he could the better tolerate his aches and incommodities, his dull ears and dim eyes, his remoteness from human intercourse within the crust of indurated years, the cold temperature that kept him always shivering and sad, the heavy burden that invisibly bent down his shoulders, — that all these intolerable things might bring a kind of enjoyment to Grandsir Dolliver, as the life-long conditions of his peculiar existence.

But, alas! it was a terrible mistake. This weight of years had a perennial novelty for the poor sufferer. He never grew accustomed to it, but, long as he had now borne the fretful torpor of his waning life, and patient as he seemed, he still retained an inward consciousness that these stiffened shoulders, these quailing knees, this cloudiness of sight and brain, this confused forgetfulness of men and affairs, were troublesome accidents that did not really belong to him. He possibly cherished a half-recognized idea that they might pass away. Youth, however eclipsed for a season, is undoubtedly the proper, permanent, and genuine condition of man; and if we look closely into this dreary delusion of growing old, we shall find that it never absolutely succeeds in laying hold of our innermost convictions. A sombre garment, woven of life's unrealities, has muffled us from our true self, but within it smiles the young man whom we knew; the ashes of many perishable things have fallen upon our youthful fire, but beneath them lurk the seeds of inextinguishable flame. So powerful is this instinctive faith that men of simple modes of character are prone to antedate its consummation. And thus it happened with poor Grandsir Dolliver, who often awoke from an old man's fitful sleep with a sense that his senile predicament was but a dream of the past night; and hobbling hastily across the cold floor to the looking-glass, he would be grievously disappointed at beholding the white hair, the wrinkles and furrows, the ashen visage and bent form, the melancholy mask of Age, in which, as he now remembered, some strange and sad enchantment had involved him for years gone by!

To other eyes than his own, however, the shrivelled old gentleman looked as if there were little hope of his throwing off this too artfully wrought disguise, until, at no distant day, his stooping figure should be straightened out, his hoary locks be smoothed over his brows, and his much enduring bones be laid safely away, with a green coverlet spread over them, beside his Bessie, who doubtless would recognize her youthful companion in spite of his ugly garniture of decay. He longed to be gazed at by the loving eyes now closed; he shrank from the hard stare of them that loved him not. Walking the streets seldom and reluctantly, he felt a dreary impulse to elude the people's observation, as if with a sense that he had gone irrevocably out of fashion, and broken his connecting links with the network of human life; or else it was that nightmare-feeling which we sometimes have in dreams, when we seem to find ourselves wandering through a crowded avenue, with the noonday sun upon us, in some wild extravagance of dress or nudity. He was conscious of estrangement from his towns-people, but did not always know how nor wherefore, nor why he should be thus groping through the twilight mist in solitude. If they spoke loudly to him, with cheery voices, the greeting translated itself faintly and mournfully to his ears; if they shook him by the hand, it was as if a thick, insensible glove absorbed the kindly pressure and the warmth. When little Pansie was the companion of his walk, her childish gayety and freedom did not avail to bring him into closer relationship with men, but seemed to follow him into that region of indefinable remoteness, that dismal Fairy-Land of aged fancy, into which old Grandsir Dolliver had so strangely crept away.

Yet there were moments, as many persons had noticed, when the great-grandpapa would suddenly take stronger hues of life. It was as if his faded figure had been colored over anew, or at least, as he and Pansie moved along the street, as if a sunbeam had fallen across him, instead of the gray gloom of an instant before. His chilled sensibilities had probably been touched and quickened by the warm contiguity of his little companion through the medium of her hand, as it stirred within his own, or some inflection of her voice that set his memory ringing and chiming with forgotten sounds. While that music lasted, the old man was alive and happy. And there were seasons, it might be, happier than even these, when Pansie had been kissed and put to bed, and Grandsir Dolliver sat by his fireside gazing in among the massive coals, and absorbing their glow into those cavernous abysses with which all men communicate. Hence come angels or fiends into our twilight musings, according as we may have peopled them in by-gone years. Over our friend's face, in the rosy flicker of the fire-gleam, stole an expression of repose and perfect trust that made him as beautiful to look at, in his high-backed chair, as the child Pansie on her pillow; and sometimes the spirits that were watching him beheld a calm surprise draw slowly over his features and brighten into joy, yet not so vividly as to break his evening quietude. The gate of heaven had been kindly left ajar, that this forlorn old creature might catch a glimpse within. All the night afterwards, he would be semi-conscious of an intangible bliss diffused through the fitful lapses of an old man's slumber, and would awake, at early dawn, with a faint thrilling of the heartstrings, as if there had been music just now wandering over them.

PALINGENESIS.

By H. W. LONGFELLOW.

I LAY upon the headland-height, and listened
To the incessant sobbing of the sea
    In caverns under me,
And watched the waves, that tossed and fled and glistened,
Until the rolling meadows of amethyst
    Melted away in mist.

Then suddenly, as one from sleep, I started;
For round about me all the sunny capes
    Seemed peopled with the shapes
Of those whom I had known in days departed,
Apparelled in the loveliness which gleams
    On faces seen in dreams.

A moment only, and the light and glory
Faded away, and the disconsolate shore
    Stood lonely as before;
And the wild roses of the promontory
Around me shuddered in the wind, and shed
    Their petals of pale red.

There was an old belief that in the embers
Of all things their primordial form exists,
    And cunning alchemists

Could recreate the rose with all its members
From its own ashes, but without the bloom,
　　Without the lost perfume.

Ah, me! what wonder-working, occult science
Can from the ashes in our hearts once more
　　The rose of youth restore?
What craft of alchemy can bid defiance
To time and change, and for a single hour
　　Renew this phantom-flower?

"Oh, give me back," I cried, "the vanished splendors,
The breath of morn, and the exultant strife,
　　When the swift stream of life
Bounds o'er its rocky channel, and surrenders
The pond, with all its lilies, for the leap
　　Into the unknown deep!"

And the sea answered, with a lamentation,
Like some old prophet wailing, and it said,
　　"Alas! thy youth is dead!
It breathes no more, its heart has no pulsation,
In the dark places with the dead of old
　　It lies forever cold!"

Then said I, "From its consecrated cerements
I will not drag this sacred dust again,
　　Only to give me pain;
But, still remembering all the lost endearments,
Go on thy way, like one who looks before,
　　And turns to weep no more."

Into what land of harvests, what plantations
Bright with autumnal foliage and the glow
　　Of sunsets burning low;

Beneath what midnight skies, whose constellations
Light up the spacious avenues between
 This world and the unseen!

Amid what friendly greetings and caresses,
What households, though not alien, yet not mine,
 What bowers of rest divine;
To what temptations in lone wildernesses,
What famine of the heart, what pain and loss,
 The bearing of what cross!

I do not know; nor will I vainly question
Those pages of the mystic book which hold
 The story still untold,
But without rash conjecture or suggestion
Turn its last leaves in reverence and good heed,
 Until "The End" I read.

MY CHILDHOOD.

By SIR WALTER SCOTT.

IT was at Sandy-Knowe, in the residence of my paternal grandfather, that I had the first consciousness of existence; and I recollect distinctly that my situation and appearance were a little whimsical. Among the odd remedies recurred to to aid my lameness, some one had recommended that so often as a sheep was killed for the use of the family, I should be stripped, and swathed up in the skin, warm as it was flayed from the carcass of the animal. In this Tartar-like habiliment I well remember lying upon the floor of the little parlor in the farm-house, while my grandfather, a venerable old man with white hair, used every excitement to make me try to crawl. I also distinctly remember the late Sir George MacDougal of Makerstoun, father of the present Sir Henry Hay MacDougal, joining in this kindly attempt. He was, God knows how, a relation of ours, and I still recollect him in his old-fashioned military habit (he had been colonel of the Greys), with a small cocked hat, deeply laced, an embroidered scarlet waistcoat, and a light-colored coat, with milk-white locks tied in a military fashion, kneeling on the ground before me, and dragging his watch along the carpet to induce me to follow it. The benevolent old soldier and the infant wrapped in his sheepskin would have afforded an odd group to uninterested spectators. This must have happened about my third year, for

Sir George MacDougal and my grandfather both died shortly after that period.

My grandmother continued for some years to take charge of the farm, assisted by my father's second brother, Mr. Thomas Scott, who resided at Crailing, as factor or landsteward for Mr. Scott of Danesfield, then proprietor of that estate. This was during the heat of the American war, and I remember being as anxious on my uncle's weekly visits (for we heard news at no other time) to hear of the defeat of Washington, as if I had had some deep and personal cause of antipathy to him. I know not how this was combined with a very strong prejudice in favor of the Stuart family, which I had originally imbibed from the songs and tales of the Jacobites. This latter political propensity was deeply confirmed by the stories told in my hearing of the cruelties exercised in the executions at Carlisle, and in the Highlands, after the battle of Culloden. One or two of our own distant relations had fallen on that occasion, and I remember of detesting the name of Cumberland with more than infant hatred. Mr. Curle, farmer at Yetbyre, husband of one of my aunts, had been present at their execution; and it was probably from him that I first heard these tragic tales which made so great an impression on me. The local information, which I conceive had some share in forming my future taste and pursuits, I derived from the old songs and tales which then formed the amusement of a retired country family. My grandmother, in whose youth the old Border depredations were matter of recent tradition, used to tell me many a tale of Watt of Harden, Wight Willie of Aikwood, Jamie Telfer of the fair Dodhead, and other heroes,— merrymen all of the persuasion and calling of Robin Hood and Little John. A more recent hero, but not of less note, was the celebrated *Diel of Littledean*, whom she well remembered, as he had married her mother's sister. Of this extraordinary person I learned many a story, grave and gay, comic and warlike. Two or three old books which lay in the window-seat were explored for my amusement in the tedious winter-days. Automathes, and Ramsay's Tea-table Miscellany, were my favorites, although at a later period an odd volume of Josephus's Wars of the Jews divided my partiality.

My kind and affectionate aunt, Miss Janet Scott, whose memory will ever be dear to me, used to read these works to me with admirable patience, until I could repeat long passages by heart. The ballad of Hardyknute I was early master of, to the great annoyance of almost our only visiter, the worthy clergyman of the parish, Dr. Duncan, who had not patience to have a sober chat interrupted by my shouting forth this ditty. Methinks I now see his tall thin emaciated figure, his legs cased in clasped gambadoes, and his face of a length that would have rivalled the Knight of La Mancha's, and hear him exclaiming, " One may as well speak in the mouth of a cannon as where that child is." With this little acidity, which was natural to him, he was a most excellent and benevolent man, a gentleman in every feeling, and altogether different from those of his order who cringe at the tables of the gentry, or domineer and riot at those of the yeomanry. In his youth he had been chaplain in the family of Lord Marchmont — had seen Pope — and could talk familiarly of many characters who had survived the Augustan age of Queen Anne. Though valetudinary, he lived to be nearly ninety, and to welcome to Scotland his son, Colonel William Duncan, who, with the highest character for military and civil merit, had made a considerable fortune in India. In [1795], a few days before his death, I paid him a visit, to inquire after his health. I found him emaciated to the last degree, wrapped in a tartan night-gown, and employed with all the activity of health and youth in correcting a history of the Revolution, which he intended should be given to the public when he was no more. He read me several passages with a voice naturally strong, and which the feelings of an author then raised above the depression of age and declining health. I begged him to spare this fatigue, which could not but injure his health. His answer was remarkable. "I know," he said, "that I cannot survive a fortnight — and what signifies an exertion that can at worst only accelerate my death a few days?" I marvelled at the composure of this reply, for his appearance sufficiently vouched the truth of his prophecy, and rode home to my uncle's (then my abode), musing what there could be in the spirit of authorship that could inspire its votaries with the courage of martyrs. He died within less than the period he assigned,— with which event I close my digression.

I was in my fourth year when my father was advised that the Bath waters might be of some advantage to my lameness. My affectionate aunt, although such a journey promised to a person of her retired habits anything but pleasure or amusement, undertook as readily to accompany me to the wells of Bladud, as if she had expected all the delight that ever the prospect of a watering-place held out to its most impatient visitants. My health was by this time a good deal confirmed by the country air, and the influence of that imperceptible and unfatiguing exercise to which the good sense of my grandfather had subjected me; for when the day was fine, I was usually carried out and laid down beside the old shepherd, among the crags or rocks round which he fed his sheep. The impatience of a child soon inclined me to struggle with my infirmity, and I began by degrees to stand, to walk, and to run. Although the limb affected was much shrunk and contracted, my general health, which was of more importance, was much strengthened by being frequently in the open air, and, in a word, I who in a city had probably been condemned to hopeless and helpless decrepitude, was now a healthy, high-spirited, and, my lameness apart, a sturdy child,— *non sine diis animosus infans.*

We went to London by sea, and it may gratify the curiosity of minute biographers to learn, that our voyage was performed in the Duchess of Buccleuch, Captain Beatson, master. At London we made a short stay, and saw some of the common shows exhibited to strangers. When, twenty-five years afterwards, I visited the Tower of London and Westminster Abbey, I was astonished to find how accurate my recollections of these celebrated places of visitation proved to be, and I have ever since trusted more implicitly to my juvenile reminiscences. At Bath, where I lived about a year, I went through all the usual discipline of the pump-room and baths, but I believe without the least advantage to my lameness. During my residence at Bath, I acquired the rudiments of reading at a day-school, kept by an old dame near our lodgings, and I had never a more regular teacher, although I think I did not attend her a quarter of a year. An occasional lesson from my aunt supplied the rest. Afterwards, when grown a big boy, I had a few lessons from Mr. Stalker of Edinburgh, and finally from the Rev. Mr. Cleeve. But I never acquired a just pronunciation, nor could I read with much propriety.

In other respects my residence at Bath is marked by very pleasing recollections. The venerable John Home, author of Douglas, was then at the watering-place, and paid much attention to my aunt and to me. His wife, who has survived him, was then an invalid, and used to take the air in her carriage on the Downs, when I was often invited to accompany her. But the most delightful recollections of Bath are dated after the arrival of my uncle, Captain Robert Scott, who introduced me to all the little amusements which suited my age, and above all, to the theatre. The play was As You Like It; and the witchery of the whole scene is alive in my mind at this moment. I made, I believe, noise more than enough, and remember being so much scandalized at the quarrel between Orlando and his brother in the first scene, that I screamed out, "Ain't they brothers?" A few weeks' residence at home convinced me, who had till then been an only child in the house of my grandfather, that a quarrel between brothers was a very natural event.

The other circumstances I recollect of my residence in Bath are but trifling, yet I never recall them without a feeling of pleasure. The beauties of the parade (which of them I know not), with the river Avon winding around it, and the lowing of the cattle from the opposite hills, are warm in my recollection, and are only rivalled by the splendors of a toyshop somewhere near the Orange Grove. I had acquired, I know not by what means, a kind of superstitious terror for statuary of all kinds. No ancient Iconoclast or modern Calvinist could have looked on the outside of the Abbey church (if I mistake not, the principal church at Bath is so called) with more horror than the image of Jacob's Ladder, with all its angels, presented to my infant eye. My uncle effectually combated my terrors, and formally introduced me to a statue of Neptune, which perhaps still keeps guard at the side of the Avon, where a pleasure-boat crosses to Spring Gardens.

After being a year at Bath, I returned first to Edinburgh, and afterwards for a season to Sandy-Knowe; — and thus the time whiled away till about my eighth year, when it was thought sea-bathing might be of service to my lameness.

For this purpose, still under my aunt's protection, I remained some weeks at Prestonpans, a circumstance not worth mentioning, excepting to record my juvenile intimacy with an old military veteran, Dalgetty by name, who had pitched his tent in that little village, after all his campaigns, subsisting upon an ensign's half-pay, though called by courtesy a Captain. As this old gentleman, who had been in all the German wars, found very few to listen to his tales of military feats, he formed a sort of alliance with me, and I used invariably to attend him for the pleasure of hearing those communications. Sometimes our conversation turned on the American war, which was then raging. It was about the time of Burgoyne's unfortunate expedition, to which my Captain and I augured different conclusions. Somebody had showed me a map of North America, and, struck with the rugged appearance of the country, and the quantity of lakes, I expressed some doubts on the subject of the General's arriving safely at the end of his journey, which were very indignantly refuted by the Captain. The news of the Saratoga disaster, while it gave me a little triumph, rather shook my intimacy with the veteran.

From Prestonpans, I was transported back to my father's house in George's Square, which continued to be my most established place of residence, until my marriage in 1797. I felt the change from being a single indulged brat, to becoming a member of a large family, very severely; for under the gentle government of my kind grandmother, who was meekness itself, and of my aunt, who, though of a higher temper, was exceedingly attached to me, I had acquired a degree of license which could not be permitted in a large family. I had sense enough, however, to bend my temper to my new circumstances; but such was the agony which I internally experienced, that I have guarded against nothing more in the education of my own family, than against their acquiring habits of self-willed caprice and domination. I found much consolation during this period of mortification, in the partiality of my mother. She joined to a light and happy temper of mind, a strong turn to study poetry and works of imagination. She was sincerely devout, but her religion was, as became her sex, of a cast less austere than my father's. Still, the discipline of the Presbyterian Sabbath was severely strict, and I think injudiciously so. Although Bunyan's Pilgrim, Gesner's Death of Abel, Rowe's Letters, and one or two other books, which, for that reason, I still have a favor for, were admitted to relieve the gloom of one dull sermon succeeding to another, — there was far too much tedium annexed to the duties of the day; and in the end it did none of us any good.

My week-day tasks were more agreeable. My lameness and my solitary habits had made me a tolerable reader, and my hours of leisure were usually spent in reading aloud to my mother Pope's translation of Homer, which, excepting a few traditionary ballads, and the songs in Allan Ramsay's Evergreen, was the first poetry which I perused. My mother had good natural taste and great feeling; she used to make me pause upon those passages which expressed generous and worthy sentiments, and if she could not divert me from those which were descriptive of battle and tumult, she contrived at least to divide my attention between them. My own enthusiasm, however, was chiefly awakened by the wonderful and the terrible, — the common taste of children, but in which I have remained a child even unto this day. I got by heart, not as a task, but almost without intending it, the passages with which I was most pleased, and used to recite them aloud, both when alone and to others, — more willingly, however, in my hours of solitude, for I had observed some auditors smile, and I dreaded ridicule at that time of life more than I have ever done since.

In [1778] I was sent to the second class of the Grammar School, or High School of Edinburgh, then taught by Mr. Luke Fraser, a good Latin scholar and a very worthy man. Though I had received, with my brothers, in private, lessons of Latin from Mr. James French, now a minister of the Kirk of Scotland, I was nevertheless rather behind the class in which I was placed both in years and in progress. This was a real disadvantage, and one to which a boy of lively temper and talents ought to be as little exposed as one who might be less expected to make up his lee-way, as it is called. The situation has the unfortunate effect of reconciling a boy of the former character (which in a posthumous work I may claim for my own) to holding a subordinate station among his class-fellows,— to which he would otherwise affix disgrace. There is also, from the constitution of the High School, a certain danger not sufficiently attended to. The boys take precedence in their *places*, as they are called, according to their merit, and it requires a long while, in general, before even a clever boy, if he falls behind the class, or is put into one for which he is not quite ready, can force his way to the situation which his abilities really entitle him to hold. But, in the meanwhile, he is necessarily led to be the associate and companion of those inferior spirits with whom he is placed; for the system of precedence, though it does not limit the general intercourse among the boys, has nevertheless the effect of throwing them into clubs and coteries, according to the vicinity of the seats they hold. A boy of good talents, therefore, placed even for a time among his inferiors, especially if they be also his elders, learns to participate in their pursuits and objects of ambition, which are usually very distinct from the acquisition of learning; and it will be well if he does not also imitate them in that indifference which is contented with bustling over a lesson so as to avoid punishment, without affecting superiority or aiming at reward. It was probably owing to this circumstance, that, although at a more advanced period of life I have enjoyed considerable facility in acquiring languages, I did not make any great figure at the High School,— or, at least, any exertions which I made were desultory and little to be depended on.

Our class contained some very excellent scholars. The first *Dux* was James Buchan, who retained his honored place, almost without a day's interval, all the while we were at the High School. He was afterwards at the head of the medical staff in Egypt, and in exposing himself to the plague infection, by attending the hospitals there, displayed the same well-regulated and gentle, yet determined perseverance, which placed him most worthily at the head of his school-fellows, while many lads of livelier parts and dispositions held an inferior station. The next best scholars (*sed longo intervallo*) were my friend David Douglas, the heir and *élève* of the celebrated Adam Smith, and James Hope, now a Writer to the Signet, both since well known and distinguished in their departments of the law. As for myself, I glanced like a meteor from one end of the class to the other, and commonly disgusted my kind master as much by negligence and frivolity, as I occasionally pleased him by flashes of intellect and talent. Among my companions, my good-nature and a flow of ready imagination rendered me very popular. Boys are uncommonly just in their feelings, and at least equally generous. My lameness, and the efforts which I made to supply that disadvantage, by making up in address what I wanted in activity, engaged the latter principle in my favor; and in the winter play hours, when hard exercise was impossible, my tales used to assemble an admiring audience round Lucky Brown's fireside, and happy was he that could sit next to the inexhaustible narrator. I was also, though often negligent of my own task, always ready to assist my friends, and hence I had a little party of stanch partisans and adherents, stout of hand and heart, though somewhat dull of head, — the very tools for raising a hero to eminence. So, on the whole, I made a brighter figure in the *yards* than in the *class*.

My father did not trust our education solely to our High School lessons. We had a tutor at home, a young man of an excellent disposition, and a laborious student. He was bred to the Kirk, but unfortunately took such a very strong turn to fanaticism that he afterwards resigned an excellent living in a seaport town, merely because he could not persuade the mariners of the guilt of setting sail of a Sabbath, — in which, by the by, he was less likely to be successful, as, *cæteris paribus*, sailors, from an opinion that it is a fortunate omen, always choose to weigh anchor on that day.

The calibre of this young man's understanding may be judged of by this anecdote; but in other respects, he was a faithful and active instructor; and from him chiefly I learned writing and arithmetic. I repeated to him my French lessons, and studied with him my themes in the classics, but not classically. I also acquired, by disputing with him, (for this he readily permitted,) some knowledge of school-divinity and church-history, and a great acquaintance in particular with the old books describing the early history of the Church of Scotland, the wars and sufferings of the Covenanters, and so forth. I, with a head on fire for chivalry, was a Cavalier; my friend was a Roundhead: I was a Tory, and he was a Whig. I hated Presbyterians, and admired Montrose with his victorious Highlanders; he liked the Presbyterian Ulysses, the dark and politic Argyle: so that we never wanted subjects of dispute; but our disputes were always amicable. In all these tenets there was no real conviction on my part, arising out of acquaintance with the views or principles of either party; nor had my antagonist address enough to turn the debate on such topics. I took up my politics at that period, as King Charles II. did his religion, from an idea that the Cavalier creed was the more gentlemanlike persuasion of the two.

After having been three years under Mr. Fraser, our class was, in the usual routine of the school, turned over to Dr. Adam, the Rector. It was from this respectable man that I first learned the value of the knowledge I had hitherto considered only as a burdensome task. It was the fashion to remain two years at his class, where we read Cæsar, and Livy, and Sallust, in prose; Virgil, Horace, and Terence, in verse. I had by this time mastered, in some degree, the difficulties of the language, and began to be sensible of its beauties. This was really gathering grapes from thistles; nor shall I soon forget the swelling of my little pride when the Rector pronounced, that though many of my school-fellows understood the Latin better, *Gualterus Scott* was behind few in following and enjoying the author's meaning. Thus encouraged, I distinguished myself by some attempts at poetical versions from Horace and Virgil. Dr. Adam used to invite his scholars to such essays, but never made them tasks. I gained some distinction upon these occasions, and the Rector in future took much notice of me; and his judicious mixture of censure and praise went far to counterbalance my habits of indolence and inattention. I saw I was expected to do well, and I was piqued in honor to vindicate my master's favorable opinion. I climbed, therefore, to the first form; and, though I never made a first-rate Latinist, my school-fellows, and what was of more consequence, I myself, considered that I had a character for learning to maintain. Dr. Adam, to whom I owed so much, never failed to remind me of my obligations when I had made some figure in the literary world. He was, indeed, deeply imbued with that fortunate vanity which alone could induce a man who has arms to pare and burn a muir, to submit to the yet more toilsome task of cultivating youth. As Catholics confide in the imputed righteousness of their saints, so did the good old Doctor plume himself upon the success of his scholars in life, all of which he never failed (and often justly) to claim as the creation, or at least the fruits, of his early instructions. He remembered the fate of every boy at his school during the fifty years he had superintended it, and always traced their success or misfortunes entirely to their attention or negligence when under his care. His "noisy mansion," which to others would have been a melancholy bedlam, was the pride of his heart; and the only fatigues he felt, amidst din and tumult, and the necessity of reading themes, hearing lessons, and maintaining some degree of order at the same time, were relieved by comparing himself to Cæsar, who could dictate to three secretaries at once; — so ready is vanity to lighten the labors of duty.

It is a pity that a man so learned, so admirably adapted for his station, so useful, so simple, so easily contented, should have had other subjects of mortification. But the magistrates of Edinburgh, not knowing the treasure they possessed in Dr. Adam, encouraged a savage fellow, called Nicol, one of the undermasters, in insulting his person and authority. This man was an excellent classical scholar, and an admirable convivial humorist (which latter quality recommended him to the friendship of Burns); but worthless, drunken, and inhumanly cruel to the boys under his charge. He carried his feud against the Rector within an inch of assassination, for he waylaid and knocked him down in the dark. The favor which this worthless rival obtained in the town-council led to other consequences, which for some time clouded poor Adam's happiness and fair fame. When the French Revolution broke out, and parties ran high in approving or condemning it, the Doctor incautiously joined the former. This was very natural, for as all his ideas of existing governments were derived from his experience of the town-council of Edinburgh, it must be admitted they scarce brooked comparison with the free states of Rome and Greece, from which he borrowed his opinions concerning republics. His want of caution in speaking on the political topics of the day lost him the respect of the boys, most of whom were accustomed to hear very different opinions on those matters in the bosom of their families. This, however (which was long after my time), passed away with other heats of the period, and the Doctor continued his labors till about a year since, when he was struck with palsy while teaching his class. He survived a few days, but becoming delirious before his dissolution, conceived he was still in school, and after some expressions of applause or censure, he said, "But it grows dark, — the boys may dismiss," — and instantly expired.

From Dr. Adam's class I should, according to the usual

routine, have proceeded immediately to college. But, fortunately, I was not yet to lose, by a total dismission from constraint, the acquaintance with the Latin which I had acquired. My health had become rather delicate from rapid growth, and my father was easily persuaded to allow me to spend half a year at Kelso with my kind aunt, Miss Janet Scott, whose inmate I again became. It was hardly worth mentioning that I had frequently visited her during our short vacations.

At this time she resided in a small house, situated very pleasantly in a large garden, to the eastward of the churchyard of Kelso, which extended down to the Tweed. It was then my father's property, from whom it was afterwards purchased by my uncle. My grandmother was now dead, and my aunt's only companion, besides an old maid-servant, was my cousin, Miss Barbara Scott, now Mrs. Meik. My time was here left entirely to my own disposal, excepting for about four hours in the day, when I was expected to attend the Grammar School of the village. The teacher, at that time, was Mr. Lancelot Whale, an excellent classical scholar, a humorist, and a worthy man. He had a supreme antipathy to the puns which his very uncommon name frequently gave rise to; insomuch, that he made his son spell the word *Wale*, which only occasioned the young man being nicknamed *the Prince of Wales* by the military mess to which he belonged. As for Whale, senior, the least allusion to Jonah, or the terming him an odd fish, or any similar quibble, was sure to put him beside himself. In point of knowledge and taste, he was far too good for the situation he held, which only required that he should give his scholars a rough foundation in the Latin language. My time with him, though short, was spent greatly to my advantage and his gratification. He was glad to escape to Persius and Tacitus from the eternal Rudiments and Cornelius Nepos; and as perusing these authors with one who began to understand them was to him a labor of love, I made considerable progress under his instructions. I suspect, indeed, that some of the time dedicated to me was withdrawn from the instruction of his more regular scholars; but I was as grateful as I could. I acted as usher, and heard the inferior classes, and I spouted the speech of Galgacus at the public examination, which did not make the less impression on the audience that few of them probably understood one word of it.

In the mean while my acquaintance with English literature was gradually extending itself. In the intervals of my school hours I had always perused with avidity such books of history or poetry or voyages and travels as chance presented to me — not forgetting the usual, or rather ten times the usual, quantity of fairy tales, eastern stories, romances, &c. These studies were totally unregulated and undirected. My tutor thought it almost a sin to open a profane play or poem; and my mother, besides that she might be in some degree trammelled by the religious scruples which he suggested, had no longer the opportunity to hear me read poetry as formerly. I found, however, in her dressing-room (where I slept at one time) some odd volumes of Shakespeare, nor can I easily forget the rapture with which I sat up in my shirt reading them by the light of a fire in her apartment, until the bustle of the family rising from supper warned me it was time to creep back to my bed, where I was supposed to have been safely deposited since nine o'clock. Chance, however, threw in my way a poetical preceptor. This was no other than the excellent and benevolent Dr. Blacklock, well known at that time as a literary character. I know not how I attracted his attention, and that of some of the young men who boarded in his family; but so it was that I became a frequent and favored guest. The kind old man opened to me the stores of his library, and through his recommendation I became intimate with Ossian and Spenser. I was delighted with both, yet I think chiefly with the latter poet. The tawdry repetitions of the Ossianic phraseology disgusted me rather sooner than might have been expected from my age. But Spenser I could have read forever. Too young to trouble myself about the allegory, I considered all the knights and ladies and dragons and giants in their outward and exoteric sense, and God only knows how delighted I was to find myself in such society. As I had always a wonderful facility in retaining in my memory whatever verses pleased me, the quantity of Spenser's stanzas which I could repeat was really marvellous. But this memory of mine was a very fickle ally, and has through my whole life acted merely upon its own capricious motion, and might have enabled me to adopt old Beattie of Meikledale's answer, when complimented by a certain reverend divine on the strength of the same faculty: — "No, sir," answered the old Borderer, "I have no command of my memory. It only retains what hits my fancy; and probably, sir, if you were to preach to me for two hours, I would not be able when you finished to remember a word you had been saying." My memory was precisely of the same kind: it seldom failed to preserve most tenaciously a favorite passage of poetry, a play-house ditty, or, above all, a Border-raid ballad; but names, dates, and the other technicalities of history, escaped me in a most melancholy degree. The philosophy of history, a much more important subject, was also a sealed book at this period of my life; but I gradually assembled much of what was striking and picturesque in historical narrative; and when, in riper years, I attended more to the deduction of general principles, I was furnished with a powerful host of examples in illustration of them. I was, in short, like an ignorant gamester, who kept up a good hand until he knew how to play it.

I left the High School, therefore, with a great quantity of general information, ill arranged, indeed, and collected without system, yet deeply impressed upon my mind; readily assorted by my power of connection and memory, and gilded, if I may be permitted to say so, by a vivid and active imagination. If my studies were not under any direction at Edinburgh, in the country, it may be well imagined, they were less so. A respectable subscription library, a circulating library of ancient standing, and some private bookshelves, were open to my random perusal, and I waded into the stream like a blind man into a ford, without the power of searching my way, unless by groping for it. My appetite for books was as ample and indiscriminating as it was indefatigable, and I since have had too frequently reason to repent that few ever read so much, and to so little purpose.

Among the valuable acquisitions I made about this time, was an acquaintance with Tasso's Jerusalem Delivered, through the flat medium of Mr. Hoole's translation. But above all, I then first became acquainted with Bishop Percy's Reliques of Ancient Poetry. As I had been from infancy devoted to legendary lore of this nature, and only reluctantly withdrew my attention, from the scarcity of materials and the rudeness of those which I possessed, it may be imagined, but cannot be described, with what delight I saw pieces of the same kind which had amused my childhood, and still continued in secret the Delilahs of my imagination, considered as the subject of sober research, grave commentary, and apt illustration, by an editor who showed his poetical genius was capable of emulating the best qualities of what his pious labor preserved. I remember well the spot where I read these volumes for the first time. It was beneath a huge platanus-tree, in the ruins of what had been intended for an old-fashioned arbor in the *garden* I have mentioned. The summer-day sped onward so fast, that notwithstanding the sharp appetite of thirteen, I forgot the hour of dinner, was sought for with anxiety, and was still found entranced in my intellectual banquet. To read and to remember was in this instance the same thing, and henceforth I overwhelmed my school-fellows, and all who would hearken to me, with tragical recitations from the ballads of Bishop Percy. The first time, too, I could scrape a few shillings together, which were not common occurrences with me, I bought unto myself a copy of these beloved volumes; nor do I believe I ever read a book half so frequently, or with half the enthusiasm. About this period also I became acquainted with the works of Richardson, and those of Mackenzie (whom in later years I became entitled to call my friend), — with Fielding, Smollett, and some others of our best novelists.

To this period also I can trace distinctly the awaking of that delightful feeling for the beauties of natural objects which has never since deserted me. The neighborhood of Kelso, the most beautiful, if not the most romantic village in Scotland, is eminently calculated to awaken these ideas. It presents objects, not only grand in themselves, but venerable from their association. The meeting of two superb rivers, the Tweed and the Teviot, both renowned in song, — the ruins of an ancient Abbey, — the more distant vestiges of Roxburgh Castle, — the modern mansion of Fleurs, which is so situated as to combine the ideas of ancient baronial grandeur with those of modern taste, — are in themselves objects of the first class; yet are so mixed, united, and melted among a thousand other beauties of a less prominent description, that they harmonize into one general picture, and please rather by unison than by concord. I believe I have written unintelligibly upon this subject, but it is fitter for the pencil than the pen. The romantic feelings which I have described as predominating in my mind natutally rested upon and associated themselves with these grand features of the landscape around me; and the historical incidents, or traditional legends connected with many of them, gave to my admiration a sort of intense impression of reverence, which at times made my heart feel too big for its bosom. From this time the love of natural beauty, more especially when combined with ancient ruins or remains of our fathers' piety or splendor, became with me an insatiable passion, which, if circumstances had permitted, I would willingly have gratified by travelling over half the globe.

THE END.

www.ingramcontent.com/pod-product-compliance
Lightning Source LLC
Chambersburg PA
CBHW020232240426
43672CB00006B/494